Television Operations
A Handbook of Technical Operations for
TV Broadcast, On Air, Cable, Mobile and Internet

Frederick M. Baumgartner, CPBE
and
Nicholas A. Grbac, CBT, CTO

© 2015, the Society of Broadcast Engineers, inc.
ISBN: 978-0-9853589-4-5

PREFACE

Some Things Worth Knowing

What you see at home on your flat-screen or possibly your mobile device, computer, or just about anything displaying live TV kind of programing, has gone through a master control room (or at least a master control process) where multiple *elements* are brought together. While details may change from one facility to another, the function of a master control room is the same: it is the control point for assembling all the program segments along with other elements (commercials, promotions, public service announcements, interstitials, and graphics), monitoring their quality and then sending them to the viewer.

To our knowledge, it has been a very long time since anyone has published a reference book on master control operations. The Society of Broadcast Engineers (SBE) has had a certification program for television operators (CTO) and a study guide for certification is available. This book is an extension of that course of study, and is intended to be the definitive text on the subject.

However, it is critically important that broadcast engineers, station management, and to a lesser degree anyone working in Broadcasting have an understanding of broadcast operations... something apart from but integral to the technology and business of broadcasting. With any luck, many managers and engineers will find this a good read and something that markedly improves their decisions and ability to communicate with the operational staff they work with.

So why write a book on master control operations, and why release it now? As with many industries, the business model of broadcast media has changed dramatically in recent years. Automation is everywhere, staffs have been reduced as part of the digital revolution, personnel reassigned -- technology is changing and stations are combining activities such as master control with other stations. Television station owners, management and staffers, in particular students looking to receive their SBE CTO certification, requested a reference for this specialized job function. With the advent of digital television and Web-based TV everywhere delivery, the SBE recognized the broad need for such a reference across the board.

In 2012, Nick Grbac met with Fred Baumgartner, and the book you're holding came to be. Technology, regulations, new trends and economic considerations all point to the evolution in master control operations. This book attempts to not only provide background and some insight into the job, but also give those new to master control operations a solid foundation of theory on which to build.

Realizing readers will come from a diverse knowledge base, essential information is presented first. In some cases, optional material is included for those more advanced – while not critical material for day-to-day operation, it is added to give deeper insight into certain topics. This extra information will be presented with gray boxes around the text.

Italicized script indicates that a term is widely used, and in order to work as a master control operator, you will need to know what it means. Most of these terms are intuitive, defined in the context of its use, or in some cases we felt parenthetical (in parentheses) support was needed. Some are also in the glossary.

Most repetition of definitions and concepts is intentional. Most readers will sample the book, skipping back and forth, and may refer back to the text at a later date. Rather than a series of see-also directions, we think many explanations are brief enough that it's faster and easier to readdress them than to refer to another section.

The construction of the book is to look at master control from several perspectives: workflow, architecture, operations, etc. This too means that we will travel the same ground from different directions.

And finally, we determined to avoid using history to explain the present for the obvious reason: This is not a history book. The biggest recent event, historically, is that analog became digital, distribution moved away from over the air transmission to satellite and cable and soon probably Internet, and what was staff-intensive became IT-centric. There are many books and stories on how broadcasting grew up. We will only cover the history when we deem it necessary to understand the present.

The SBE serves the professional needs of broadcast engineers. Part of this service is to provide well-respected educational materials to broadcast engineers, with several levels that reflect the engineer's growing capabilities in the industry. If this is your first SBE publication and first exposure to the SBE, welcome. If you are just starting in broadcast, the two of us are sure you will find it a fascinating career with many places to go, grow and hopefully enjoy.

Please Read the Following Disclaimer

This book is supplied solely as a teaching aid for individuals wishing to acquaint themselves with master control operations. It is not intended to be an authoritative source of information on current rules and regulations. Federal Communications Commission rules and broadcast technology are constantly changing. For these reasons, the reader is cautioned to refer to the current Code of Federal Regulations for up-to-date and detailed information.

Every effort has been made to ensure the accuracy of the information provided herein. The authors and the Society of Broadcast Engineers, Inc. make no warranty of any kind and will not be held liable for any errors or omissions.

Likewise, we cover *standard operating practices* (SOP), which a given facility may or may not follow. For the most part, the industry uses the same language and practices from one facility to another.

Purpose of this Book - Obligations

Almost every "broadcaster" has the obligation and objective of assuring that their facility is in compliance with government regulations and industry standards -- and puts out a product that provides a good viewer experience. The purpose of this book is to cover the basics of TV master control operation, so that the operator is familiar with the concepts, practices and the regulations inherent in the job. And unlike other texts, this book is specifically designed for those with a minimum to moderate amount of master control exposure. No doubt, experienced operators and non-technical managers will also benefit from this text.

Some readers may already be working in the field and seek certification of their skills. An increasing number of facilities have required SBE TV Operator Certification as a prerequisite to hiring or staffing a master control shift. Some 6,000 master control operators have been certified to date. Others might be students where the program requires SBE TV Operator Certification as part of the graduation requirements, or highly recommend certification before seeking work in the industry. We strongly urge you to look into certification through the SBE website (www.sbe.org). While there is no legal requirement for certification, we are aware that many, if not most facilities, require certification as evidence of your qualification to serve as an operator in their facility. The SBE always takes education seriously, at all levels.

About the SBE

The Society of Broadcast Engineers, Inc. (SBE) is a non-profit organization serving the interests of broadcast engineers. It is the only national organization devoted to all levels of broadcast engineering.

Membership is international in scope and consists of studio and transmitter operators, technicians, supervisors, chief engineers, engineering managers, directors of engineering, consultants, field service engineers and sales engineers. Engineers from recording studios, schools, CCTV and CATV systems, production houses and related technologies and industries are members also.

The SBE provides educational programs and a certification program, maintains a training tape library and provides educational material for the broadcast engineering community. There are many other services provided by the Society, including employment services with JobsOnline and a Resume Service, computer and amateur radio communications, life and health insurance and more. The SBE also represents the technical interests of broadcast engineers and their stations before the FCC and other governmental bodies. The SBE publishes a bimonthly newsletter, *The Signal*, for its more than 5,400 members in more than 100 chapters.

If you would like information about becoming a member of the SBE, or if you would like to inquire about SBE services, please contact: Society of Broadcast Engineers, Inc.; 9102 North Meridian Street, Suite 150; Indianapolis, IN 46260; phone: 317-846-9000; fax 317-846-9120; www.sbe.org

The Ennes Educational Foundation Trust

The Ennes Educational Foundation Trust, Inc. is devoted to the advancement of the science of broadcast engineering through educational programs. The trust, which focused initially on granting scholarships to those interested in careers in broadcast engineering, was originally created by Indianapolis SBE Chapter 25 in 1980, in honor of the memory of chapter member, Harold Ennes.

Ennes was a noted author of many textbooks on the subject of broadcast engineering at a time when there was little other information available. He was a member of the SBE National Certification Committee and made many contributions to the early development of the SBE program.

In 1981, Chapter 25 asked the Society of Broadcast Engineers to assume operation of the trust to give it exposure on a national level. Several years later, three former SBE presidents: Roger Johnson, Jack McKain and Jim Wulliman, expanded the educational aspects of the trust to include educational programs and projects benefiting broadcast engineers and the field of broadcast engineering.

Since that time, the Ennes Educational Foundation Trust has grown to provide several Ennes Workshops at regional and national industry events each year, covering a wide variety of broadcast engineering topics. The Ennes Trust also works to encourage the entry of minorities and women into the technical broadcast field, evaluates educational courses and works with other industry organizations to develop and enhance common technical training courses.

The Ennes Trust is designated a 501(c)3 charitable organization by the IRS and is supported solely from donations by individuals and businesses. Tax deductible contributions may be made payable to "Ennes Educational Foundation Trust" and mailed to Society of Broadcast Engineers; 9102 N. Meridian Street, Suite 150; Indianapolis, IN 46260; Attn: Ennes Trust.

Authors

Frederick M. Baumgartner, CPBE, is a Fellow of the Society of Broadcast Engineers, a trustee of the Ennes Educational Foundation Trust, and has served the SBE in several roles since joining in 1972. Fred currently is the television product manager for Nautel. He has also worked for KMGH-TV, and Harris Broadcast on two occasions in a variety of roles. Fred was also director of broadcast engineering for Qualcomm's MediaFLO, which broadcasted a multichannel TV service nationwide to mobile devices. Previously, he served as director of engineering for the Comcast Media Center in Denver, as its director of new product development through the center's AT&T ownership and before that as director of broadcast satellite operations during its TCI ownership era. Before joining the satellite and cable origination world, he held the position of engineering manager at KDVR-TV and KFCT-TV, Denver; WTTV-TV, WTTK-TV, Indianapolis; KHOW AM & FM, Denver; WIBA AM & FM, Madison, WI; operations manager at KWGN-TV, Denver; and others beginning with the overnight gig and a newly minted FCC 1st Class license at WBIZ AM & FM, Eau Claire, WI. Fred was also heavily involved with the development of EAS, has authored several hundred articles on radio and TV engineering, and operates amateur radio station KØFMB. Jody and Fred are empty nesters and live outside of Denver on a 35-acre "ranchette" with horses, dogs, cats and antennas.

Nicholas A. Grbac, CBT, CTO, has more than 30 years of television experience, specializing in on air operations. Performing on air operations and production duties in both small- and large-market facilities, Nick has had the opportunity to see various working philosophies and to observe what does and does not work successfully. Over time, he has worked at KGSC-TV/KICU and KNTV (both in San Jose, CA) as well as KTLA/Golden West Videotape in Hollywood, and finally KRON-TV in San Francisco. Serving as master control crew chief for several years at KRON-TV, he has taken a special interest in the education and training of new operators and demystifying television engineering. Nick lives in South San Francisco, currently works for KRON-TV; his interests include dogs, music, and television history and memorabilia.

Acknowledgements

It's impossible to acknowledge everyone who had a part in this book, but we are nonetheless grateful. The authors are especially grateful to the following:

Craig Beardsley, CPBE; Imagine
    Communications
Ray Benedict, CPBE; CBS Radio
Richard Chernock; Triveni
Mildred Ellison; Raytheon
Doug Garlinger, CPBE, 8-VSB; SBE/Ennes
    Educational Foundation Trust
Richard Goett; Harmonic
Ralph Hogan, CPBE, DRB, CBNE; SBE
Shawn Maynard; Florical Systems

Wayne Pecena, CPBE, 8-VSB, AMD, DRB, CBNE;
    SBE
Tony Peterle, CPBE; WorldCast Systems
John Poray, CAE; SBE
Craig Porter; Young Broadcasting
Joe Snelson, CPBE, 8-VSB; SBE
Jim Starzynski; NBCUniversal
Bob Stroup, CSRE, AMD, CBNT; iHeartMedia
Patrick Waddell; Harmonic

Cover
Photo of KMGH-TV control room by Fred Baumgartner.

Layout
Chriss Scherer, CPBE, CBNT; Society of Broadcast Engineers

A Handbook of Technical Operations for TV Broadcast, On Air, Cable, Mobile and Internet

Contents

1
THE BASICS OF MASTER CONTROL

What a Master Control Operator Does

The ***master control operator*** (***MCO***) is the last person to have control over what the viewers see and hear...literally the eyes and ears of the *station*. Every department in the station's (or other broadcast facility's) effort comes together with the MCO. The operator's job is detailed to the fraction of a second and requires a great deal of mental and occasionally physical dexterity. It is often said that it can be fairly boring, punctuated by moments of terror. Part of being a good or even great MCO is an ethic of high engagement and great skill with detailed work. Not everyone can do this well. The job comes with both a certain amount of stress as well as its own rewards. Master control may be a life's career, an entry point for other careers, or the day job that pays the bills while working on productions such as sports. In any case, it is easily one of the more interesting and challenging roles within broadcasting.

What Happens in a Master Control Room

While master control room (MCR) is the most common term, it is not uncommon to have an equipment control room (ECR) or an operations control, technical operations center (TOC, pronounced "tock") or rarely network operations center (NOC, pronounced "knock"). There may be other terms to describe this function.

Regardless of your facility's size, master control rooms serve three specific functions:

1. A reception point for all programming, commercial and other interstitial material,

2. A location to check, modify, ingest, time and otherwise massage material to fit the facilities' needs, and,

3. A control point to distribute programming.

You'll find a number of ways to receive material into the facility: fiber-optic link, Internet, satellite, microwave, production control rooms and studios, and even the U.S. Postal Service.

Once material is in-house, MCOs can use MCR equipment to spot check shows and screen commercials, ingest material into the video server system, and time and segment shows.

Finally, MCR acts as the control point to monitor, sometimes edit, and distribute material. This output may be uplinked via satellite, distributed by fiber-optic link, carried via IP connections, or transmitted via microwave (even laser) or fiber to a transmitter. The Federal Communications Commission picks up regulatory responsibility.

Federal Communications Commission

All United States ***over-the-air*** (*OTA*) broadcast stations are licensed by the *Federal Communications Commission* (*FCC*). The FCC was created by Congress to implement the Communications Act of 1934, which regulates the private use of *radio frequency* spectrum. The FCC sets the ground rules for what is acceptable, especially for over-the-air broadcasters. The FCC also regulates some aspects of a ***multichannel video program distributor*** (***MVPD***) operation – that is, program distributors such as cable, satellite, phone companies and, now, the Internet. Of greatest concern are the guidelines of power output of transmitters, a station's capability to broadcast or re-broadcast emergency announcements of a local, state or national nature, as well as issues like access to television for the hearing-impaired, commercial time in children's programming and indecency concerns.

This book will cover the more universal FCC Rules and technical information needed for a typical broadcast day. It's possible your facility will have an operations manual with necessary information on your specific station available to master control operators. The FCC rules are all contained in Title 47 of the Code of Federal Regulations (CFR). There are several parts to Title 47, which cover various services. Part 73 is the primary section concerned with broadcast services. Part 76 addresses multichannel operations. There are related regulations in Part 74-79. The website is www.fcc.gov.

Facility Requirements

Facility requirements will largely be dependent on the programming emanating from the plant. The most common example, a traditional television station, involves programming running in real-time. Many stations invest heavily in having "backup" sources for programming and commercials. Most stations have news departments, necessitating "live" programming requirements. On the other hand, a cable network running only pre-recorded material has more flexibility. If a cable network won't be breaking into programming with live news, this allows them to run their air product off-air and record it into a video server, then play it at the scheduled time to assure an error-free product. As protection, facilities doing this will frequently have a backup on a separate list running in real time. All-news networks are mostly live, but do pre-record some pre-produced material (or *elements*), in particular news packages.

Operators must be aware of their company's needs and expectations and know how to fulfill them. Say your station feels strongly about airing only family-oriented programming, you are spot-checking a syndicated show and you become aware of questionable dialogue. What do you do? Ideally, a facility will have some written guidelines that specifies what is expected of the staff, and who to contact (generally in management) for what issues. This is becoming especially important as temporary/part-time staffing is more prevalent than in the past.

With consistency being vital in a 24/7 operation, some facilities take an active role in preparing their staff: a training checklist of common tasks can be very helpful, both to new staff as well as their trainers. Then, correspondingly, the supervisor can revisit the checklist at evaluation time and measure how the employee matches the objective standard. Also, tasks that are less common (not daily events) should be included in a binder in the MCR. Obvious things to include: powering up/down transmitters, switching to a backup transmitter or antenna, perhaps directions to get to the transmitter if it is at a remote location, restarting servers, who to call when systems fail, etc. Some facilities prefer to have all duties outlined, so new staff have a clear idea of what is expected of them, and know the station's way of doing tasks.

As a practical matter, much of what is expected is common sense, and some is tribal knowledge passed from person to person rather than committed to paper. It takes a minimum of four and a half MCOs to cover a 24/7 operation. It is a small enough group that some communication is best passed from one to another (hand-off time is often brief, and not everyone sees everyone else very often). In this regard, because you're dealing with the bottom line of the facility, it's best to err more on the side of printed communication and rely less on tribal knowledge for the most critical issues.

Many facilities have an MCO message board where notes can be passed from shift to shift. Small things can have a big impact.

Co-workers

Operators have a duty to be aware of their own crew's needs. The broadcast industry is very much a group effort, so an operator should not only be prepared to complete their own shift duties, but also start to prepare for at least an hour or so into the next shift. It is not only common courtesy, but it's the professional thing to do. Always be thinking of what is on air now, what is next, and then what follows. For instance, leaving equipment configured in an expected way should become routine (for example, your satellite receiver #3 is usually on CNN: when you use it for something else, returning it to the expected settings is most helpful).

Awareness of crew needs means: being on time, verifying in advance that material is available for air on each channel for which you are responsible, and preparing for the next shift. Typically, this is done by checking your on air *schedule*, shows and spots. Most stations have an overlap of shifts, and some even have a *standard operating practice* (*SOP*) where each operator checks the shows for the next shift (some check both their own and the next shift).

A white board with exceptions, warnings, status and other information about the content and systems can be very helpful as each MCO passes messages on to the next as they come to mind. A spot that does something weird (looking like you are off the air or flashing color bars and tone) can be jarring, and lead to a panic recovery when none is needed...that's useful information. Also helpful are notes regarding equipment that is not functioning properly.

Interviewing for a Master Control Job

This is all basic stuff; still, some potential MCOs fail to prepare to get hired.

MCR staffs are often assembled from several sources: those who've worked elsewhere as MCOs, sometimes those having been laid-off in other departments, still others working in adjacent departments, such as production.

For the sake of this discussion, we will assume an applicant is coming in from the outside with some MCR background, and discuss how a typical interview might proceed. Naturally, your experiences will vary, but the purpose of this is to give you an idea of what to expect.

Prior to the interview, have extra resumes prepared. You might also have a sheet ready that lists your references (usually three references are sufficient): their names, titles, phone numbers, and how the references know you. (Naturally, get permission to use them as references, first!) Bring copies of both your resume and reference sheet to the interview. If you have one, carry your resumes, references and whatever else in a business-like portfolio. If you don't have one or can't afford one, a new manila envelope will work, also.

Online application processes are the norm in most group owned situations and large companies. These can be fairly straightforward or require several hours to complete calling upon information that isn't likely in your memory. Keeping a spread sheet of answers to likely questions such as the email address and phone number of previous employers, web sites of companies, physical addresses, dates, income, reasons for leaving, and more; can make the process faster. Online applications generally do not receive any other than an occasional automated reply. Your social media is part of your resume, in particular Linked-In, and face-book. Having a poor Internet presence or none at all is likely a disqualifier. Networking is by far the most fruitful means of obtaining that right job. Nonetheless, MCO in a small market isn't lucrative and often it is difficult to find candidates, which makes it fertile ground for that first job.

When you make it to the interview stage, you may receive directions to the facility from the company but it doesn't hurt to go online and get directions there also. It wouldn't be the first time an applicant got lost going by the directions they were given. Almost anything that gives you confidence before your interview is the thing to do. Make a test drive if possible. You cannot over-prepare for interviews!

Give yourself plenty of time to get to the interview – a good time to arrive is about 15-minutes before the interview. This gives you an opportunity to pop into the restroom – check that your hair is brushed and your clothes look neat. And then while you're waiting in the lobby for someone to come and get you, take a deep breath and relax! MCOs shouldn't stress-out easily.

The Interview Itself

OK, you've done the pleasantries in the lobby with the interviewer, and you ride the elevator a couple of floors. Think of a very general comment you can make if the need arises, such as "I've been looking forward to seeing this facility," or "I enjoyed our phone conversation the other day." Some interviewers are not great conversationalists and can be apprehensive about the interview they're about to begin with you. Having something to say during an awkward pause will put you both at ease.

The goal is to have this interview be a totally positive experience: no criticisms of present or past employers, no disparaging remarks; you want the interviewer to leave the interview thinking, "That went well." If you're asked why are you looking for another job, your response should be more along the lines of "I've contributed all I can where I am," not *I gotta get out of there!*

You'll usually get a tour of the facility; often this is before the interview. It provides a good getting-to-know-you period between the interviewer and you, and can be a good source for questions later in the interview. Some interviewers use it as a test to see how familiar you are with the equipment and work environment. And remember: look the interviewer in the eye during the interview.

It is very important to think about your focus while sitting across from the interviewer. As a job applicant, we tend to be focused on ourselves: "Wouldn't it be great if I got this job..." or "I'd really like working for the such-and-such company..." But the fact is, a potential employer has a problem: an open position. He is thinking about how you as the applicant can solve *his* problem. By hiring you, will it make his life easier? What do you bring to the table? You need to communicate this answer to the interviewer.

It's a pretty safe bet the first question you'll be asked is something like, "Tell me about yourself." or, more bluntly, "Why should I hire you for this job?" To answer, you must compare your skills to those requested in the job description. Then, try to enhance your argument by giving details of what you've done: how *much* time the new process you initiated at your current job saves? How did you reduce on air discrepancies? As a segue, you might end this by saying, "Because of this, I think I'd be an asset to your department." Keep this little speech to about 60-90 seconds – two minutes, maximum. Again, what *can* you do for the station's department?

As you get to the middle of the interview, you'll get a sense whether the interviewer has actually read your resume or not. Don't be surprised if you feel he or she has not. If he begins to ramble or not address specifics of your background, think about *very gently* guiding the interview back to why you would be a good fit for this job (the station job requirements versus your background).

Towards the end, the interviewer will likely ask if you have any question. Yes, you do! Never say, "I think that about covers it." Ask work-related questions that show you have an interest in the job, and that you were listening to what was said during the interview. If you freeze up, here are some suggestions to get you started:

• "As a new employee, will there be some shift orientation, and for how long?" (Try not to say "training," as this implies they need to train you, and that involves an added cost.) Every facility will need to orient you to the way it does things, what is the station's routine, etc.

• "What is the biggest challenge you face regarding the master control staff?"

• "As a new hire, what can I do that would make life easier for you?"

This would be a good time to ask questions prompted by the tour you may have been given earlier.

After a few questions, thank the interviewer for seeing you, and you will be looking forward to hearing from him or her soon. You want to say thank you, and the "looking forward to hearing from you" comment may prompt the interviewer to say when he or she expects a decision to be made (if that decision hasn't already been made).

Finally, send a follow-up thank you note or email to your interviewer after your interview. Use this opportunity to not only thank him or her, but also use it to reinforce why you'd be a good hire. And keep this note brief: one line of thanks, a second line reinforcing your background, and then a brief "I look forward to hearing from you."

2
HOW TV FACILITIES WORK

For the most part, all television stations and their direct descendants, *central-casting* and multi-channel facilities, *cable* channels, and webcasters, operate more alike than differently. Master control operators moving from one facility to another generally require little retraining. The basic television station or the like is a small business with a basic objective: content is acquired or created at some cost, and revenue is obtained by either selling advertisers access to the viewers, seeking funding from the private and public sector, or collecting fees directly from the viewers (pay-per-view, subscription TV, cable TV, satellite TV, Web TV, mobile TV, etc.) or some combination of these revenue sources. Retransmission fees ("retrans") from cable and satellite are a big contributor to some TV stations revenue.

In a commercial station, the salespeople only get paid when their commercials run and they collect the payment. Obviously they don't want to see spots missed. No one wants to see the station off the air, or a show air badly, and no one wants to refund pay-per-view revenues when a show fails to be played correctly. There are a lot of people in the facility who want the MCO to do well.

Content can be distributed via *over-the-air* (*OTA*) transmitters, or *multichannel video program distributors* (*MVPDs*) such as *cable TV* (*CATV*), Satellite, and the Internet as *real-time streaming* broadcasts, or repurposed into downloadable on-demand media files. In most cases, there is some combination of distribution means.

Television Markets

Traditional television stations operate with an OTA transmitter at the center of their distribution system. The Federal Communications Commission licenses the transmitter, and there is finite spectrum; Thus there are a limited number of transmitters that can be licensed in a market. There are 210 television markets or *Designated Market Areas* (*DMAs*) in the United States, and they are ranked. New York, with 7,387,810 TV households and 6.4% of the country's population is market one. Los Angeles is market number two, but most markets are more like Eau Claire – La Crosse, WI, at 128. Glendive, MT, with 4,180 TV households is 210. There is no 211th market...yet. The market ranking is determined by the Nielsen organization that provides ratings information. The list changes periodically based upon population shifts and viewership habits (viewers who can receive two markets might shift their viewing from one to another and a whole county might flip). You can search "DMA, market ranking" for the current list.

Markets are called major, medium, and small. While both New York and Los Angeles are major markets, not everyone would include Chicago (#3, with less than half the viewers of New York), Philadelphia (#4), or Dallas-Fort Worth (#5) in that same group. The definition of a medium market ranges anywhere from market three to market 50 (probably depending more on which market the observer is working in than anything else). Small markets are definitely any market over 100, though most include everything over 50, and some would claim markets 26 on down are small market TV. National advertising buyers will sometimes buy just the top 100 markets, so 600 homes, the difference between market 99 and 100, can make a lot of difference in a station's income.

The only real purpose for this vague and arbitrary convention is that the income and the viewers in major markets are orders of magnitude more than in the small markets. There is often a desire to work in the major markets, or at least medium markets for the newer equipment, better income, and maybe the challenge. But a small market can have other rewards.

One often hears the goal of many new operators is to begin working in the largest markets. However, some feel it's wiser to begin in a smaller market. Why? In smaller markets, you're exposed to more learning opportunities, you get to do more, and most importantly you can make your mistakes in a place where the stakes, the revenue and the number of viewers are lower compared to a major market facility. Larger markets also tend to be more specialized in job duties and may have union restrictions.

There are a couple of helpful things to know about TV stations. Those starting with a K tend to be west of the Mississippi, while the W's are east. The stations with networks in their call letters tend to be in major markets (KCBS-TV, KABC-TV and KNBC-TV are in Los Angeles; WCBS-TV, WABC-TV and WNBC-TV are in New York City). Those with three call letters can trace their history back to the early radio stations in the 1920s (KGO-TV in San Francisco, WBZ-TV in Boston and WGN-TV in Chicago).

Some television facilities (or stations) have no *OTA* transmitter, and operate only over cable, satellite, Internet, or other distribution system. So when we use the phrase "play-to-air" or "broadcast" we recognize that there may not be a transmitter to place the signal into the air at many facilities.

This is an important distinction, as OTA stations that operate with an FCC license have certain regulations that they must comply with. Cable systems, satellite *direct-to-home* (*DTH*), telephone systems, and even the Internet all operate under the umbrella of FCC regulation. In general, the OTA rules are the most stringent, and other distribution systems operate with less exacting requirements. Facilities that do not require an FCC license will not have these restrictions. For example, profanity and nudity are restrained on OTA distribution, but not so much elsewhere. Likewise, OTA stations have some public service obligation, but again not so much for cable or satellite.

Current Broadcast Trends

If you have a basic knowledge of television, you might be surprised at the current business model of the average television station compared to how it was not long after the dawn of the 21st century. Not so long ago, a station broadcast a single channel to the public, and that was that. As time, technology and the economy moved forward, the paradigm changed. Technology allowed more channels to be multiplexed into the same spectrum space that was previously taken up by just one channel. Relaxed regulation often allowed for the ownership of more than one station in a market, and agreements to operate another owner's station finds many TV stations clustered under one roof. This is generally referred to as *shared service agreements*. Some groups do some, if not all, of their work from centralized locations. Other companies operate scores of stations as a third party service. Most stations now have a Web presence. Broadcast equipment suppliers provide hardware and software that allows one person to operate more than one channel at a time. If you're working in a facility where more than one program entity is being aired at the same time, you are working in a "multichannel" facility.

Hubbing or *centralcasting* has become a popular operating structure for many stations. Hubs can perform one or several functions (master control operations, acquisition, traffic, graphics and possibly news and promotion) as well as housing most of the hardware, and then distribute the air product to the spokes from the hub. There are two basic configurations, and many variations of each. In one, the broadcast is assembled at the *network operations center* (*NOC*) or a better term, *broadcast operations center* (*BOC*), and carried by mostly fiber to the various transmitters. Satellite is sometimes used as backup or if many stations carry mostly the same content. The other version is the remote control or thin model where the content is at the station, and the station is largely driven by remote control.

Depending on structure, the basic drivers for *centralcasting* are operational cost savings from reduced staff, *ingest* once – use many workflow scenarios that reduce duplication of effort, and a reduction in equipment needed as all stations can share satellite antennas and receivers, servers, storage, and the like. Centralized traffic and billing, production, ingest, quality control, programming, and even news are not uncommon.

There are variations from everything-at-the-hub: where equipment stays at the station but operating staff are all at the hub, and *sharecasting*, where some operations are done at the hub, while others may be done locally; or the local station operates for a portion of the broadcast day, and the hub "shares" the workload typically by operating during overnight hours.

See Chapter 14F. Appendix: Centralcasting Notes for an in-depth discussion of centralcasting issues.

The Business Workflow

The various departments all deal with specific pieces of the station's *workflows*.

In most stations, the top of the organization is the general manager or vice president. See Figure 02-01. Ultimately, this person is responsible for the performance of the station. In most stations there are a group of managers or directors that oversee the operations of the various departments, and particularly in the case of broadcast operations, there are likely to be managers, crew chiefs and shift leaders, or an ***engineer in charge (EIC)***.

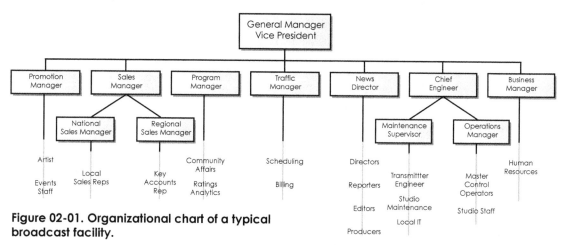

Figure 02-01. Organizational chart of a typical broadcast facility.

From the highest view we can take of most facilities: a commercial (spot) is sold, a program is scheduled, and these are turned over to the traffic department. Broadcast traffic refers to the traffic of programs, commercials, promotions and public affair announcements scheduled to air on a daily basis through master control.

The traffic department delivers a ***schedule*** to broadcast operations (and the MCOs). The schedule is a list defining every *event* for every second (sometimes every frame or $1/25$ or $1/30$ second) that a station is on the air. The traffic department (commercials) and the programming department (shows) deliver content to broadcast operations. In larger facilities, there might be an additional department or group that handles the content and its preparation for air (ingest department, in many cases) outside of master control/broadcast operations.

Broadcast operations plays the content as called for by the ***schedule***, and then produces an ***as-run log*** (or just *log*) which is typically generated by the automation system, and shows which elements played, in what order, and the exact time each ***element*** aired. Generally, traffic takes the as-run log and ***reconciles*** it against the schedule. If the station is for-profit, this information is sent to Accounts Receivable in the Business Department and is used for billing the clients. Traffic may reschedule missed spots discovered during reconciliation.

Engineering maintains the equipment of the station. Engineering is generally led by a ***chief engineer***, *engineering manager,* ***director of engineering and operations*** or *operations manager*, and in some larger markets, it is a vice president title. In most cases, broadcast operations and the master control operators report through engineering in some manner. There are facilities where the operations are large enough to report directly to the general manager/vice president. In the rare case where a station does a lot of live programming, Broadcast operations may report through the production department. Many stations are so small that very few people do everything and no departmentalization makes any sense at all.

In an *OTA* station, there is a designated *chief operator* under the FCC rules. This person assumes the primary responsibility for the technical operation, especially keeping the documentation of the station in FCC compliance, and may be any employee or designated person.

Marketing, news, fund raising, quality assurance and production departments may exist at your facility. Less common are the departments that serve a specialized need; for example, a home shopping *network*, military network, and the major networks all have departments that handle specific functions. For instance, customer service phone banks would probably be found at home shopping networks. A *standards and practices* department, which controls the acceptableness of program content, exists at the major and more sensitive networks, but few other places. Each specialized department is likely to have some integration with broadcast operations. Figure 02-02 shows a typical station business workflow.

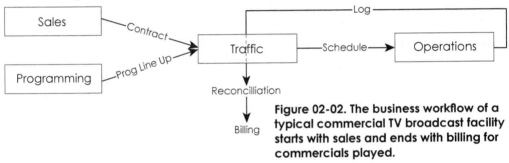

Figure 02-02. The business workflow of a typical commercial TV broadcast facility starts with sales and ends with billing for commercials played.

The Content Workflow

The content workflow is of chief concern to broadcast operations. Key to this is the method of storing content, and where and how any live or pre-produced content comes into the facility. There are typically two ways stations receive (or *acquire*) content: media or content *files* sent over the Internet, satellite, microwave, wireless *networks*, or dedicated data circuits (often stored in *the cloud*); and *transportable or physical media*, including DVDs, disc drives, solid state memory, and the ever-rarer videotape and virtually nonexistent film. *Archives* might still contain long retired tape formats such as two-inch wide quadruplex videotape and 16mm or rarely 35mm film.

The cloud is a relatively recent concept within the computer world. Cloud computing refers to services, storage and/or applications accomplished at another, often distant, location. The idea is that you can gain capabilities: storage capacity, computing resources, etc. without buying hardware, investing in overhead, training, and then maintaining software updates generally found within an on-site IT infrastructure. Many broadcast functions can happen in the cloud.

Acquisition is the step where the content is brought into the facility. In the case of an *MVPD*, this might be rooms of satellite receivers and fiber fed decoders. In broadcast stations especially, there are *catch servers* attached to satellite antennas and the Internet, or a live network feed via satellite. Boxes of storage drives (or flash memory cards), DVDs or tapes delivered via mail or courier work also.

Files sent over the Internet often use *File Transport Protocol* (*FTP*) as a means of transfer, while satellite systems often use a *pitcher* at the hub and *catchers* at the receiving sites to move content files and verify that they have arrived intact. The process delivers a *proof of delivery*.

In either case, with the increasingly rare exception of an analog tape, all **non-real-time** content is moved, stored and played as a digital media file. **Real-time** content, or *live* content, is received as a continuous stream from cameras, satellite, microwave, graphics devices, branding equipment, and the like. Sometimes a continuous program stream is referred to as a *linear* or *live linear* program. An **OTA** program is linear programming.

Stations can only reasonably directly playback a limited number of the possible content mediums and formats, and there are many resolutions, screen sizes, **compression** formats, and various other configurations. Hence, format conversion -- **transcoding** from one format to another -- or simply *dubbing* a piece of content from one physical media to another is a key function of broadcast operations. **Dubbing** involves playing back a piece of content in real-time and recording it or **ingesting** it in the desired format. Transcoding is a file conversion process that occurs out of view and can be slower or faster than real-time, depending on the speed of the equipment and complexity of the conversion.

Whether a file transfer, transcoding, or dubbing is involved, the process is referred to as **ingest** and the workspace is an **ingest station**. The ingest process includes validating that the audio and video levels are correct, trimming the content for time if necessary (tops and tails), validating that the content is correct, and maybe making simple adjustments to levels. Additional *quality control* (QC) or *quality assurance* (QA) processes are generally applied after the content is ingested to verify that the content is ready for use. This may be largely automated to determine that things like audio levels, video levels, times (length or duration and in and out points), are correct, and other portions, such as closed caption and additional audio tracks are present. Automated QA/QC can't tell if the content is correct (it can't distinguish a soda pop can from a car ad) so an operator generally looks and listens before the material is released for on air use.

Generally there are some **metadata** captured, or at least validated as part of the ingest process. We will go into greater detail on metadata later; at this point, know that metadata refers to a collection (usually detailed and very specific) of data related to a broadcast signal or a file in a server. Time-specific content must have kill dates (a date when a spot or promotion should stop airing). It is also a good idea to identify airdates for programs, especially if they are *topical* (an example would be the many daily entertainment news shows available in syndication).

Video file servers, or simply video servers, form the core of virtually all facilities. In most facilities, a video server handles stored **non-real-time** content playback. Some facilities will integrate live programming, or outside programming in real-time from a network, sporting event or news organization, with what is played back from the file server. In some facilities, only spot announcements are placed on

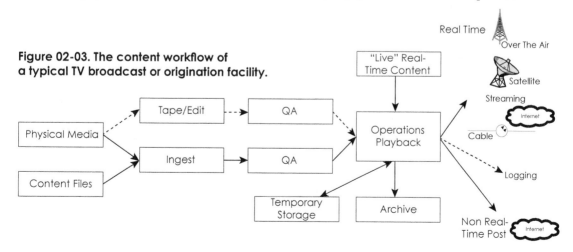

Figure 02-03. The content workflow of a typical TV broadcast or origination facility.

the video server, and tape or other mediums form the bulk of the playback. This is especially true for syndicated programming that may be bicycled (when one station is done with the program, it ships it to the next station) from one facility to another, though as the cost of digital distribution comes down, this too is becoming increasingly rare. Figure 02-03 outlines the station workflow.

The Roles of the Key Departments
• Operations and Engineering

This is the department where *master control operators* (*MCOs*) work. In some cases, mostly very large facilities, operations and engineering are separated functions, however most operations and engineering departments are composed of master control operators (typically 5 to 7 for an individual television station, a number that allows 24-hour coverage, vacations, and support functions) and maintenance engineers or technicians. There may be one or more transmitter engineers as needed. The technical team is likely to be SBE certified at some level from Certified Television Operator, Broadcast Technologist or Broadcast Engineer to some higher level.

Leading the operations and engineering department is a *chief engineer* or a manager or *director of engineering and operations*. As a practical matter, the technical staff does a fairly poor job of operations and the operations staff generally is not as technically proficient as the broadcast engineers. Rarely is a person skillful at both operations and engineering, so as a practical matter a division of responsibilities and developing different proficiencies is more efficient and most common.

The relationship between master control and the technical staff is usually rather close. The engineering staff frequently is maintaining and servicing equipment. Sometimes it is because the operating staff has reported a failure (by opening a *trouble ticket* in many facilities). Other work is more every day. Both MCOs and technical staff can occupy the same room for hours on end, doing different tasks on the same equipment. Needless to say, some ballet of cooperation is needed.

Occasionally, operations and engineering are widely separated. In this case, engineering maintains any transmitter, facility equipment, and manages the *networks* (unless IT is separated from engineering, which happens mostly in IT- centric and large facilities). Operators may contact engineering through a more formal structure and process in this case.

• News

There is a certain informal hierarchy in television facilities. If there is a news department, it is almost a given they are the station's focus and given a high priority. The news department tends to use the most resources, and accounts for most of the station's revenues. They also have the most needs served from broadcast operations to support live shots, ingest content, and handle live shows and breaking news situations with rapidly changing elements. Broadcast operations may have a large number of duties tied to news support.

• Sales

If it's not the news department, it is likely the sales department that drives the station. Often (unless revenue comes from subscription, donations, or other sources) they produce the cash flow and profit, and may bring last minute changes in content (a new commercial) and schedule to broadcast engineering. Sales may need copies of content for their customers, production of spots, tagging, and customization of commercials, remote production, and more.

Most sales are predicated on the delivery of an audience to an advertiser. The more viewers watching, the more a commercial playback can demand in station revenue. Sales departments work from a *rate-card* that gives a rough idea of what a spot sells for. We say rough because discounts are often given for quantity, special circumstances, and other marketing deals.

In commercial **OTA** television, the Nielsen *ratings* typically drive the value of a commercial. While the *share* refers to the percentage of people watching your program versus all the other programs available, the *rating* refers to the number of households viewing the program. Broadcast television enjoys the highest *cost-per-thousand* (CPM) of any mass media ($28 in 2012, radio and cable are about $10). That's $28 for a thousand viewers watching a given 30-second commercial.

Sweeps are special ratings periods that are used to set the value of air time. Sweeps are generally November, February, May and July. Most stations restrict vacations during sweeps, and many *stunt* (air a promotional event) and run their best programming in sweep periods.

Prime Time (the evening hours after dinner for most facilities as this is the most watched *day-part*) are often the time of peak viewing and thus revenue, although news, sporting events, or other special programming often demands a premium and may have more opportunities for the station to insert commercials. Most broadcast operations will schedule their most experienced and able people in the prime-time shifts. There is often competition among master control operators to work the prime-time or news shifts. Why? Because they are the most engaging and stimulating shifts, and naturally, the facility would want the best operators in the higher-profile (and higher-revenue) time periods and special events.

You may also hear of *Prime Access* – this is the hour just before Prime Time. Typically, local stations run topical entertainment news shows, newer sitcoms or game shows in this time period. Prime access shows are often the costliest shows for the station to gain rights to air, and correspondingly, charge a premium amount for commercials. This hour can be just as critical as Prime Time.

Time periods are classically referred to as *day-parts*. The day-parts for many stations are: early morning (4 a.m. - 7 a.m.), daytime (7 a.m. -4 p.m.), news (4 p.m.- 7 p.m.), Prime Access (7 p.m.- 8 p.m.), Prime Time (8 p.m.- 11 p.m.), and late night (11 p.m. - 4 a.m.). Eastern and Central time zones generally air network programming at the same time (11 p.m. news in New York is the 10 p.m. news in Chicago). The Pacific region has its own time zone, and the networks are sometimes run out of Los Angeles with programs delayed from New York by three hours. The Mountain Time zone is a world of its own, generally following the news at 10 p.m. convention as the Central time zone does, but delays can be anything from one or two hours or more, and some local breaks are often offset by a few minutes to create the Rocky Mountain Minute where an extra spot or two can be slipped into prime time. The Mountain Time zone delays almost everything, and this can be done at the station or for a group of stations out of a hub traditionally in Denver or Phoenix, though this practice seems to come and go.

A station's spot inventory is called its *availabilities* or more commonly *avails*. There are many kinds of contracts for advertising. A typical contract specifies a given number of spots in rather defined shows or time periods. *Run of Schedule* (ROS) means that spots are spread throughout the contract period. *Co-op* spots have a local business buying time with the help of a product supplier looking to improve the sales of their product through that dealer. *Paid inquiry* (PI) spots are often shows (*program length commercials*) where the station gets paid only when the advertiser receives an inquiry from a viewer. PIs are sometimes used to fill unsold or unscheduled time slots or when a program isn't received or has a problem in playback.

General managers tend to be understandably sympathetic to the sales effort, given that a major portion of their responsibility is the financial performance of the station. Most general managers come from sales backgrounds. Making money is important to nearly everyone in most facilities.

• Promotions, Creative Services and/or Marketing

The promotions department is often next in the day-to-day view of broadcast operations. It is their job to increase revenue by holding a viewer longer and convincing them to come back for later programs. Promotions often require pieces of content, copies, and other support from broadcast operations. Many stations have a policy of filling any last minute air time that might become available with promotions, which usually is a last minute task for the broadcast operations staff. For this reason, it's a good idea to have a *hot list* available of generic promos that can be run at a moment's notice to fill what might otherwise be *dead air*. One promotional element that has more recently become more prevalent is the snipe. Snipes are graphics superimposed over program material promoting a show, sub-channel, contest, and sometimes a commercial client. Typically seen as a graphic – animating or sliding onto the screen in the screen's lower-third – over programming, it usually remains on screen 10 to 20 seconds, then animates off the screen.

Promotions (creative services, or marketing in some facilities) also control the *prize closet*. In small stations, contest winners come in at all hours to collect their prizes, and MCOs might be asked to answer the night bell and retrieve winnings for visiting viewers, in particular after normal business hours. Currying the favor of the Promotions Department can often be good for *swag, chits* (gifts), or even an event ticket or dinner out every now and again. This department takes its job seriously and is often competing with the sales department for available air time.

• Public Affairs

In some facilities, there is also a public affairs department, which may be a staff of one, or a part of someone's duties. If there is a public service requirement, these people will schedule public service announcements (PSAs), public affairs shows, sponsorships and events. Frequently, public affairs conducts community ascertainments. These are surveys of public issues and may affect how the station serves the public as part of the station's FCC obligations. All station staff may be asked to assist in the effort especially in smaller markets.

• Traffic

Traffic is the most connected department to broadcast operations, so it's worth discussing in detail. As we mentioned at the beginning of this book, it is traffic that provides the **schedule** for all on air programming, retrieves the log, and are accountable for every $1/_{30}$ of a second (a single video frame) of what is to go to air. It also takes the as-run log and reconciles it against the schedule to generate billing.

Let's stop for a minute to review and elaborate on **schedules**, **logs** and **reconciliation**. This is a core function of broadcast operations. The traffic department developsschedules, usually using a computer-based traffic system built on a *plotter*. The plotter juggles the ads and other events to maximize profit while following all of the rules for placement. Once the data is entered, it might take several hours for the plotter to complete the schedule, and another couple of hours for checking and manual adjustment. Because plotters have little to do until needed, and then it's computationally intense work, they tend to be an ideal *cloud* computing or virtual machine candidate.

Ads have a series of rules. Times they can run, times they can't, placement next to certain events, minimum separations from competing advertisers, and certain ads can't run after weather events. Political ads often have elaborate restrictions. Airlines almost always have an automatic cancellation clause in their contracts in the event of an air disaster. There are too many rules for an MCO to know them all, or have the time to go back to read contracts (if they are available) to understand what can and can't be done. MCOs will often try for a **make-good** of a missed spot, and given the rules, it may or may not work, or worse, it might ruin something else. The make-good policies of a station are the best effort to recover lost revenue without causing problems elsewhere. They are often not intuitive.

Generally, traffic schedules are 24-hour periods that mirror the broadcast day. In most stations the broadcast day starts and ends at 5 a.m., however it can be midnight to midnight or any other time of day. Before the end of the broadcast day, the next day's schedule is *appended*, or attached to the currently running day's schedule; which is to say it is attached for a seamless transition from one day to the next. There are some broadcast workflows that are continuous where the schedule is assembled constantly well into the future. This is desirable, but complex, because the traffic department can (in most of these systems) make changes to the schedule even moments before air, or weeks in advance.

This takes us to the concepts of *day of air* and *moment of air* and introduces the concept of **archive**. More broadcast operations are moving to a workflow that allows changes right up to the moment of air. Any number of automation and traffic systems have branded their products that will do continuous programming. The master control operator's most immediate focus is generally the moment of air.

Archive is deep storage that is not always instantly accessible, used for content that may or may not ever air again. **Archives** may be *purged* of now useless material periodically to make room for more content. As the cost of storage continues to go down, the need to manage storage also becomes more relaxed. The master control operator often has duties to manage the storage; archiving material as needed and purging dead content to free up storage as needed. Think of the **archive system** as an extra storage space, just as many people have external hard drives on their personal computers for additional storage and backup protection. Retrieving content from the archive is referred to as *restoration* or *restoral* to the system that can play it back. Restoring archived content may take some time and often involves some complexity. The IT department, which is also backing up other files, often handles archiving. Often the largest challenge to archived material retrieval is simply locating it. *Media asset management systems* (MAMs) help search for archived material.

In any case, the schedule drives the on air product. In very few circumstances, the schedule is in fact aired perfectly without adjustments. Last minute changes, the variables introduced by live sports, news, and other live and unpredictable content, and errors all conspire to make the actual events differ from the **schedule**. What actually ran is captured in the **as-run log**. Logs may be a *manual log* (that is, on paper), but that is becoming increasingly rare. Most logs are now captured by the automation and playback systems. The log has a legal dimension in that it is the official record of what the station actually aired. The master control operator will be required to certify (sometimes with a signature, sometimes an electronic signature, sometimes implied) that the log is the accurate representation of what actually aired on the station to the best of their knowledge.

Logs are often supplemented with the use of *loggers*. Loggers record the on-air product and can be replayed to verify that the written log is correct. Loggers record the on air product at some reasonable level of quality and also display the date and time. Modern loggers are based upon hard drives and are searchable by a Web-based or other application – the same kind of equipment used for surveillance cameras. Loggers are especially useful after a major problem: they give you the chance to see what the viewers saw, and what, in fact, did or did not air. In the midst of a problem, it can be difficult determining exactly what aired and at what time; the task at hand is to fix the problem *first,* then piece together what happened later by viewing the logger.

Reconciliation is the process of taking the log and comparing it to the schedule (a.k.a., the program log in some settings). Comparing what actually played (or ran as in the **as-run log**) with what traffic scheduled to run. In some cases, the two are identical, but more often than not, a technical failure (the server failed during playback), a last minute schedule change (in almost all sporting events, most live events and sometimes news; some unexpected event will change the expected event and require that some scheduled event be delayed, dropped or added). A piece of content that didn't arrive in time or an operator error may cause a **discrepancy**. Reconciliation catalogs all of the discrepancies (commonly abbreviated as discreps or DRs – the bits of a discrepancy report) so that traffic can adjust billing or reschedule commercials (a **make-good**) or other program elements.

Sometimes a master control operator can reschedule a make-good inside the time period where the make-good will be accepted as good. A make-good doesn't always work as some commercials are fixed time, tied to a program, or restricted to a certain time period. Master control and traffic generally work together to understand how to handle a missed or defective commercial playback. The ways stations handle make-goods and discrepancies vary widely. Sometimes, master control has access to the contracts that the sales department executes that instruct the traffic department or parts of the contract that sets the times and conditions a commercial must meet, and is expected to make informed decisions concerning rescheduling. Stations have make-good rules for MCOs that are generalized, but it's not uncommon to have to call traffic after hours or on a weekend to approve a substitution or late add. Sales may make a last minute add, but most stations have learned that this is dangerous and difficult to deal with at all levels, so are discouraged, if not prohibited.

Part of this concept is to shorten the path between the traffic department and on-air operations. In some systems, the master control operator is tightly tied to traffic, maybe even with traffic duties. During less intense periods of the day, where there are few last minute changes, the master control operator may have a very minor role with the on air product, and be focused on preparing material for air, traffic or other duties.

As mentioned, traffic and master control work very tightly together in any successful facility. That said, the most likely places for tension in a facility is usually between operations and traffic or news. Needless to say, good working relationships here pay off in many ways.

• Production

A production department may or may not exist in your facility. Some facilities have limited or no studio facilities, and may not even possess any cameras or microphones. Some have extensive production departments that produce everything from commercials to daily programs. Operations staff may or may not have occasional production duties. Usually, production is one of the more exciting parts of the job.

• Programming

Programming departments range from a task done at corporate headquarters to a group of people who conduct research and determine what programs the facility runs, and maybe even what happens within some programs. Operations have few interactions with programming although tasks such as dubbing or copying content for the programming department's use might be required. Likewise, being the eyes and ears of the station, the master control operator may be asked to notify the programming department if certain events occur, particularly in programming that comes from outside the station. This department may have a significant interest in how to respond to sporting events that run very long, or any event that has a major impact on the station's programming.

3

ARCHITECTURES and DISTRIBUTION

The possible architectures for where the program starts, is stored, switched, processed, delayed, inserted, captioned, etc., and how that is distributed are endless. In the case of ***cable***, the miles travelled and the complexity of the systems that bring us our immense selection of programming is beyond the imagination of most people and the actual architecture a comfortable repetition of key components that are organized to produce the desired end product for others. Satellite and OTA delivery architectures might be a bit simpler, but still rather complex.

As a master control operator, and a number of other roles in broadcasting, you are or will become familiar with the technical architecture of your workplace, and likely have opinions about how to improve the design. There are no systems that can't be improved on or does not involve compromise no matter how well it is done or how much money is invested. These systems are complex enough that virtually every change results in some unintended consequence. Besides, needs and technology are always changing, so physical plants tend to be composed of legacy (old equipment and content that can't be thrown out and reasonably replaced) components as well as new, cutting edge equipment with their own issues.

Player-inserter

There is no single word or phrase for this, so we'll invent one just to get through this concept: player-inserter.

A player-inserter is more of a function than a device. Both of those terms have meanings; a player is a device or a piece of software that takes elements from tapes, discs, files, or whatever form content comes in, physical media, or data and plays them out to a video screen and speakers or headphones. Inserters can be hardware or software and may be tightly integrated to the player. Inserters insert any number of things from audio to graphics to whole content elements into a program. If you look at the way broadcast works, from the point of origin to the viewer, we have a string of player-inserters. There is at least one player-inserter function, often two, and sometimes three and four between the origin and the viewer. With the trend towards more, each moving closer to the viewer, allowing customizing the program to smaller and smaller groups of viewers until we reach a point where each viewer has his or her own player-inserter – just for the individual – which allows *dynamic advertising* where everyone gets his or her own commercials and other elements.

A broadcast master control is a player-inserter, generally with advanced functionality. It is difficult and expensive to work with real time video with high quality and precision – what we have come to call broadcast quality. Master controls are often a special, expensive, highly capable form of inserter-player. However, some are very simple, capable of inserting or splicing in different elements in cuts only fashion and without graphics or audio enhancements like snipes and voice-overs. These are often used for services that need little enhancement or customization such as home shopping and news carousels.

The basic content flow in any broadcast environment is from some point of origination to the viewer/listener. The basic means of financing (or *localizing*) this mostly long-form content is to pause periodically (at breaks or in the case of network feeds, station breaks) and insert short-form content (commercials). From the beginning, this pause and insertion was often done first at the national (broadcast ***network***) level, and then at the local, station level. During much of the day, and almost all of the time for *independent* stations (e.g.: WGN, KTLA, WTTV – stations without a regional or major national network affiliation), the long form content was produced or played back at the local station level.

For the most part, one could buy a national spot that covered the country, or a local spot that reached the coverage area of the given station. This is good for advertisers who market to wide areas, but very inefficient for advertising customers that have smaller marketing areas. Neighborhood businesses find that broadcast advertising is *inefficient*. For this reason, local and regional companies don't advertise nationally.

The most valuable advertising is the most *efficient*, meaning that it reaches only those who are prospective customers at the lowest price. *Impact* requires some work and good data to quantify, but television receives a higher CPM because the spots have more impact than other mediums. A good spot is worth the cost of production if the impact is increased.

Advertising impact and efficiency is largely a matter of reach and frequency: how many people see it, and how often. As an MCO, it's not always a mistake or a make good when you see the same spot or sponsor twice in the same break. Bookends are when an advertiser has a spot in the front of a break and the end, similar to having advertising on the covers of a printed magazine; it is more likely to have more impact.

This is where the concept of player-inserters applies. An individual viewer is looking all the way back to the originating source through a series of player-inserters. If I'm watching a sporting event on a handheld device or computer, I'm more likely looking at a player-inserter in the device that can insert a spot just for me, rather than a local station inserting spots just for devices in a given area, to a network inserting spots for the nation or region, and finally to a remote truck actually capturing the event and inserting content that is seen by everyone, everywhere (even internationally) – one player-inserter after another.

Player-inserters that operate at the *cable* headend, *MVPD*, set-top-box (STB) or device level tend to be simpler and less expensive. Broadcast networks and OTA broadcast stations' master control might be a player-inserter in function, but they can run under automation, insert *triggers* and other commands for downstream players, adjust audio and video, mix in complex layer after layer of graphics, do effects, transitions and more. The closer to the origination, the more capable the player-inserter is likely to be. A high quality, fully redundant master control is the ultimate player-inserter. An application on a device that stream switches to pick up personalized spots or overlays the local weather data being the unadorned down-to-earth minimum.

The contemporary station-level master control receives the content and triggers from an originating master control (or <u>is</u> the originating master control when running syndicated programs or local programming such as news), and passes that program output to player-inserters at various levels in the distribution chain that further *localize* the program. As this is written, most stations do at least a little of this for a Web feed, and others have separate derivative feeds for their MVPDs. That said, as this is written, this is early in the transition.

Proper insertion requires *triggers* that are standardized. Traditionally, DTMF (touch tone) sequences (usually a very fast 123# to start and 123* to stop ["#" is pronounced "pound" and "*" is pronounced "star") were and often still are used, preferably on a separate ("out of band" so it cannot be seen or heard) audio channel, but your station might take in *SCTE-35* triggers and hand off SCTE-35 triggers to downstream player-inserters at *cable* head-ends, and repeaters. Your station may also send Web based triggers like IAB-VAST. There is a great deal of complexity in a world where your master control is no longer the last player-inserter in the chain. At this point, what is required on the MCO's part is an awareness and understanding of this development in the broadcast business, and of course, if your facility does distribute in such ways, how to drive this part of your facility.

Local, *hyper-local*, and personalized playbacks allow more efficient advertising, being able to target the ads to smaller groups, and not reaching those who are not in the target group. Directing this ever more personalized content requires elaborate systems that dynamically adapts to the viewer and the advertisers *campaign*.

Sub-Channels: Digi-Nets or Dot-twos

The arrival of digital television also allowed stations the ability to distribute multiple program sources within the 6MHz of RF bandwidth (in North America) allotted to them. The two principle issues with sub-channels have been: how do you program these sub-channels, and how do you operate them technically and cost-efficiently?

Initially, the most common programming on sub-channels was local weather: stations could buy black boxes that would convert data from the local weather service to digital graphics that could be aired 24/7. Over time, more groups came into the picture providing various types of programming to be used specifically on sub-channels.

The most popular programming categories that have developed to date are: nostalgia (1950s-1970s) television, foreign language programming, music videos, as well as various forms of all-news and information programming. Most news is carouselled, meaning the last newscast is repeated over and over. With some effort, new spots might be rotated through and with even more effort, updated weather segments etc., might be inserted. With substantial effort, an existing news department can take portions of their local newscasts, news product, and some live or at least updated material, and piece them together to form a local headline news service that is fresher.

Channel-In-A-Box

The next logical progression from the player-inserter concept is the channel-in-a-box concept. For several years, broadcasting facilities would tie together many different pieces of hardware, each having a link to the master control automation system. Ten or 15 years ago, this was a practical way of equipping a traditional facility and controlling its various elements. Many of these systems are still on air albeit with upgrades.

In the last decade or so, regulatory, economic and staffing reduction pressures dictated the industry come up with a quick, cost-efficient way of being able to add channels to an existing plant. The solution was creating an all-in-one software application running on off-the-shelf hardware. This concept makes it easier for a broadcast facility to add sub-channels to their existing lineup efficiently and without a huge investment in either equipment or staff. Depending on the vendors, some are opting to use the channel-in-a-box hardware/software for not only their sub-channels, but also their primary channel as well.

Mostly these boxes are reduced sized versions of the hardware and software that make up traditional automation, graphics and playback systems. Others are *virtualized* in that they are entirely software running on common computing platforms. Ultimately, a television station's entire work and content flow is simply a computer program.

Channel-in-a-box systems have a real advantage in some disaster recovery scenarios. One can operate two systems, miles apart (typically one at a studio and the other at the transmitter) and mirror them, so the loss of one system does not take you off the air. The scenario is a bit more complicated than that in real life, but easier and more cost effective than other approaches.

Stepping On

When a program has *availabilities* for commercial insertions, there are two ways of approaching it: Either break the program into segments and let master control ingest each segment and play out the segments between breaks, or send this as a continuous *sustaining program*.

A sustaining program doesn't stop, and it doesn't have discrete segments. If you play it off storage or run it live, the program continues from start to finish. Within the program, availabilities for insertions are either *black holes*, or filled with default content. Black holes are sometimes just a blank screen for the duration of the break. Sometimes black holes are filled with a *slate* (an on-screen text box) to indicate what break this is, sometimes with a countdown clock.

Most network programs arrive as sustaining content. Certainly anything live is. Black holes are not popular, so even if the program supplier anticipates that an insertion will *step on* the *built in* break, they will still put in some default break with promotions, public service, and if billable, commercials. An average hour of network programming allows for roughly 90 seconds of local break at the mid-point, and perhaps 60 or 90 seconds at the end. Some networks will have their logo moving around on the feed, similar to a computer screensaver. Be aware there might be times you will need to cover a network spot or promo for various reasons. Make sure you're using the most recent ***timing sheet*** for the show.

Timing needs to be *tight* as when one inserts by *stepping on* or *covering* running content, even a small timing error will give a *flash frame*, just a snippet of the spot being *covered*, or an *up cut*. A *down cut* is also possible with timing errors of just a frame (in the US, $1/30$ second, others nations and systems may be $1/25$ or $1/60$ second for other typical frame rates) when a spot rolls just a little early, down cutting the last frames of the program content.

The Air Chain

In ***OTA*** facilities, the *air chain* almost always is composed of the same kinds of pieces in nearly the same order, and it's a mostly a straight line, one piece hooked to another; hence the term *air chain*. In other facilities, the similarities fade.

The air chain starts with the master control position, the output of which is the properly switched program elements playing back from whatever source or storage. The master control position adds program elements: bugs (the channel name or number you see in the lower-third of the screen), effects, graphics, and voice-overs. They exercise control over the starting and stopping of the program, and monitor audio and video levels. ***Emergency Alert System (EAS)*** equipment is either adjacent to, or just after the MCR switcher output.

This must go in turn to a ***multiplexer*** where it is combined with other master control and program outputs, ***PSIP (Program and System Information Protocol***; more on this later), and other data and formatting to create the ***transport stream (TS)***. The TS is the combined packetized data streams necessary to carry one or more video outputs plus related and unrelated audio programming as well as the information needed by the television or other display device to present this properly (the right audio with the right video, the right video and audio formats, the right guide data, etc.).

That is all complicated and detailed, but the important part is that the TS is the end product of the facility, and it all comes together as packets of data multiplexed into a transmission stream.

In most ***OTA*** stations, the transmission stream is sent over a ***studio-to-transmitter link (STL)*** to the transmitter(s) from the ***control point***. The STL might be a microwave link, fiber, or less often, an Internet connection or satellite.

TS Technical Details

All transmission streams have packet identifiers (PIDs) that call out the purpose of each packet. They also have a *program map table* (PMT) that indicates all of the PIDs in use, and a *program association table* (PAT) that lists all the programs in the TS. There is even a *program clock reference* (PCR) necessary to create and use the TS. Most of these are more or less fixed and operate out of view, however, the *Program and System Information Protocol* (PSIP) is dynamic and the MCO might interact with this portion of the TS that carries program schedule data. PSIP also carries rating data, the terrestrial *virtual* channel table (TVCT), the *master guide table* (MGT) and *event information tables* (EIT) that are necessary for a television receiver to know where to tune, what to display, ratings, and more.

The TS can be carried as an *ASI*, SMPTE 310 (typically a short coaxial cable), and sometimesTS on IP (TSoIP) from the multiplexer to the *STL* or *exciter*, though SMPTE 310 is the most common. This is of note to the MCO in so far that only specialized test equipment can decode the TS directly as the format for the TS is unique and different from the SDI used just about everywhere else in the facility, even though *ASI* and SMPTE 310 are on coax with BNC connectors just like video.

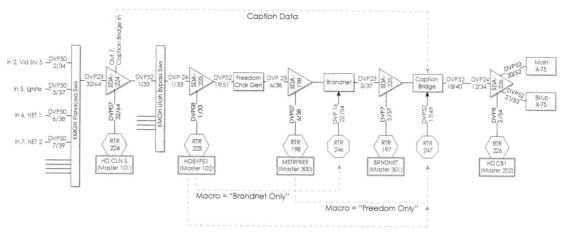

Figure 03-01. A typical OTA air chain; in this case, the KMGH-TV air chain. The origination path is above. The transmission path is below. Note that signals go into and out of routers and patch bays. Virtually every piece of the air chain can be bypassed if it fails, which results in a loss of function. Note too that a router or switcher under automation control and driven from a hub is used to select the playback source. In some cases the bypass router is activated to take manual control of the air source, shunting the hub and automation out of the loop. Breaking news and weather are typically done on the bypass router.

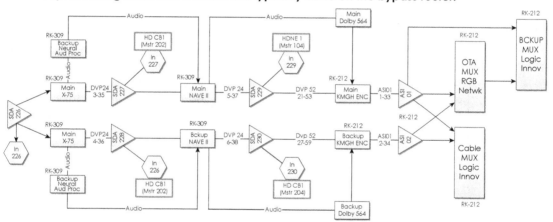

At the transmitter, the TS is modulated into a ***radio frequency*** (***RF***) signal by an ***exciter*** (a *modulator* with enough output to drive the transmitter), and amplified by the transmitter and radiated by the antenna. Frequently, the ***MCO*** will have some responsibility for monitoring the pieces of the air chain. Most OTA stations have backup STLs, transmitters, and even antennas that the MCO might be required to put on line in the event of a failure. There should be a process and part of your station training to know when and how to execute these moves. And because several transmitter functions are relatively uncommon activities, a nearby binder should contain easy-to-follow instructions for most commands. Figure 03-01 shows a typical station air chain.

Monitoring the air chain can be as simple as a TV set tuned to the OTA service, or if the transmitter can't be seen from the studio (or master control location), a more elaborate ***transmitter-to-studio link*** (***TSL***) might return *confidence* video to a monitor and transmitter data to the remote control. In order to save bandwidth, confidence video is low bandwidth video, just good enough to know that the transmitter is working, but not good enough for *critical viewing*.

When stations made the transition to digital transmission, it was decided most stations using VHF spectrum move to the higher frequency UHF band or decidedly better coverage especially in urban settings and where indoor antennas were anticipated. To keep their *brands* and their channel numbers the same, a method was devised to shift the actual broadcast frequency channel to the UHF range, but continue to have the televisions display the legacy (*virtual*) channel number as it always had been. In other words, if a channel 5 was shifted to RF channel 29, TV receivers would still access it as channel 5; the means of doing this is a PSIP element that contains important data about the channel and plays a major role in the DTV signal. If PSIP codes are missing or wrong, most digital TV receivers won't recognize the presence of an otherwise usable DTV signal. It is the PSIP that identifies an over-the-air signal that may be transmitted from digital channel 29 but appears on a home receiver as virtual Channel 5.1, and establishes the sub channels 5.2, 5.3 and so on.

Centralcasting Architecture

As mentioned earlier, *centralcasting* comes in two basic forms: remote control or thin, or the more intensely centralized full bandwidth. In the remote control version, the programming, network receive antennas, spots, file servers, etc., are located at the station and controlled via a narrow bandwidth connection from the central location (*NOC* or *BOC*). The thin bandwidth approach may permit unattended operation for most of the day at the stations but requires local file servers and a considerable amount of equipment on site at the station location.

The full bandwidth approach makes sense where enough affordable connectivity is available. In the example below, two on-air servers provide two multiplexed content streams to operate two stations on a commonly available circuit (MPLS or a dedicated DS-3 are typical telecom standards in the U.S. for circuits with suitable bandwidth and reliability).

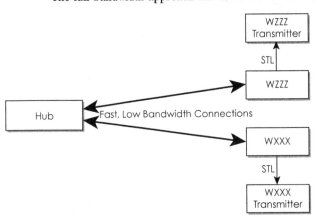

It also allows programming from the station site back to the BOC to be switched into the program stream to be broadcast. Here, all the heavy lifting is done at the BOC. There are far fewer timing issues with this configuration given that all the latencies and delays are known and don't change and the BOC is controlling something it can see without latency.

Figure 03-02. Thin centralcast model essentially remote controls a station from a distant broadcast operations center. Generally, the thin model works best in smaller markets with limited connectivity, but the thin connection also makes monitoring, accurate switching, and some fancier master control operations more difficult.

Another way of describing centralcasting architectures is *hub and spoke* or distributed, and several other unique configurations. Thin or full bandwidth, most architectures have a hub, *BOC*, or *NOC* as a core, with connections (spokes) to each station or distribution point.

The BOC, the broadcast operations center, is where master control and content-oriented operations are performed. A NOC, the *network operations center*, is where the distribution network, physical plant, computer centers, equipment, and services are monitored and overseen. If they are combined, one might use the term NOC/BOC, pronounced "knock-bock."

It is widely believed that *centralcasting* will continue to be the future of the business. Centralcasting can be done by cooperatives (stations in a city or region that join together), third-party (out-sourced

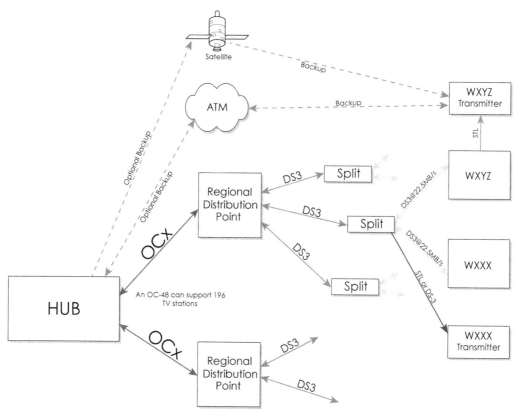

Figure 03-03. The full bandwidth centralcasting model sends complete and ready for broadcast programming from the BOC to the transmitter. It requires fatter pipes and higher quality of service (QOS) connectivity.

to a service provider), or group (a group owner centralcasts their own stations). Many broadcasters realize that it isn't necessary to have the master control operation in their building in order to completely control what is broadcast. The issue of program stream reliability is a major factor. Expensive redundant program feeds or local backup operators can impact the economic incentives offered by centralcasting.

Refer to Chapter 14F for an in-depth discussion of centralcasting issues.

Cable

The **head end** is the center of a **cable** system. Here all the program streams are placed on a cable in mostly 6MHz-wide slots. Most cable systems have 750MHz or more of bandwidth, though this bandwidth also serves data, security, telephone and other services. A series of amplifiers continue to boost the signal as it is attenuated by the cable, bringing it eventually to a customer. Current cable systems are composed of **QAM** (quadrature amplitude modulation, pronounced "kwahm") digital signals that can carry many more services in the same digital spectrum slot; usually 10 or 12 standard-definition or four high-definition services in a 6MHz bandwidth, or more with advanced compression and higher data rates. QAM allows cable to carry **4K** ultrahigh definition movie-like content where other distribution cannot do so well. Ever fewer systems also have a few legacy analog signals where older television sets can see a few basic services. Television stations often have a small analog system for internal use, mostly because analog modulators cost almost nothing, while even low-end digital modulators and encoders are at least hundreds of dollars per channel.

Centralcasting Technical Details

Many traditional master control functions are difficult without decoding the video from the TS and re-encoding it after the master control functions are complete. This is expensive and clumsy, and degrades the quality by requiring the additional encoding step. *Stream splicing* is popular where no real master control functions are required other than cutting from one element to another, and all the content is already encoded. Cable systems and some broadcasters with centralcasting use this technique. More advanced stream splicers can do more, but as of this writing, the state of the art doesn't quite duplicate what a baseband master control can do in terms of audio and video control and processing. Complicated digital video effects (DVE) moves and layers of graphics have yet to be done well enough and economically enough to replace baseband master control functions where the level of performance is high.

Where downstream commercial insertion is desired, the MCO might also have to be aware of triggers sent to the downstream equipment to set off the insertion. Traditionally, the MCO or the automation generates a touch-tone command (DTMF), which is sent on an audio channel to the insertion gear. A digital trigger, *SCTE-35*, is popular for stream insertion systems, and some use a trigger placed in the video (*ancillary data* is provided for in digital video, and a similar *vertical interval signaling* can be used in analog TV; however, compression systems and some processing removes these triggers placed in video) and retrieved by special equipment. Triggers are often sent exactly five-seconds or one-second in advance of the insertion. This *dead-roll* time can vary from one user to another, but accounts for the time a playback machine might need to come up to speed and play.

Most of the full bandwidth centralcasting schemes are based on using terrestrial fiber DS-3 circuits, or MPLS (Multiprotocol Label Switching is a protocol that allows less expensive higher adjustable bandwidths on **IP** networks with low latency and high quality, so it useful for sending video as well as other traffic). A DS-3 circuit can carry 45Mb/s in both directions. This bi-directional capacity allows the station to send commercials, news, and other content back to the centralcasting facility for use on the air. Program schedules and other information, including communications and sometimes computer control, EAS, and other functions can also be carried. A United States DTV station transmits 19.4Mb/s thus a single common DS-3 circuit can carry two DTV stations at once.

Timing is the great challenge, in that all of the pieces tend to delay signals. The MCO needs to switch in real time, but that might mean a live element from the station is *pre-cued* maybe seconds in advance of the switching point. Likewise monitoring the transmitter's output is going to be seconds delayed from when it left master control.

Others have moved to largely IP delivery (probably the end game). The digital signals are not the same as OTA broadcast, and need a separate *set top box (STB)* or *smart TV,* or *connected TV.* Services on cable are often encrypted and the STB or suitable display decrypts the program when supplied the correct authorization data through the cable. Cable can also carry *video on demand* (VOD) and other services. Local *franchise* agreements may require that the cable system provide certain services, like community programming.

Many cable systems program local news, sports, and other entertainment, which is where again master control comes into play. Even if the system does only limited commercial insertion, there are master control functions such as *ingest* and quality control that need to be done. On a larger scale, there are regional and national cable networks, in particular for sports, which are functionally and essentially the same as an OTA station. About as many MCOs work in cable stations or for cable networks (sometimes called netlets), than work in OTA stations.

Satellite DTH

Satellite shows up in two places in the MCOs world. The first is the ***direct to home (DTH)*** satellite providers. These services bring the local television station into the home via small dish satellite systems. *Spot beams* allow satellites to reuse the same ***transponder*** frequencies in several areas allowing *local into local* carriage of local television stations via satellite to customers in the ***DMA***. DTH Satellite looks and feel a lot like cable systems, but without an inherent return path, and no way to subdivide distribution more finely than a spot beam, there is no ***IP*** or VOD, etc. without effort beyond what cable does. Some DTH satellite services use Internet, wireless service, or even telephone to establish a return path. While the use of multiple satellites can allow DTH to have far more bandwidth than cable has, that bandwidth has to be shared by all of the services and users. Cable can break IP services down to the neighborhood or even home, making large numbers of very individualized feeds possible.

DTH falls under ***MVPD*** rules, so while they have access to a wide variety of programming, they also have to pay TV stations for retransmission, and are subject to must carry.

Over The Air Viewers vs. Cable & Satellite Viewers

In almost all cases, there are far fewer people watching an ***OTA*** station via its OTA transmitter than watching via cable and satellite. Many master controls monitor the output of local cable, DTH and MVPD providers with as much interest as the OTA transmitters, and move to remedy any loss of programming with as much vigor as if it was the station's legacy OTA transmitter.

Because of this fact, should the over-the-air transmitter either go off-air totally or intermittently, most stations feed direct-to-home satellite systems and cable systems directly, rather than via the transmitter. Stopping the program will disrupt those non-OTA viewers needlessly and lead later to program timing problems. Even more than that, you really have no idea when transmission will be restored, so rolling programming simply turns into a *join in progress*, which is likely easier to deal with than stopping and starting playback.

Satellite Intermediate Distribution

The second way MCOs deal with satellites are ***TV receive-only (TVRO)*** systems. TV receive-only dish antennas or systems is a term that generally refers to larger dish antenna systems, more often used by TV facilities to receive the lower power (than DTH) *fixed satellite service* (FSS) programming, generally distributing content for rebroadcast. Cable nets will also often distribute their programs to cable headends via FSS satellites; hence the reason one sees larger dish antennas near most broadcast facilities and cable headends. In general, satellite is a more efficient distribution system when many receive locations are involved, or locations that don't have viable terrestrial connectivity. As the name implies, TVROs don't uplink and have no transmit capabilities.

Individuals, households, hotels, sports bars, venues, cruise ships and the like may use *BUDs* (Big Ugly Dish, more of a nickname than an actual term, but broadly used to indicate a TVRO not used for intermediate distribution to a headend or broadcast facility) to receive broadcast services under some conditions, though in many parts of the world these are becoming rarer in favor of DTH delivery.

Internet Distribution

TV anywhere is both a concept and a mantra. As this is written, the amount of broadcast content viewed on the Internet is growing. This may be ***real-time***, or ***non-real-time*** *video on demand*.

There are dozens of video formats, even more screen sizes, and more than a handful of ***compression*** and packaging formats. For the MCOs purpose, we'll draw a line here and say that in this distribution, content goes not to a transmitter but to a *platform*. Web services are bi-directional (and thus capable of being interactive), where as broadcast television alone is not. This means the viewer can and may come to expect interaction with the Web content; select the content, fast forward, replay, pause on one device and resume on another. There may be rights involved, targeted advertising that knows who is watching and what to show them, billing functions, click-throughs, geo-located and geo-restricted services. In short, this distribution medium is much more complex and capable than OTA broadcasting. Just a survey of Web delivery would take a book this size, and given that it's a child of the Web, constantly shifting, it is best studied on the Web.

Still, the **MCO** has to service this distribution, largely by *repurposing* content. There may be different edits of news stories that take advantage of the longer times viewing a Web viewer might have for some particular item. There might be shows and spots that can't be shown on the Web because of rights issues. There are Web-specific ads that aren't necessarily video.

Most facilities automate as much of this Web repurposing as they can, but as automation has limited the number of people working in broadcast, the Web seems to be demanding more MCOs or Web workers, or whatever moniker they are or will be given.

Some stations have a digital or Web group that manages and creates this content, and there may be a digital sales group also.

A Web platform has two key components, and potentially thousands of other important components. Content is given to a *publisher* that then turns it over to one or more **content delivery networks (CDN)**. A good deal of the work can be done by the CDN *in the cloud*.

Virtually everything MCO-wise, from QA to prepping, needs to be done for the Web services, hence the job opportunities.

There is one term that currently has the industry's attention: *over-the-top* or OTT. OTT is a special version of Internet delivery that currently relies on *multirate encoding* and *HTML chunking* to deliver video over both good and not-so-good connections over-the-top of firewalls. As this is written, OTT is sometimes used to refer to Web distribution generically, because OTT enables direct distribution to home television via *Internet service providers* (ISPs). While the terms Web distribution and OTT are not synonymous, for now they seem closely tied, and are often used interchangeably.

It is impossible to finish this chapter without noting that OTT distributors may someday receive MVPD status and be allowed to compete on an even basis with the other MVPDs, without having to build a distribution network or maintain satellites. [As I edit this book for the last time before layout, Aereo, probably the most recognized OTT broadcast supplier, has announced its plans to seek such status following a Supreme Court loss of its case to operate as a subscription DVR service in the cloud. By time this is published, the regulatory environment for OTT distribution will have changed, which is the constant. Media changes.] It's not so big of an advantage in and of itself as the OTT provider needs to pay for the content distribution (more later), but it seems unlikely that OTT, or whatever Web service this develops into will not have a major impact on how this business works, and how an MCO works in the business.

As a side note, some stations also have outdoor (billboard) advertising and *digital out of home* (DOOH) or digital signage businesses. Some of these have a video component, even live video. There is plenty of creativity in broadcasting. Not all of it finds a *business plan* that produces revenue.

4
WORKFLOW

A broadcast facility is all about *workflow*, and the master control operator is the critical human element that drives that workflow. As much as we would like to focus on the creative, entertainment and educational aspects of the work; the process boils down to getting content into the facility, conforming it to a consistent standard or a select group of useful (supported by the facilities equipment) standards and playing it out in the desired order at the correct time, with all the correct elements.

Content flow is the steps content takes through the facility from acquisition to distribution to the audience. *Workflow* is very similar, but looks not only at the steps the content takes, but the additional work involved in organizing and managing the content. Workflow may also look back into the sales and traffic systems where the workflow includes the *sales campaign* and *business analytics*, *orders* and *contracts*. Workflow can even include staff scheduling and resource *reservation* and *delegation* (a server might be reserved for a news cast, then control delegated to it from the news control room for the duration of the newscast, then returned).

For our purposes, workflow and content flow are nearly identical in the master control piece of the broadcast system. Figure 04-01 outlines the basic workflow of a TV station.

Workflow is a gigantic topic, and there are many ways to assemble a workflow. Again, for our purposes, we'll go through the pieces and processes that are the building blocks of any facility's workflow.

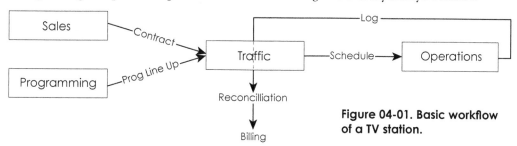

Figure 04-01. Basic workflow of a TV station.

Video, IP Routers & Video Mixers

Broadcast facilities are built around at least two routers, a video (and often audio) *baseband* router and an ***Internet Protocol*** (***IP***) router, or a system of routers.

To be fair, there is an emerging *Audio Video Bridge (AVB)* technology, SMPTE 2022, and some proprietary data protocols that combine a lot of the characteristics of *Ethernet* and baseband video and audio. Most do more than carry video and audio with other data for command, control and timing, all improvements to the art of moving video and audio around. This convergence seems to be driving architecture to a single Ethernet based router system. Ethernet, those eight wire cables and connectors (and their optical equivalents) can carry more than just Internet Protocol (IP).

A video router is a real-time device and the video and audio it switches are most often synchronous. Video routers may be analog, but most are digital utilizing ***Serial Digital Interface*** (***SDI***) that carries standard definition (SD), high definition (HD), and various higher definition (UHD, 4K) video and audio.

The reason the video is synchronized is so that it can be mixed; which is to say combined. For example, a video feed might have a *graphic overlay* or be part of an effect such as a *squeeze-back* or *cross-fade*. To work with video in this manner, the video signals must arrive at the mixing or effects device at the same time (or within the timing range of the equipment) and it is most convenient at this time to do this work in baseband form. If *sync* is lost, the images shift and audio clicks, or the equipment simply stops processing the signal.

Video mixers can be called a master control switcher, or just referred to as "the switcher." These can be large or small and may include any number of built-in effects, audio controls, and machine interfaces (to start and stop equipment for example). If one operates in manual mode, it almost always is done by pushing the buttons of the master control switcher. These switchers are an elaborate control for what is basically a video router, and often are physically built into sections of larger video routers, though they may be separate.

SDI video is connected via coaxial cable with *BNC* connectors (as is analog video and synchronization signals) up to about 100 meters or 300 feet with good cable. Alternately, *balanced, unshielded twisted pair* (UTP is what *Ethernet* and telephones use) with *balluns* (short for balanced/unbalanced, a conversion device for coax to UTP) can be used, and much longer runs can be made with fiber. A studio camera might be more than 100-meters from master control, so some device must be installed mid-path to extend the range.

IP traffic is carried on UTP CAT-5, CAT5-E, or CAT-6 (each category is better [faster, further] than the last) Ethernet cables are composed of four unshielded twisted pairs. There are also a number of faster more sophisticated connections including Firewire and other fiber-based connections. Baseband video (SDI) is carried on coaxial cables where a single inner conductor is shielded with a wire mesh, metal foil, or both.

The *Ethernet IP* router is not necessarily real time, and may even ignore synchronization. In broadcasting there is a useful distinction between Ethernet; the physical wire and sometimes physical switching, and IP; a protocol used to move packets of data.

While IP dominates the Internet, and almost everything in the networked world, because it packetizes data into packets that don't always arrive at their destination(s) at an exact enough time for video, it limits how video and audio can be mixed and processed and encounters delays. As of this writing, most broadcast engineers believe that eventually everything in facilities will be done on UTP or fiber, whether AVB or a more proprietary (e.g., as this is written, Evertz is promoting its IPX system) supplants *SDI* and *ASI* is merely a prediction at this time.

Probably most important is that SMPTE has been working since 2007 on the SMPTE 2022 standard, which has since expanded to cover several types of IP video transport. The first two sections of the standard cover IP protocols for compressed, constant bit-rate video signals in MPEG-2 transport streams. Newer sections of the standard cover two different kinds of variable-rate compressed video signals, as well as methods for carrying uncompressed video and hitless protection switching. As this is written, it is too early to tell how this develops and how quickly or widely it is accepted.

One other small detail about Ethernet: it can supply up to 51 watts with power over Ethernet (PoE). That might seem like a small detail, but AVB with PoE means a single wire can provide input content, take output content, synchronize it, control the device, and even power small devices that might otherwise have wall-warts (those often black plastic blob power supplies that take up plug space, fall out with devastating consequences, often have thin breakable connecting wire, easy to pull out power connectors and are often inefficient and not very long lived). Anytime a lot of wires, power supplies and weaknesses can be easily and cheaply eliminated, broadcast engineering is interested.

Relatively short delays of even seconds encountered in distribution are generally not an issue, but delays of fractions of a second in the playout, production, and master control environment pose serious limitations. For example, inserting a graphic into video requires that the *pixel* (one dot of video) to be inserted, arrives exactly in time to replace the pixel it is being laid over – millionths of one second – or it will land in the wrong place on the screen. There are ways to correct for delays, buffers that hold the early arriving video until ready for use, but if the delays are too long, the correction a buffer makes may have noticeable consequences.

Frame Synchronizers are the ultimate buffer. Often they are used to synchronize the video coming from outside of the facility to the synchronous video inside. The price is that the each frame synchronizer will delay the video by some indeterminate fraction of a frame (zero to 1/30 second). The benefit is that the resulting video will be timed for switching and processing, and it will be *stable*, which is to say a hit upstream is cleaned up so the output is unconditionally stable even if the source video fails completely. An MCO will often have to adjust frame synchronizers and audio delays (generally built into the frame synchronizer) to get the audio levels and timing (*lip sync*) correct, and maybe even video levels or format conversion (e.g., *SD* to *HD*, 720p to 1080i). Usually the largest issue is delaying the audio to match the delay in the video caused by multiple frame synchronizers, compressors and players. Video being more complex, it almost always takes longer than audio to manipulate and time, so the lips move on screen after the sound is heard. More than about a 1/10 second (100ms) is noticeable, and can be irritating if it even approaches 0.5 second (the ITU and others have suggested that the thresholds of timing detectability are about -125ms to +45ms, and the thresholds of acceptability are about -185ms to +90ms; note that sound leading video is more of an issue than when sound is late).

Video files, most often compressed by *video encoders*, and control and administrative messages and even email and telephone and intercom data flows through the IP switches. This router is perfect for transferring content for the video server to play back, logs, schedules, and controls to start and stop various functions. As this is written, there have been several years of work on equipment to mix video in a compressed IP environment, and some of this work can be done, however it is difficult to approach the capability of the baseband, uncompressed video router and environment.

The two routing systems form the heart of the broadcast facility. *IP* routers are generally redundant, often *dual homing* connections (two wires from each *network interface card* (NIC) located on each computer and device to each of the routers) between two IP routers that are load balanced in such a way that if part of one fails, the other redundant path and router will pick up the traffic. Managing this is generally not an MCO role, but reporting alarms and failures often is.

Video routers may be internally redundant and are generally wrapped in patch bays. One can generally (although not all facilities have *patch bays*) *patch around* a video router in an emergency just to keep something on the air. Video routers may contain monitoring equipment and generate multiviewer displays. Patch bays have a number of *jacks* that a patch cord with a plug on each end can plug into.

Most jacks in patch bays are *normalled* to something, so that *throwing a patch* will disconnect the normal source from a destination and replace it with the patched-in source. To patch around a router or any other device, the patch cord breaks the normal path into the router and inserts it in place of the normal path out. One reason for not having patches is that it's easy for an MCO or engineer to make mistakes and take things off the air or put things that shouldn't be on the air. Also patch bays age and will eventually fail in particular if used in uncontrolled (too wet or dry and too hot or cold) environments. Your station may have SOPs that involve MCO's throwing or making patches, but generally this is rare, either to recover something or deal with a special event such as maintenance, playing an old tape from a machine not on the router, patching in an *IRD* that was shipped overnight for a special event are typical rare patching events.

By convention, the top row of a patch bay has sources that are normalled to the patch slots and destinations directly below them. Plugging into the top patch steals that source from the destination below it. Plugging into a bottom row patch replaces the source above with what is on the cord. Sources and destinations can also be unpaired in patch bays (or a single slot) without normals. For example, a destination may not have a normalled source and is open waiting a patch cord to complete the circuit.

Analog audio patches are often the exception in that they can be half-normalled, where plugging into a source doesn't break the connection to the destination below, but bridges (parallels, like two plugs in an ac outlet) the audio from the top row to make a copy. It's useful because a source can be copied to a second destination without a distribution amplifier.

Broadcast engineers have many options when designing their facilities, and while *SDI* and *IP* are the norm for infrastructure, there is a class of facility whose primary purpose is transmission (distribution). Some large part of their purpose is pass-through, which may include some automated commercial insertion. In this environment, it may be that keeping the content in a compressed format is ideal for cost and quality reasons. ***Asynchronous Serial Interface*** (***ASI***) is electrically the same as ***Serial Digital Interface*** (***SDI***) with two important differences: It is polarity-sensitive, and the content is compressed, *not* baseband. Some distribution amplifiers and other devices invert the signal polarity, which has no effect on *SDI*, but will not pass *ASI* (many distribution amplifiers have half of their outputs inverted and the other half not). The data, however, is considerably different; *ASI* carries compressed content, sometimes as many as 100-services, on a single wire. Equipment can drop and add video, splice video into a stream, and decode *ASI* back to baseband *SDI*. In a multichannel facility where most content is rarely manipulated, you can see the advantage. In most facilities, there is a combination of many signal interconnects.

Integrated Receiver/Decoders (***IRDs***), often put out an *ASI* signal and or an *IP*, with all of the programs on a given satellite ***transponder,*** multiplexed into one stream. File servers can take this ASI or IP in, pick the right programs (identified by program identifiers) and *capture* (record) the video without ever decompressing or otherwise processing the content.

Compression

Serial Digital Interface (***SDI***) video (SMPTE 259M) is baseband video, as is analog video, meaning that there is no ***compression*** of the video. Every pixel of information is sent as either a discrete analog or digital value. Standard definition SDI requires 270Mb/s and *HD* requires 360Mb/s. High quality may require two wires or for 4K/UHD, four wires. A satellite transponder typically carries only 27Mb/s (60Mb/s is also popular, but many transponders carry less than 27Mb/s). Hence the video has to be compressed so that as many as 14 *SD* reasonable quality services in ***MPEG-2*** can be carried on a typical 36MHz-wide satellite transponder. Double or triple that for MPEG-4. This requires more than a 100:1 compression of the data. Storage presents the same issue. While $100,000 of storage might be affordable, $10 million for uncompressed video is probably not. There are many compression algorithms available and encoders of varying efficiency and cost; however, the two most common are the MPEG-2 and the MPEG-4 family (AVC, H.264, etc., are all in the MPEG-4 family). As this is written, H.265 is only becoming available, and it does represent continuing advancement in efficiency.

MPEG-2 is widely used for transport, storage and over-the-air broadcast. MPEG-4 is more efficient (requires less bandwidth for a given quality) and includes many features that favor IP ***streaming*** and is used everywhere there are no large legacy issues. Just because a file or stream is compressed in one of these families, does not mean that every device can play it. The file *wrappers* (an overhead that contains information about playback, interactivity, content, security, and more) and other subtle differences in the files or streams may make them unplayable by a given device without *transcoding* (flipping one flavor of file or stream to another).

The simplest way to transcode is to decode the video to baseband and re-encode in the desired formats. Broadcast facilities do this on large and small scales. Compressed video is often too processing intensive to work with directly economically, although compressed feeds can be stream-spliced to insert commercials or the like and stream processors continue to improve to the point where work can be done in the *compressed domain*. Staying compressed avoids *concatenation*, which is what happens when video is encoded, decoded, and re-encoded. At each *lossy* encoding step, the video quality suffers, so ideally one would like to avoid as many lossy compression steps as possible. Lossless compression doesn't offer the compression ratios desired for most applications. The effects of concatenation vary based on the types of compression and *depth* (compression ratio) in the chain. Transcoding MPEG-2 to MPEG-4 is generally benign enough that cable and satellite routinely take broadcast MPEG-2 services and transcode them to MPEG-4 to save bandwidth in distribution. If you compare the video from cable or satellite to OTA broadcast video, the superiority of the OTA signal is obvious. Some viewers with cable or satellite will also keep an OTA antenna for just this reason. Some MVPDs integrate OTA antennas into their STBs for an additional reason. There are no retransmission fees for signals received OTA.

Automation

The primary purpose of automation is to control some section of the video router or master control switcher, directing the right video to air and starting the playbacks following the on air schedule determined by the traffic department.

Not all facilities operate with automation…it is possible to broadcast entirely manually. In fact it can be fun to do so for a while simply because an operator can keep their hands on every piece of the process and arguably, a live person can make subtle adjustments to timing and the like that make the playback look better. Schools and community access stations are more inclined to run manually both for the educational value and to avoid the expense and complexity of automation.

As a practical matter, automation allows a single operator to run many services at once, where manually, several operators would be needed to run a single service for any length of time. Also, automation generally results in fewer on air mistakes.

As this book is written, there are no less than 50 automation companies in the world and no less than 200 automation systems available (some proprietary) to be configured in almost an infinite number of ways. Nonetheless, there is much in common from one automation system to another. There are exceptions to every rule, so please insert the phrase in most cases in front of every claim in this section. While automation is the core of the facilities workflow and the central tool, there are too many variations to cover them all here, and there are new features and functions being added to many systems regularly.

Automation systems provide *machine control* to operate a facility's content storage and acquisition equipment. The automation may cause more than just a playback to occur. "Recordings," steering satellite antennas, retuning and configuring satellite *integrated receiver/decoders* (*IRDs*), making video routes, timing program segments, moving cameras, are all tasks that may be accomplished automatically.

Automation Hardware

The heart of most automation systems is a *device controller* (Figure 04-02). Device controllers are basically a computer designed to give frame accurate commands to devices via *general-purpose interface (GPI)*, *serial communication*, or *Ethernet*.

Most systems have two device controllers for reliability. In most situations, the backup system is *warm*, meaning it's ready to go on line, but will need to have the schedule and other things loaded and started, be switched online, and restarted. More advanced systems will have some form of *hot* backup, meaning that very little needs to be done to switch over, because the backup is already loaded and up to date. Hot backups are considerably more difficult to design and build, and thus more expensive because of the need to keep two systems in lock-step. There are various approaches to backup. An MCO should know what to do in the case of an automation failure, and there should be an SOP and some practice switching to a backup system. Many stations rotate systems for training and assurance that both systems are fully functional.

Automation vendors often have product names for their products that accomplish the warm and hot backup functions. It may be called parallel list or some other name, but in the end, it has to follow the conventions cold,

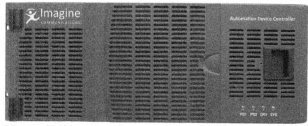

Figure 04-02. A device controller.
Courtesy of Imagine Communications.

A GPI is a single-wire (two connections with ground) circuit that can give only one simple command, such as start. They are often found triggering a simple device to insert a bug or turn on an indicator to warn an operator. Most systems use serial communication or Ethernet, although dealing with timing and being able to talk to multiple devices at exactly the same time are a challenge. More devices now expect Ethernet control.

Serial communication has been around the longest, but has quickly become rare (RS-422 and to a lesser degree RS-232, using DB9, 9-pin connectors, RJ-45 modular or special connectors to save space, attach one machine to one device), although it is still common to find device controllers with up to 32 (64 in big installations) serial ports attached to as many devices.

A persistent issue that an MCO will almost certainly deal with is that there are often many conversion devices to go between various control interfaces. It's not uncommon for a serial to Ethernet, or USB to serial, or USB to Ethernet, or Firewire, etc., not to mention various digital video converters to hang up. Resetting the converters when control and communications are lost to a device is common enough. Usually this involves unplugging a devices power, often a wall-wart and repowering it after a few seconds and then waiting for it to come back to life.

warm, and hot backups, and there will be a *recovery* procedure. Figure 04-03 shows a typical automation system operating screen.

Many systems have *clients* that often run on other computers that perform other tasks. The most important are the on *air clients* that process the schedule and interface with the operator. These can appear as simple lists with some control to move content, and start and stop devices. More advanced systems can display a timeline similar to an editor including secondary events and even video thumbnails.

Other clients will manage records, record keeping, and other workflows like transcoding and ingest.

There are essentially three elements to any automation system: ingest, the system database, and playout. Internal functions support one or all of these three tasks. All of this runs on a computer or a series of computers and database file servers, that in turn control video servers, switchers, graphics generators, tape machines, and video file servers and storage. The three basic elements control the functions that range from ingest to editing and involve metadata, compression, transcoding and other workflows.

Figure 04-03. Screen shot of a typical automation system. Courtesy of Florical Systems, Inc.

Ingest Element of Automation

Even in modest automation configurations where programming is run from external sources, somewhere around 95% of systems in the world have a video server for commercial playback. In more and more facilities, all of the on air elements (commercials, shows, etc.) live in the video server. The alternative is to store the content on tapes or even older technology like film.

The means of taking a spot and ingesting it (or recording it into a server) must start the process. Typically, the spot is played back to verify audio and video levels, also checking the *slate* information preceding the spot (client, spot duration, agency number). There will be a process to *cue* the spot (where the source of the spot is set to the beginning of the spot, ready to play), and then tell the automation system to ingest or record the spot into the server. After transferring the spot into the server, generally the newly ingested spot *recues* (as if rewinding a tape to the *head*) itself to be spot-checked. You want to verify the start and end of the spot aren't clipped or there are too many frames of black. Many facilities place a few frames of black at the beginning and end of each element so when they are played each element transition dips briefly to black. Also check that all audio and video levels are acceptable.

Ingest stations are work areas that run an ingest application that can take in tape, live, or data files, and sometimes legacy playback equipment like film and long-retired tape formats. To make this easier and faster, most ingest stations can cue tape decks and communicate with some sources and hardware to start and stop the feed.

Some ingest is automated. If a station routinely delays a program for later playback or reuses a program, an ingest server might be set up to capture the feed based on time of day. Automation may even select video router sources, retune satellite receivers, generate metadata, time the segments and more. The MCO is likely required to check on these automated feed ingests, and maybe *reorder* (ask the supplier to resend the content) a feed, file or a tape if the ingest fails.

Re-feeds are a fact of life. Many distributors are surprisingly sloppy and errors and degradations are common. Some groups have a central ingest facility simply so that content is conformed, and quality checked only once. Re-feeds and fixing programs is time consuming but part of the business.

Some ingest systems are capable of automated timing. Here the automation involved can identify test signals (usually bars), and black segments, and use them to make initial ingest decisions and timing. The MCO might check these automated decisions and make adjustments as needed. Unlike cutting physical tape, most ingest processes allow a *trim* to be undone should a mistake be made, or another in or out point is desired.

The actual length of the piece must be captured and in some cases a piece of content needs to be trimmed to fit, for example, a 29:29 (29-seconds and 29-frames) standard spot slot. By the way, this gives a one-frame dip to black between each spot. Some facilities require no break or a frame or two more to achieve a desired look. This trimming and timing is informally called *tops and tails*, the top being the first frame and the tail being the last frame of the element. Often this is done by viewing a *low-resolution proxy* and may be done miles away from the storage or playout location.

A *low-resolution proxy* (or *low-res proxy*) is a duplicate, lower-quality file, allowing operators and other staff to view content or make start/*end of message* (EOM) decisions at a location other than the ingest station, or allow someone from Sales to view a spot at their desk or at a sales call using a laptop computer.

Programs require additional steps since they generally include multiple segments within the show. Here you record, for example, a half-hour show with several segments. Most systems will have you identify the 30-minute or so piece of server time with a house number generally assigned by traffic (*e.g.* SHOW1234). This is often called the *parent clip*. Once completed, you call up the parent clip using the house number and begin the process of *marking* the in- and out-points of each segment (where the segment fades up from black and later fades back to black). Subsequently, each segment is given a corresponding number (*e.g.* SHOW1234-1, SHOW1234-2).

Editing

Edit bays (a place to edit video content, usually a tiny, sound-proofed room) are found in most facilities, and the function of editing (even if it's just trimming a spot to meet the length required for *tops and tails*) exist in just about every scenario. Editing happens on-line, meaning one is manipulating the full resolution content, or *off-line*, where one is manipulating a low-resolution *proxy*.

Apple's video editor Final Cut Pro family including the newer Final Cut Pro X (or just FCP and FCPX) is probably the most commonly used editing software. Many stations take content in directly to the editing station, and simply *mark in* and *mark out* the *start of message* (SOM) and *end of message* (EOM) respectively.

MCOs often edit and mark low-resolution proxies. Generally, when ingested, a full resolution encode for playback and a low resolution encode for review and marking is made. The low-resolution proxy is easier and faster to manipulate, *jog, and shuttle* (move around the timeline as in fast or slow forward, reverse and pause), but it's not useful for judging video quality or for use on air. Jog and shuttle features are found on most editors and some physical storage (tape especially). Thumbnails on a timeline are especially useful, especially if intelligently placed at the beginning of scene changes, for locating breaks and particular locations in a video file.

Video Servers

Most facility **real-time** video systems are built around two key components: the video (and audio) router we spoke of above, and a video server. It doesn't have to be so, and video servers didn't exist until television was fairly mature. Computer and digital speeds reached a point where they became useful and economical in the early 1990s. From that point on, digital ability has continued to increase rapidly replacing virtually every form of storage (film is almost completely gone and tape is fast following film) and processing in broadcast facilities, and consumer electronics. Digital has enabled higher resolutions in video and audio, lower loss of quality with each *generation* (copy or dub) and is becoming more capable. Tape hasn't gone away, but more often it is high density data tapes (linear data tape, in particular the LTO family (LTO-2, LTO-3) is the most popular format) that are used to compactly archive content, typically in a robotic archive system as part of a *hierarchical* storage system feeding video servers, rather than videotapes that are used in a tape recorder.

Video servers are simply servers optimized for ingesting and playing back content fast enough and accurately enough that the viewer experience is perfect. There are other issues that are somewhat video-centric. Security of the content is important, so some of the better schemes to protect the data through encryption are often employed. The server can also be the platform upon which format conversion, quality assurance, and editing occurs.

In most facilities, there is more than one video server *domain*. The news department, production department, promotion department, and any other specialized group may all have their own server domains isolated from the commercial and playback domain.

The on-air servers are likely composed of a set of more-or-less identical, and (usually) fully redundant servers. The reason is simple; if one server fails, the other can take over. The cost of the second server is often more than covered by the risks of failure and the desirability of having a system where maintenance can be performed on one system while the other is unaffected. Often too, servers are sometimes divided between **day-of-air** and/or *play-to-air* and **ingest**. Any of these terms are a bit flexible, but the point is that there are separate servers for receiving the freshly encoded or transferred content, and the servers to which content is moved to playout on line.

Video servers usually use a high speed *switching fabric* utilizing typically fiber connections to allow faster than real time and multiple simultaneous transfers.

Catch Servers and Watch Folders

Special functions, such as program or news distribution via Internet or data satellite employ **catch servers.** DG Systems/Spot Box, Pathfire, Pitch Blue, and Extreme Reach, CNN Oasis are common as of this writing in the US, but the companies and ownership are often in flux. Catch servers receive content from a central *pitch server* that distributes it and checks to make sure the content is received intact at the *catch servers* of the facilities served. These use combinations of satellite and/or public Internet or private **IP** networks for connectivity. Along the same lines, there can be process servers that hold *watch folders* (where one puts a file waiting transcoding or preparation) or hold content and/or *metadata* (information about the content, such as: duration, name, and format) awaiting some process usually driven by automation.

Once placed on the ingest server, there may be a *quality assurance* step (QA) where, in some cases, another operator at another time verifies that all is correct (right length, audio and video levels, *metadata,* end date (*kill date*), and any other important information) before release to the air server or servers.

The air servers play out the content, which remains on those servers for the length of time they are useful. As we mentioned previously, once the content is no longer needed, it may be placed in an *archive* system, or it may simply be *purged.* If the content is needed again at a later date, it is restored to the air server sometime before it is required to play. Archiving can be to digital tape, disk, DVDs or any number of storage options, while material needed quickly is more likely to be stored on *spinning disk, solid state storage,* or the like.

The actual organization of the storage and servers varies widely and preferences change with the costs and speed of the various storage devices. It is not uncommon for a video *clip* to be stored only once in one place (often a redundant ***RAID*** *array* of disks of some sort for reliability), nor is it uncommon for the clip to be moved many times between ingest, air, and archive. The structure and processes depend on the facility's workflow.

Arguably the most visible piece of the servers in a master control is the array of video monitors attached to the process. The video servers, along with live and content feeds from cameras, tape machines, or other devices are selected at the master control switcher and sent to the transmitter and/or other distribution systems. A *source monitor* looks at all of the incoming sources, usually on a *multiviewer* where many *windows* on a single large monitor serve the purpose of a group of dedicated monitors. A *preview monitor* allows looking at content before it is switched to air. A *line monitor* shows the output from the switcher (the finished product). An *off-air* or *air monitor* presents the signal after it is transmitted (usually delayed by several seconds) and received at the facility. Typically the last three have a dedicated monitor of some quality, or a multiviewer with few but high-resolution windows.

> The most common on-line or near-line storage structure is either a simple single level storage system, usually a storage attached network (SAN) or network attached storage (NAS) unless a single RAID array (redundant array of independent disks, originally redundant array of inexpensive disks) is big enough for the facility's needs. As systems get bigger, a hierarchical management system (HMS) can place what is needed *moment of air* on playback storage; what will be needed *day of air* goes to intermediate storage; and what will not be needed soon, if ever, on archival storage. Each deeper storage level in an HMS becomes slower, cheaper, and larger as it moves farther from the moment of air to deep storage.

Automation Database

A key piece of any automation system is the content database. If the facility has no automation, it almost certainly maintains some sort of content database even if it's limited to a small *db* (as opposed to dB, the abbreviation for decibel) coexisting on the video server.

Once programs, spots and other elements are ingested into the system (video into the video file server, and metadata into the automation database) there is an *index* of each item ingested. At the time of ingest one typically has the opportunity to include at least the following data:

- House number: generally a multi-digit number assigned to any element intended for air; program, commercial, PSA, or promo. Assigned by traffic department.
- Ingest date: when the element was put into the system--often entered automatically.
- Kill date: date the element should no longer air.
- Ingest operator: the operator responsible for ingesting the show, commercial, etc.
- Account number: AD-ID, UMID, or in-house production number of spot or program.
- Duration: the overall length of the spot or program segments.
- Last date aired: self-explanatory (and usually entered and updated automatically).

The content database is critical to the facility's operation and most make great efforts to maintain and secure the database. The database can be queried to answer any number of questions, from "Do we have this?" to "How many spots do we have that are out of date?"

Metadata

Metadata means "data about data." Years ago, a spot would arrive at the station on film or tape in a box with a label including the sponsor's name, duration and perhaps a start/kill date. Now, with content (both spots and programming) going into a video server – and often with no physical media to be touched by human hands – there is no more sticky label or even a barcode to read or modify. Once ingested, content goes into this black box and may be tough to locate. Typical metadata for a spot might include: the sponsor, duration, kill date, date the spot was ingested, the last time it played, how many times it has aired, ad agency information, etc., and sometimes technical information such as format, audio track configuration, and the like. A simple error in the metadata can render a *clip* lost, or worse, the wrong clip might play many times before being caught, if ever.

There are other identification schemes for content, some that involve registries, and others that simply generate a number based on time and GPS location of a camera. UMIDs are from SMPTE standard 330M, and contain 32 octets or 64 for extended UMID, and can be parsed for time and other information. Registries are usually kept in Internet accessible clouds and accessible by any authorized party, which may mean that they are available to everyone. The benefit of this is that the metadata for a given piece of content can be modified at will, and each user going to the registry will have the latest information.

For example, extending a kill date is made easy and universal. It works like this: an ad comes up for playback and the system goes out to grab the UMID data. The last time it was played, the spot was to expire that day, but the campaign has been extended. The old metadata would prohibit the playback, or at least flag the spot as out of date. The updated UMID data says it's still active, so without any fanfare, the spot plays. Rather than a hundred faxes or emails to a hundred traffic departments to extend the kill date, a hundred silent inquires of the UMID db take place.

When a piece of content comes to the facility, it is first ingested, along with all of the metadata necessary to identify the content, it's length, where it lands in a sequence if it is a series of segments that make up a larger program, and possibly other metadata that can be used to populate program schedules or indicate where a voiceover or super might be inserted. In some facilities, some content is ingested in a central facility and propagated out to the place of air. There are many variations of the centralized broadcast operations scheme, with various tasks being performed at the central facility, and others at the broadcast facility.

Most facilities use *house numbers* to identify content. Facilities vary widely in the length and structure of the house numbers and reuse policies. It's not uncommon to have a house number for a *topical* spot or promotion where the actual content is replaced periodically but the number remains the same. House numbers are often assigned before the video asset is produced. House numbers are frequently tied to *ad-IDs* or *universal material identifiers* (UMID).

Ad-IDs come from the ***American Association of Advertising Agencies***, also known as the *4-As* or AAAA, and the *Association of National Advertisers (ANA)* that keeps a master list of ad-IDs. Ad-IDs are four alpha characters that represent the advertising agency, followed by eight alphanumeric characters that represent the unique content identifier. A typical ad-ID might be: "ABCD1234XYZ5." Local spots, in particular spots made by a television station, can't have ad-IDs, so other schemes are used.

Knowing what *metadata* is available can help you greatly. Suppose a sales person comes to you and asks which Marina Pet Shop spots were ingested within the last two weeks. By going into the automation system's database, you can retrieve all the Marina Pet Shop spots, and then query the database to sort these by ingest dates.

On a more practical level, consider that you just ingested a spot or program earlier in the day and realized you may have entered an incorrect house number that identifies that spot or program, and you can't recall what house number you actually gave it. Now what? Call the list of all the elements in the server and then sort them by ingest date. You now have an accurate list of each and every element ingested into the server today (and the order in which they were ingested). You can see a spot that was supposed to be ingested as 4064 earlier that day was actually entered as 6064. Simply correct the error and the problem is solved.

Transcoder

A ***transcoder*** (or ***flip server*** or *transcode appliance*) is often necessary to convert one server's video format to another. For various reasons and purposes, it is virtually impossible to build a facility with just one compressed video format. ***Catch servers*** all seem to use different formats, as does camera storage, tapes, and imported files. Typically, some automated process take the incoming files, and places them in a ***watch folder*** (or some other process is evoked) where a transcoder converts the video into the desired storage and playout format. This can happen faster than real time, much slower than real time, or anywhere in between, depending on the speed (power) of the transcoder and the complexity of the video being transcoded. If it's going live to air, it obviously needs to be a real-time transcode, although there can be even several seconds of *latency* or delay caused by processing and moving video.

The transcoder may also produce a ***low-resolution proxy***. The low-res proxy is sufficient enough quality to see what the spot content is (often lets traffic and sales see the spot over a network connection) and find the *start of message* (SOM) and *end of message* (EOM) times (allowing staff to time shows in several locations) without having to use a lot of bandwidth.

Non-Real-Time (NRT) and Fast Transfers

Slower than ***real-time*** transfer of content is a concept where content ***clips*** are transported at a speed less than what would be necessary to play them out in real-time. News, commercial, and occasionally program content are transported via satellite circuits, telecom or ***IP*** distribution, and sometimes slower storage devices which are too slow to accommodate direct playback. A 30-second spot that takes ten minutes to move over a media distribution network might be justified by the savings in connectivity costs.

Some facilities also send their content directly to the viewers as downloadable files, which are not necessarily sent fast enough for ***streaming*** live on a computer or media player, and never played at the same time they were released or published.

Opportunistic data presents an interesting use case. Video is best sent with a variable bit rate (VBR) so that it uses more bits when the video is intense and very few when the video is idle. Transmission paths for VBR content have periodic slow periods where the capacity exceeds demand. Normally this leftover data space is filled with *null packets*, basically strings of zeros or their equivalent. These null packets can be replaced with opportunistic data that dribbles content or any other useful and time insensitive data out into the field when it can. This can be used on anything from broadcast transmitters to Internet connections to pre-place everything from spots to edge servers and STBs to whole movies for on demand access by the customer.

Sometimes a clip can be sent faster than real time. This is especially important to editing, where it's inconvenient to wait until all of the content loads on the workstation before work can start. The faster it can load, the faster one can begin working on it.

The connectivity is such between some servers that a transfer can occur much faster than real time. All of this has an impact on the workflow of the facility. In news-intensive facilities, and other fast paced facilities, there may be a period of time during a day where many transfers occur simultaneously. In these cases the bandwidth must accommodate the peak speeds, or other provisions such as delaying selected transfers must occur. MCOs may have a hand in managing these transfers so as to best utilize the facility's bandwidth.

Automation of Playout

As we have discussed earlier, the traffic department creates the *schedule*, which is then translated by software and converted to an automation playlist. In small facilities, the raw schedule may be entered by hand by the MCO. The playlist is then loaded into the automation, is previewed, possibly edited, and saved for future use. Later, tomorrow's schedule will be attached or appended to the current day's schedule so there is a seamless transition from one day to the next. Each element on the program log has a corresponding element in the playout list.

As an example: if the first element of the day is a segment from a syndicated show, the first element on the playlist would be segment one of the show followed by the first local break. If it is a four-spot break, following segment one of the show you'll see four commercials. The automation gets the data from the log and matches it with the information from the system's database. This, in turn, rolls each program segment or commercial. This process is repeated *ad infinitum*.

If an item is not in either the video server or automation database, the system will generally alert the operator to this. The errored line in the playlist might turn red or flash, depending on the system. Many systems are set up so certain colors in the playlist will represent certain conditions. Red is typically a warning, another color may represent dated material, secondary events, or perhaps an entirely different color scheme may represent another channel run from the same facility.

In automation, *primary events* are the major events in a playlist. *Secondary events* are elements related to primary events: *Voice-overs* (VO), effects, graphics, animations, crawls, etc. It is not uncommon to see far more secondary events than primary events. For example, it is not uncommon for a news channel to have a five to ten minute segment as a primary event, with somewhere around 30 secondary events – mostly bugs and animations being dropped in and out. Secondary events are always *tied* to a primary event. If you move or duplicate a primary event, more often than not, one also wishes to bring the secondary events that are tied to it with it.

Automation does one thing for machine playback very well, and that is the **pre-roll**. Mechanical playback devices (videotape machines, for example) typically require a few seconds to come up to speed after the play command. Some video servers also require a pre-roll. *Cuing* the tape and *pre-rolling* the machine several seconds before its content is needed can be particularly challenging for an MCO operating manually.

Another term you'll hear is *dead roll*. This is the process of rolling a program off-air starting at a specified time. Example: a live sports program runs long; it is to be followed by a recorded show. When the overtime sports show eventually ends, you would like to **join in progress** (*JIP*) the recorded show as though it began on time (and sports ended on time). Some automation systems allow you to program the show to be *JIP'd* automatically.

JIPs and sports where there are several options for the next spot (baseball is probably the worst as there may be a rain delay, pitcher change, station ID, or end of inning at any point requiring one of four spot sequences to air) are among the hardest things for automation to do and log correctly. Automation systems that can handle the more intense operations are considerably more expensive, complex and difficult to run than simple spot playing automation. Consider that even when it comes to JIPs, that there are scenarios where one won't JIP a program in the last few minutes, so the entire JIP program gets blown out in favor of filling the short gap. There are times too when rolling two JIP scenarios is desired, one if it's a short delay, another if it's a longer delay. Likewise some roll a different program given the outcome of a game or election. These scenarios are complicated to begin with, and a real challenge for automation.

Broadcast Exchange Format (BXF)

Likewise, the direction of the automation industry is to standardize and increase the level of integration between the traffic systems and the on air operation's automation. One standardization protocol is the

Broadcast Exchange Format (BXF), or SMPTE Standard 2021.

BXF makes it easier to integrate the automation system to the traffic system and use any BXF-compliant traffic system with any BXF-compliant playback automation system. In software, this is referred to as *interoperability*. Vendors sometimes gather on neutral ground to test and demonstrate interoperability between their products and others.

Automation in General

These examples are just the basics of automation. Depending on your system, you might have a fairly simple screen before you (the screen look is referred to as the *graphical user interface (GUI,* pronounced "GOO-ey"), or one that is rather complex – all dependent upon the complexity of your facility's end product.

Finally, the goal of automation is to collect each element logged for air, seamlessly playout each and every event in the correct order, then note whether each element aired or not. Human error and technical failures can cause impairments of the on air product. The two phrases often seen or heard regarding commercial **discrepancies** are *up cut* and *down cut*. Something is up cut if the beginning of the element in question wasn't seen fully from the start. Conversely, down cuts are when the end of a segment or spot is clipped or cut short. You've probably experienced commercials where, at the end of the spot you heard, "...call us to-d." You didn't hear the last syllable of "today!" Advertisers, the station's customers, usually do not pay for commercial messages that are incomplete.

OPERATIONS WORKFLOW

In the end, MCOs execute *events*. For the most part, a schedule is being executed one event after another under automation, and many processes that are mostly automatic in most facilities. If that were all there was to it, master control operations would be simple and boring. And some days it is. MCOs however are required to do much more, often with little notice.

Executing News Cut-ins & Special Reports

If your station has any form of a news department, at some point you can expect to break into programming to air a *special report, breaking news* or *news bulletin* from MCR. This is typically an unplanned event with very little preparation time. An MCO must be ready to execute program interruptions at a moment's notice. Many operations managers feel news *cut-ins* are the most difficult events to execute cleanly.

Before we discuss the details, let's break down the elements of typical news cut-ins:

1. There will likely be an *open*, with audio such as, "The following is a WAAA-TV News Bulletin." This may be a pre-produced clip on a video server, a still-store graphic with an audio source, or perhaps something on a videocassette that can be run as needed. An MCO needs to know what elements are needed and what the SOP is.

2. Typically, the SOP is to cut to a camera in the newsroom called a flash cam, drop cam or newsroom cam, perhaps with a lower-third graphic keyed over the flash cam identifying this as *breaking news.*

3. In some situations, you may have the capability to go to a remote source (live camera from a news van or helicopter, special network news feed, weather radar, seismograph, etc.).

4. Finally, there is likely a *close*, "This was a WAAA news bulletin, stay tuned for more details on our next newscast." Or, if each program has its own *standby graphic*, you might go to the standby graphic of the show you will be joining along with an audio announcement saying, "We now join our regularly scheduled program, already in progress"

At the time we want to do our news cut-in, we also wish to keep normal programming (and spots) running in the background. This way, once you've finished the cut-in and return to regular programming,

The MCO Mindset

Up to now, we've outlined workflows that dealt with other elements: hardware, software, station management, and staff who share the work area. The human element is the MCO, and there is a mindset involved beyond the mechanics.

The role of an MCO is that of a problem-solver. In the course of a day, several issues will present themselves; it could involve doing some research, or it may mean making a split-second decision, the results of which the operator will have to live with for the rest of that day's shift. The goal of this section is to help an operator to think like a master control operator – how to deal with the day-to-day challenges one encounters. What is the decision making process?

Things to Memorize

To begin, there are certain facts MCOs should commit to memory; these are points that should be instinctive:

• The signal path of the transmission stream: have at least a basic understanding of how your facility gets its signal from MCR to its various distribution points. This used to mean just the *studio-to-transmitter link (STL)* and transmitter; now we're talking about not only one or more STLs and transmitters, but also cable, satellite, plus Web/mobile applications. If an MCR monitor is labeled OFF AIR, is that from an antenna on the station's roof, or is it a cable or a satellite feed? In other words, *exactly* what are you seeing and hearing? And at what point is it in the transmission stream? Should something go wrong within the transmission stream, you need to be able to quickly narrow down where the problem might be.

• Know the major adjustable controls in MCR: things like the on-air audio levels, graphics for MCR, bypass switcher functions, essential transmitter controls and critical items like EAS hardware and procedures (for both weekly and monthly tests, and other occurrences such as weather and AMBER alerts). How-to notes placed nearby are a great idea.

• As a network affiliate or O&O, there should be a telephone number or two to call in New York or Los Angeles, etc. to confirm certain network program information, transmission data and the occasional special request. Currently, most network operations have their main control centers in New York City. Either memorize this number or have the number(s) handy by your MCR phone. *(DO NOT abuse this telephone number! You are likely just one of more than 200 stations in a network that are supported by a surprisingly small staff.)*

• Of course, network affiliates should *always* have a backup plan should they lose their network feed. This will likely vary from station to station; nevertheless, loss of the network signal, especially in prime time, is serious business. You won't have the luxury of time to think about this. Know *ahead of time* what your options are (alternate satellite dishes, a link to another affiliate, etc.). You might also want to write details down for this. *If you prepare for nothing else, prepare for this possibility.*

• Next is a subject we mentioned earlier, that of fill material. At a moment's notice, you should be able to get your hands on *time fillers*. Both short (from :05-:60 seconds up to 3-4 minutes) as well as long, program-length shows.

• Over time, you should also memorize *quirks* in the automation software, and *restart and switchover steps* for automation, video server hardware, transmitter operation, and have adequate familiarity of major tasks done on shifts other than yours. When someone calls in sick, or be delayed getting to work you will need to fill in for them.

the current show you interrupted will end on time and the following show will begin on time.

Recall that some facilities use servers for just their commercials, promos, and PSAs, but an increasing number use them for both commercials and programming. Given that; a facility will have at least one server output channel designated as the air channel (and possibly a second one as backup). Ideally, there will be an additional server channel as an all-purpose, catch-all output for various uses. Utilizing this extra channel to run the special report open is a normal SOP.

Whether the switcher and automation are separate products, or everything is a channel-in-a-box, there should be some means of engaging or disengaging the automation from controlling the switcher. Often the button is labeled auto(mation) or auto engage. This plays a key role in allowing you to do two things at once. Turning off (or disengaging) this button lets the automation continue to run (roll sources, etc.) but will *not* allow the automation to talk to the switcher and tell it to switch sources.

Alternatively, a *breakaway switcher* or *bypass router* allows switching to the news source while letting the regular playback and automation operate (although automation output goes nowhere as a breakaway switcher would normally override automation).

Here's the concept: you want to keep regular programming (and commercial breaks) airing at their scheduled time so that your program schedule remains on time while you do your cut-in. But we need to accomplish a second task: that of inserting the cut-in on air over regular programming.

The air server channel will continue to play out the regularly scheduled programming and spots, but, by disabling or disengaging the automation from controlling the switcher, the MCO can now use different sources on the master control switcher to *manually* execute the cut-in on air. In this way, the automation keeps rolling the air server (and keeping regular programming on time) *off-air* and *not* switching the switcher, thus allowing you to *manually* punch up other sources for the cut-in (which *will* be seen on air). Another server channel plays the open; the flash cam is another switcher source, and so forth. Once the cut-in is over, you manually go back to the original air server channel and re-engage the automation to start talking to the switcher again, and you rejoin regular programming.

Many automation systems have a *JIP* function: allowing you to leave regular programming, do something else, and then rejoin regular programming, all on the same *list* (schedule). At the time of this writing, JIP functions are not always user-friendly, so in the frenzy of a news cut-in, some operators and facilities simply opt to just do cut-ins manually.

The Automated JIP Function

The JIP function in most automation systems works similar to this: for example, the program airing is a pre-recorded talk show and news requests a special report following the next local break. In the earlier example, we ventured off the main air playlist to begin by rolling the open for the special report. Using the JIP command necessitates the special report come from the same playlist as air. Doing this requires indicating you want the JIP to begin at a certain point (in this case, after the next break in the talk show) and run indefinitely. At that point, the automation must calculate how long the special report runs and note this continuously changing value.

When the interruption to the playlist is over, the automation must do two things: calculate a specific time when to rejoin the playlist, and then have an adequate amount of time to physically cue the video server to the appropriate place and rejoin programming. An adequate amount of time for all this is roughly 7 to 10 seconds. To facilitate this, stations using the JIP function will tack on a prerecorded close to the end of the special report, saying something like, "With this special report from our newsroom concluded, we now return you to our regularly scheduled program" The automation system is aware of a finite duration element (the prerecorded close) will end at a certain time and "note it," then calculate when the report began and when it will end, and give a command to the video server to cue the system to that specific spot to resume the playlist.

Flash cams

Flash cams serve a very specific role in news-oriented facilities: being able to get a news bulletin on instantly. Many facilities are set up so a cut-in can be done via MCR with no studio crew (stage manager, camera operator, audio operator). Generally, flash cams are studio-quality or near studio-quality cameras permanently pointed at a desk or standup site in the corner of a newsroom and are always on.

Should there be a need for a cut-in, the on air talent needs simply to go to the desk, flip a switch to turn on lights around the flash cam, put a mic on, and put an *IFB* in his or her ear. In seconds news is ready to go on air. Usually news staff or MCR staff will communicate with flash cam talent through the IFB. Communication during these spontaneous happenings is critical and there is a near universal common issue; If there are two sets of IFBs at the flash cam, one for use during a standard news broadcast through a news production control room, and another for special cut-ins only through MCR, they must be easily distinguishable by on air talent at the flash cam desk.

If regular programming for a news cut-in is interrupted, it needs to be entered on the discrepancy report. If you used a server channel to run an open, you can later go back to note the time (from the as-run log) and jot this time down as the time you left programming to begin the special report. Once the rejoin to regular programming has occurred, remember to record the time in the log or discrep as required. Looking at the as-run log in automation won't generally give you the time you rejoined programming because you manually switched sources and the automation system likely can't see the event. Manually taking sources on the switcher usually does not get noted in the as-run log.

It is good practice to preview any news crawls or graphics you put on the air, especially if they have not been created in MCR. Often, there will be some infrastructure allowing a news staffer to input a news crawl from the newsroom and then send it to the station's character generator, allowing master control to put it on the air. Previewing not only allows you to check spelling and grammar issues but verify that there are no questionable or offensive elements to the crawl. This type of thing does happen, and the MCO is the last link in the chain to correct potential errors.

Wall-to-Wall News Coverage

At some point, an event will happen that causes your station to suspend programming for a few hours or days to bring news coverage to your audience. These events come with little or no warning. A well-prepared MCO should be ready should such an event happen on your watch.

The primary issue in MCR is to determine the effect an event has specifically on the air product. A natural disaster (flood, earthquake, tornado, fire) may cause physical issues with staff safety in the building but little else on air. In other instances, the facility may become inoperative, and unless plans have been made well in advance, operations may need to cease for an extended period.

If programming is suspended for a period, other duties (ingesting and timing shows, other daily assignments) must still be done. There may be an inclination to put some of this off, but the best practice is to take care of this other work as soon as possible. These situations are highly unpredictable, and it's impossible to tell what an MCO might be called upon to do. One never knows when news may opt (even briefly) to resume programming.

During an emergency event there will be many things you'll need to write down in order to clean up the incident later. A pile of paper or notebook is a necessity. Record anything that will help recreate the times, sources, adjustments, and other details.

Live Specials & One Time Only Events

The MCO will likely deal with a live, local program that is out of the ordinary. In this case, walk through the entire event in your mind: beginning the show: any unusual elements you need to be aware of, *air checks* to start recording beforehand? And do the requested air checks need to be recorded from a specific, out of the ordinary source (a *clean feed* – control room output minus graphics – versus a standard air check, for example)? Once in the show, are there any very short breaks? In fact, writing down a list of all break durations and the show's *off-time*, *end-time*, or *out-time* for both you and the control room is helpful. Will the show be on a video/audio delay? And what about the show's end: is it guaranteed to end on time, or could it run long? Will this present any problems with either the special program or the following program? Can the transition from one show to another be an issue?

Many facilities feature some recurring local events; annual parades, marathons, pledge drives and the like. If there are well-documented notes for these events, it helps to keep any notes for future use. A file folder or large envelope stored somewhere with these notes can be very helpful for the future, especially if the producer or director changes from year to year. It's safe to say that neatness doesn't count. It's better to have a folder full of paper scraps than nothing at all.

Perception of the Air Product

As an MCO, you not only control what airs, but how air is perceived. For example, at the end of a news segment, you've probably seen the obituary of a celebrity. Typically, the tag line the news anchor reads is along the lines of, "…and he was 95 years old," followed by a slow fade to black. There's a different perception of what you just saw if the fade to black is followed by a second or so of black (out of respect) before a commercial break begins, versus the break beginning the instant the switcher reaches black – it's jarring to the viewer. And aside from poor aesthetics, you've just distracted the viewer from the next thing he or she is about to see.

Several years ago, one of the master control authors was assigned to handle a pre-empted news block; instead of news, the station was to cover a very somber memorial service for a local child who'd been kidnapped, then later found deceased. The memorial ran long and it was decided to JIP a tabloid-type entertainment show scheduled after the service.

In this case, some tact was needed. Think of the viewer watching 2+ hours of a very emotional child's funeral, followed by an upbeat, high-energy entertainment show. To make the transition as gentle as possible, here is what was done to separate the two programs (and note what follows can easily be programmed into MCR automation, so once the MCO begins the transition, the rest can be carried out automatically).

• The control room ran the traditional slow fade-to-black concluding coverage.

• MCR programmed a slow fade from black-to-video of a static station ID graphic with a low-key audio ID (and in theory, the ID could have run silently). (This action begins a separation from one program source to another.)

• Following a brief pause, and continuing with the ID graphic, the audio JIP announcement ran ("We now join our show, already in progress.").

• After a beat, a slow fade-to-black was programmed, followed by a fade up to the entertainment show to be JIPed.

This may seem unnecessary, but remember most people watching your on air product are either alone or with just one or two other people, and they're sitting in quiet living rooms or kitchens, not in a high-energy MCR. Transitions between programs should be as smooth as possible. And even if your switcher isn't capable of doing fades (it's just a cuts-only switcher), most of this can be adapted.

Reacting to Problems

There is a double-whammy when something goes wrong, especially for people new to master control. First, there is the mistake the operator needs to address, and second, the whole world is seeing the mistake.

When you see the error, your first impulse is to react, giving 110% energy to go to the switcher and do something! When something happens we suggest this: Dial that energy back slightly to 98%, take a beat and think, "What can I do to fix this?" or even just something as simple as, "What?" In that moment of reaction time – taking a beat to think, and *then* running to fix the problem – you'll be surprised what gets processed in your brain to correct a problem.

The goal here: knowing what you need to do to start correcting the problem *before* you begin punching buttons. It is precisely for this reason many facilities have the capability to air *standby graphics*, at the very least a generic ID graphic, but ideally a graphic for each show aired (these are typically *freeze frames* taken from the programs themselves) at the touch of a *panic button*. While a static graphic is not scintillating television, at least there is something on air other than a black screen. A show graphic or other *panic slide* buys time to fix the problem. Viewers with remote controls take only a short while to tune elsewhere.

Anytime you punch something on air other than what is programmed into the automation, get into the habit of also *disengaging the automation from controlling the switcher.* Especially if you're working alone, there is nothing worse than putting a *trouble slide* on air, starting to fix a problem away from the switcher, only to have the automation trigger the next programmed source, which very likely may not be functioning, causing you to have to stop, come back to the switcher, re-punch the panic slide and then return to fixing whatever problem you were working on before. *But afterwards, remember to re-engage the automation.*

If you're in the learning process, you can also apply these techniques to others you may be working with: if they run into a challenge, pretend it's yours. How would you fix it?

This is a good time to mention it is considered very bad etiquette to reach over someone seated at a switcher (or other equipment) and punch buttons, thinking you're helping him or her during a crisis. Should something happen to another operator and you know the solution, ask if you can help or take over. And that's all you ask. Often there is more than one way out of a mess, and working two solutions at once is usually worse than any course an MCO might take on his or her own. In tense situations, keep comments or questions as brief as possible. If you're working with a partner, remember you two are a team especially when things are going badly, you *must* work as a team. There's an old saying in this business that no one dies doing TV. As focused and intense as live TV can get, it is just TV.

Show Format Book

With a few exceptions, many issues the average MCO will have to clean up are due to human error, perhaps yours, perhaps someone else's. One sees similar problems crop up again and again. A common problem centers on the mistiming of locally recorded shows. Luckily, 95% of these shows are highly formatted and routine. Whether we're talking about a to-be-trained novice or an experienced operator, both can make use of the ***show format book.***

By compiling all the information for a show, one show per page, an operator sees how each show is formatted, how many show segments there are and how many black holes or slugs between segments are there and how long they are.

Perhaps the most important piece of data is the *total running time* (TRT). This is the sum of all the show segments. For a typical half-hour program the TRT would likely be something like 22:50 (22 minutes and 50 seconds). If the TRT is 22:50 of program material then there is 7:10 (7 minutes and 10 seconds) for other material (commercials, promos, a live news update, IDs). Not only is this good information, but TRTs quickly indicate mistimed shows. Once a show's segmenting has been done most automation systems calculate the TRT automatically.

A TRT (or an element) that is longer than the time allowed is *heavy.* If it short it is called *light.*

Other variances included in format books include the occasional hold time for syndicated shows that may be recorded on Monday for release on Thursday. Certain Monday through Friday strip shows (because they fill a strip of programming time) might vary their format one day of the week. Most syndicated shows have a *trouble number* to call if there's an issue with the satellite feed, file transfer, or media. On occasion, shows will have a feed in both standard-definition and high-definition delivered on two different transponders. Both SD and HD information should be included (some facilities record the HD source as the primary feed, and the SD source as the backup. They are the same show from two different sources). Each of these details should be included in an easy-to-read format in the show format book.

Network affiliates should also include the format sheets for the network morning and late-night shows (how many local breaks, where are they, cues for weather inserts, etc.) in the show format book. Most network morning shows will run a minute or two of national weather, then say something like, "That's the national weather, here's what is happening in your world today." Local stations may break away from the network, and either air pre-produced local weather *hits* (short, recorded as live, elements) or run a live insert. Stations that do not take advantage of the local insert *availability* will ride the network while the network broadcasts a generic element. Similarly, network late-night programming has its quirks and should also have its format laid out for new or temporary operators.

Emergency Procedures Book

A collection of directions of uncommon tasks (anything not done, say, on a weekly basis) should be included with the station *SOP*s. This could include switching, resetting, powering up/down or modifying the output of an STL, transmitter, satellite uplink, generator, etc. Most SOPs include EAS instructions (done weekly, but a critical part of station operations), directions to a remote transmitter site, loading a traffic file for the next day's schedule into the automation, in short, directions for each of those extraordinary occasions.

You will no doubt have some procedures that require lots of details, directions, and data on where to find certain controls and operate or repair given equipment. The SOP book becomes infinitely more useful if there is both a detailed (wordy) explanation *and* a compact bullet point version of the same material. New MCOs and those who haven't handled a particular task in a while, if ever, will appreciate the longer, hand holding, details. Once one becomes familiar with a technique or routine, the brief version will save time and errors.

Fill Material

Most facilities have *fill* material for when extra programming is needed to fill time. This could be due to a logged commercial or promo that isn't available, or a show may have been mistimed. Fill can be long-form or (fill programming) to replace missing shows or rained out sporting events. If the news production switcher stops working five minutes before the news a station might need to fill an hour or more.

Promotional Material or Promos

Besides the typical complement of topical (for a given show that airs soon) promos present in a system, it is ideal to have generic promos for at least the syndicated shows available. They should be available in several lengths from five to 60 seconds. Syndicators frequently feed generics at or before the start of the season. If a topical promo is outdated or unavailable, you can plug-in a generic promo. Keep the generic promo list near the MCR operating position.

Public Service Announcements

Also, you should have a fairly large number of public service announcements (PSAs) for on-air use, in durations of 10, 30 and 60 seconds, and every now and again a longer form PSA will come in handy. Stations report PSA time as part of their license renewal process, so a PSA is actually good use of time on occasion.

A concept that is widely accepted is to assemble a number of existing PSAs from the PSA inventory and designating them as PSA*X* so if 30 seconds of fill is needed, one simply enters "PSA30" into the automation as the house number. In the title of "PSA30" you can include the facility's house number and title of the PSA (e.g., #92345/Heart Fund). A second set of different PSAs can be called FILL or something similar for situations where another 30 seconds is needed in short order, it's desired to avoid repeating the same PSAs too quickly.

Variable-Length Fill

For timing's sake, many stations have the need to have an element that can be used to fill an indeterminate time; for instance, to meet network exactly on time. Many top market stations never wish to see any black on the air. To assist in this regard, it is common to have an element that has a total of 10 seconds of material with only three or four seconds of actual copy, followed by a musical *pad* that can be faded out at any point. Sometimes a simple musical *bed* without any voice-over is used and a voice-over may be added at any point. *Back timing* the musical bed so that an ending punch hits at the transition to the next element is used in some live talk shows and newscasts. The element rolls so that it ends at the right time, and a transition (usually a fade up) is made to the dead rolling pad as the content (usually when the talent runs out of dialog) dictates.

Long-form Programming and Evergreen Shows

Along with generic promos, syndicators feed one or two generic shows to their stations for use if a problem arises with feeds of their show. These generic shows are often called *evergreens*. The term evergreen means the standby show is always ready to be aired. However, that doesn't mean you can air these anytime. For most entertainment-based syndicated shows, if a station contracted a certain show to air at 7 p.m. Monday through Friday, the station can only air the evergreen for that show to replace a missing show at 7 p.m. Monday through Friday. Generally, overtime, a number of usable evergreens collect.

Most traffic departments will provide alternative programs for sporting events that might be cancelled. The programming department will almost certainly have long form evergreens identified and available for any contingency. This might be very specific. The MCO will likely have to take commercials from the missing program and insert them into the replacement program.

Network Fill and Procedurals

As an affiliate, it is not uncommon to carry live network programs that vary from their estimated length. Sports programming is notorious for running short or long, holiday events (parades, tree-lighting ceremonies) or political events (State of the Union speech, conventions, elections) also tend to expand in length. Prior to the event, network operations will send contingency plans or *procedurals*, to their affiliated stations for planning purposes. Networks generally have these situations planned reasonably well.

Let's assume network is scheduled to finish a show at 9 p.m. (actually more like 8:58:25 p.m. with 1:35 for the affiliate's *terminal break*). Under normal conditions if the event ends early the network will fill to the top of the hour (in this case 8:58:25 p.m.) and will lay this out in the procedurals. If the event runs long, procedurals will specify what will happen next. The network will break down times so if the event ends between 9 p.m. and 9:14:59 p.m., network plans to end as soon as possible and run a 10 second *network identification* (NI). From 9:15:00 p.m. to 9:28:25 p.m. another set of guidelines might apply. A NI may be as simple as a static slide, to complex productions where a promo has the NI built in.

The more involved an event gets, the more detailed the procedurals are likely to be. The average length of procedurals for a regular, no-frills, football or baseball game is roughly 6-8 pages. It is good practice to print the procedurals and highlight each time period the network has broken down, and succinctly write down the outcome you need to achieve for that given time period.

Long-form Programming

There are two situations that merit special attention: airing network feeds for networks that aren't part of the Big 5 (ABC, CBS, NBC, Fox, PBS), and airing local movies. Because these two situations are longer than the usual 30- or 60-minute show, they can be more prone to timing or break issues.

Depending on your specific time zone, you might be able to receive your network feed early and record it for replay. Naturally, most East Coast and Central affiliates will have to take their network live. But for the smaller networks, it is not uncommon for stations in the Mountain and Pacific Time zones to prerecord the East Coast feed for later replay. In this case, carefully match your break lengths with those indicated on the two-hour primetime rundown sent daily by the *netlet* or *ad hoc network*.

The network may give stations 64 seconds for a local break, but for local sales purposes, you may be requested to add a 30 second local spot to one break and then deduct that time from the next break. If your network replay is recorded, you'll need to go through the process of segmenting this two-hour block of programming. For those whose network replay is coming from tape, the tape will need to be re-cued between local breaks that are adjusted for time.

Slightly more prone to errors are syndicated movies. Depending largely on the distributor, movies can have as few as six segments, or as many as 14. In some cases segments might consist of only *built-in barter spots*, or even a short five-second *bumper*. It's good practice to verify that all of the movie segments and breaks add up to the movie total running time.

Dealing with Time

Generally, automation systems will calculate times for you very efficiently. If it's not in automation, the times need to be calculated manually. Time is written out in h*ours: minutes: seconds: frames*. In practice, frames are generally rounded up to full seconds. Adding a series of times is best done on a time calculator or with a time app. Without significant practice or experience, making errors is time calculations is too easy. A few simple calculations for practice follow in this chapter.

Backtiming

Backtiming is a process to calculate times starting from a point in the future, and working backwards. If you want to get to work at 8 a.m. and it takes 40 minutes to drive to work, you back time so that you leave the house by 7:20 a.m.

Backtiming in MCR is the same equation. If you need to join the network at the top of the hour at 8 p.m., and the last local break is 2:35 long, that break needs to start at 7:57:25 p.m. Prior to that, if the final show segment is 5:26 long, it must begin at 7:51:59 p.m. to remain on time and ultimately join the network at exactly 8:00:00 p.m.

Assessing an Automation System

An automation system can have a very long life, and they are not easy to replace, so the selection of a system is very important. Receiving and evaluating MCO input on selecting a new automation system is generally a good idea. It's easy to overlook needed functions, and each facility is different.

Living with MCR

Working in MCR is *not* a 9-to-5 job. There will be several things you'll need to get used to (and perhaps rather quickly). Being the new kid on the block, you'll more than likely start training on a morning shift. There tends to be more regularity there and frankly, there are fewer eyeballs watching at that time of day. But depending on the facility, MCR morning shift times can start anywhere from 3 a.m. - 7 a.m., and you work either an 8- or 9-hour day. If you're not a morning person, here are some suggestions.

To start, think about having two alarm clocks. One would be kept near you (this is the clock you'll hit the snooze button on), and another clock on the other side of the room (that way you have to get up to shut it off). The clock closest to you might be set a little early. It starts the wakeup process. The alarm on the other side of the room is a this-is-your-last-chance-*GET-UP-NOW* alarm. Naturally, you'll need to plan in advance how much time you'll need to get ready.

Incidentally, real godsends are seven-day alarm clocks, in case you're not familiar with them. A typical alarm clock just has one, maybe two, alarm settings. The seven-day alarm clocks are great in that you can program each individual day with different wake-up times. It's possible your shift start-times may vary, so these clocks are very handy. Most have battery backups, and can be bought online.

It helps to do what you can the night before. Have all clothes ready, and whatever you plan to take for breakfast, lunch, or a snack should be packed and ready to go in the refrigerator. Charge cell phones overnight, and incidentals like keys, wallet, and any necessities should be organized and on hand. With odd shifts, it helps not to have to think when leaving the house.

Time Calculations

Considering only minutes and seconds, Let's say you want to add the last show segment (9 minutes, 17 seconds) to the terminal break of the show (2 minutes, 35 seconds).

```
    09:17
+   02:35
```

7 + 5=12, thus:

```
      1
    09:17
+   02:35
    11:52
```

This example is a simple math calculation; after getting 7+5=12, we write the 2 and carry the one, giving us the result: 11:52.

The next one requires an additional adjustment.

```
    09:51
+   03:22
    12:73
```

Twelve minutes and 73 seconds is correct but not useful. We know that 60 seconds equals one minute, so 73 seconds can be expressed as 1 minute and 13 seconds. Looking at this last calculation, 9:51 plus 3:22 actually comes to 13:13 (thirteen minutes and thirteen seconds).

Let's try another one:

```
      1
    06:23
+   08:58
    14:81
```

Again 14:81 needs to become a normal time. Taking 60 seconds from 81 seconds results in 21 seconds and one minute. Add the minute and we get 15:21.

One more.

```
    07:43
+   01:57
```

3+7 =10

```
      1
    07:43
+   01:57
       0
```

The result is 100 seconds or one minute and plus 40 seconds, thus:

```
      1
    07:43
+   01:57
    9:40
```

Management needs to determine what needs it will have both now and in the future, including expansion for additional functions, staff reductions, possible centralcasting, multichannel operation, merging with other entities, or leasing out facilities to other media groups. There may be unique issues your parent company chooses to make priorities, which, in turn, will influence their equipment purchases.

That being said, each automation system should initially be assessed with the following criteria:

• The automation company's history, reputation, recommendations.
• Technical/customer support and product line support.
• Cost and ease of installation and integration with existing hardware/software.
• Operator interface and peripheral programs ease of use (ingest, database, playlist).
• If a multichannel facility, ease of monitoring multiple channels at once (at a glance).
• If a centralcasting facility, ease of control of multiple operations in multiple locations.
• Most groups standardize on a system that makes sharing

Time Tip: If there can only be 60 seconds to a minute, and we're dealing with a seconds number that's 61 or above, the 60 can move over to the minutes column, and what remains becomes the seconds that are left.

everything from support and spares to content easier.

• Some small markets tend to all do the same thing because there is safety in numbers when it comes to support, and it's easier to use the same pool of freelance operators.

In any case, operators will interface with three parts of the automation system; ingest, database management, and playlist operation.

Ingest Assessment

To some, this may be the workhorse of the system. Throughout the day, programs are constantly being ingested into the system, either manually or through a file transfer process. Then, perhaps, in late afternoon or early evening, commercial ingesting begins. During certain times of the year, operators can be inundated with spots that need processing. Some systems will have two subsystems for processing: one for single elements (commercials, promos, infomercials), and another for multi-segment programs (note that most multi-segment modes can process a one-segment-only program, like an infomercial, if one chooses).

The goal of the ingest process is simple, fast and error free. A typical afternoon MCO shift may see 40 to 60 commercials. Once ingested, automation might facilitate QA by allowing immediate review. Ideally traffic will supply a *dub list* that will populate each field on the ingest interface so operators don't have to fill in each bit of metadata (title, house number, duration, agency number, etc.). This also insures data in the on air schedule and in the commercial database matches exactly. MCO keystroke errors and the time it takes to enter data are all reasons that the automation system and traffic systems should be tightly integrated.

Database Assessment

The key difference between database systems is the power of the searching functions and the usefulness of the user interface. Some systems, while allowing the MCO to see metadata for one element, won't allow you to compare it to other elements easily. Operators frequently go to the database to find elements. If the database only allows viewing limited metadata and makes it hard to compare entries, the database is less than efficient.

The more robust databases tend to look similar to a spreadsheet. You can sort by columns, and often run advanced searches based on text, dates, etc. The time it takes for changes entered in the ingest/database process to be reflected in the playlist may be an issue.

How important the database is for searching varies by facility. The database is backed up and placed on hardened equipment. Like the automation device controller, it is mission critical.

Losing the database can be a near death experience. Ideally the database is fully backed up and copies routinely stored off site. Database corruption can be as bad. There are a number of scenarios where IT systems can get out of sync or files corrupted. Having two databases that are significantly different or out of date can require a lot of manual work to restore. Most automation systems will operate at some limited level for some time without an active database. Vendors have flown staff in on an emergency basis to recover the db and other key pieces of the automation system while the system limps along. Some databases can at least be partially restored from metadata wrapped with content files on video servers.

Playlist Assessment

Most automation firms put the bulk of their resources into this portion of their systems. Playlists becomes the personality and look of the system. A good feature is being able to look at the playlist monitor from across the room and see a missing spot or an error message. Moving closer, most on-screen notations should be fairly self-explanatory. Going through the various menus, some systems will have file and edit commands very similar to a typical word processing application, others may have a more limited range of commands. Expect to see common functions like find and replace, and copy and paste. Some automation GUIs drive like most computer programs, with others one needs a cheat sheet to explain the commands. Some have special keyboards.

Questions one might ask

• How many logs can be appended together? Thanksgiving weekend is a good example. Before the staff leaves Wednesday afternoon, it's nice to confirm all shows and spots are available through the following Monday.

• How easy is it to manipulate the playlist? Can the playlist be controlled from a remote location? What security exists if controlling the list remotely?

• Are error messages clear and reasonably specific? Will automation automatically email notices to a supervisor?

• At what level does the vendor support the system? Do they routinely monitor the system? Can they be called in to remotely work on the system?

• Some systems have features similar to a clipboard, allowing operators to store standby promos/fill programming/alternate playlists. How easy is this function to access and utilize? Can you drag and drop and copy and paste those elements into your playlist easily? Does this function work similarly to a word processor?

• How does the automation system support a news operation?

Training

Throughout this book, we've stressed the idea of list-making, establishing procedures, and leaning towards keeping your operation fairly well organized.

Earlier, we mentioned a training checklist. In a perfect world, it would be great to have just one experienced staffer with great teaching skills to work with each new staffer from start to finish. Rarely do things work out that way, and it can be difficult to get continuity in training from one trainer to the next.

With the training checklist, the goal is to list each task or subject an MCO will encounter, from the most basic to the most complicated tasks. Listing them in order of difficulty builds on prior knowledge and presents a logical progression from one topic to the next.

Documenting these points does several things. It lists each point a new staffer needs to know, it gives both the trainer and trainee a consistent direction to work towards, and later, provides a standard for the manager to assess the skills of each MCO. If the training checklist is the standard to which each of the MCOs are held, then at evaluation time there is a consistent, verifiable standard the supervisor can use to determine strengths areas needing development. Because equipment and duties change over time include the date the checklist was issued or revised.

An example of a training checklist is in Chapter 14, Appendix E.

Newsroom Systems and Automated Production Control

While not a master control task, you should have some familiarity with the automation used to get many news programs assembled and executed on the air. Understanding what another crew does to accomplish their job ultimately makes you better at your job.

Prior to the newscast going to air, the newscast's producers *build* the show from start to finish. This is a sequential list of which stories and *packages* will air and in what order. Where each commercial break, package, audio, graphic, camera moves, production switcher effects, etc. that are required are all entered into a special newsroom application geared to creating a *rundown* for later use. At this writing, probably the most common newsroom systems are AP ENPS, Ross Inception, Octopus and Avid iNEWS.

Within the rundown are codes that tell the control room equipment what to do. These commands (a *Transition Macro Element* or TME in Grass Valley Ignite) are sometimes referred to as MOS (Media Object Server) commands. MOS is a protocol that either directly or through a gateway or other intervening device connects all of the controlled pieces in a newsroom together, video switchers, audio mixers, graphics, robotic cameras, prompters, servers, etc.

Earlier, we said traffic usually built the on air schedule in a special application, and that schedule is what activates each step, each element of what goes on air in MCR. Likewise, for *automated production control* (APC), the rundown built by the producer becomes what is used to program each element of a news broadcast using automated production control.

Once the rundown is complete, the control room loads the rundown into the APC system in preparation for air. When the newscast is ready to begin, the operator cues the first event and essentially pushes a button to activate the rundown, then at the right time, pushes a button to advance to the next rundown element and the next, etc. Some systems have unique pushbutton controls to execute commands while others use a traditional computer keyboard to control the system. The three most common APC systems at this writing are the Grass Valley Ignite System, the Ross Overdrive System and the Sony ELC System. All have provisions to deviate from the rundown if breaking news happens and you wish to manually call up specific camera shots and open up specific audio sources. All allow the *floating* of elements, dropping elements, and moving elements.

Newsroom and production control systems are an expanding field with many vendors with many variations of the architecture. Many news stations use products from a number of vendors, often more particularly matching their needs. Digital Broadcast's NewsBank, Autocue, Comprompter as well as any number of proprietary systems are in use. Likewise, social media interfaces and systems that do everything from repurpose content to tracking trends play a large role in some news operations.

The goal of automated production systems is to reduce staffing requirements in the control room and studio. Prior to this, a news production typically employed a director, technical director, audio operator, video control operator, a graphics/character generator operator, and possibly an assistant director to assist in timing, and coordinating live shots in the control room and camera operators and floor directors in the studio. All of the duties can be reduced to one person, though many have two or three, to assist with floor, robotic and producer, and audio duties. Some systems allow the flexibility of adding an audio operator for an audio-intensive show or camera operators for a video centric program, but the goal is to utilize fewer staff overall. One might argue that automating the processes results in a more consistent product and reduces errors. Others suggest that some show formats are too fluid and automation too difficult to make flexible enough to accommodate a fast moving, unscripted show. Virtually everything in TV is a compromise, both views are legitimate, and hence TV productions are mostly the same, but all have some uniqueness.

Summary

Workflow and content flow, no matter how the building blocks are assembled, or how many workflows there are, the basic path is the same facility to facility. Content comes in, is prepared, and played out. Everything goes to where it needs to be through routers. Storage options are many. Editing and quality assurance functions occur as needed. Adding graphics and secondary events are the norm.

Beyond the basic workflow and content flow, there are often ancillary workflows that deal with everything from Web distribution to secondary audio and language graphics.

The big elements are usually the nearly invisible router systems that connect the equipment physically and provide the paths that content and instructions travel, and the automation systems that execute most of the workflow.

With the understanding of what makes up the workflow engine that is a service (channel origination), we can look at the sources of content, and then the distribution to the audience.

5
SOURCES

Video and audio can come from almost anywhere, including studio cameras, edit bays, microwave *shots*, tape machines and more. When we talk of sources, we generally refer to a real-time video feeds that would or could run through the video router and be controlled by the master control or news production switchers. At any given time, a broadcast station has one or more *sources* switched to air.

When we say we have more than one source at a time; we may have graphics, a squeeze-back with additional video sources in windows, *voice-over* (VO) audio, etc., hence the concept of a master control switcher being a *video/audio mixer*. Alternately, the mixing can be done in a capable video server, in which case the server controls a video router to select the appropriate sources. Each source of video and audio content has its own characteristics and needs. No doubt there are more sources to be developed. We'll look at the more important sources.

Satellite

As we noted earlier, satellites are not only for reaching the audience, but are used for the distribution of programming to broadcast stations, **cable head ends**, etc. Program providers *uplink* their signal from an *earth station* to a satellite in synchronous orbit (it orbits the earth once a day at the same speed the earth rotates, so it appears continuously in the same place in the sky) 22,753.2 miles above the earth. The received signal is then transmitted back to Earth where a ground antenna will *downlink* the signal for use back on earth by stations within the satellite's *footprint* (coverage area, which is often directed to some land mass: Europe, North America, etc.).

TV stations receive satellite signals mostly on either C-band (3.7 to 4.2GHz) or Ku-band (11.7 to 12.2GHz). Dishes and receivers may receive one band or both. Everything else being equal, C-band dish antennas need to be larger than Ku-band antennas for the same quality of reception. Bigger antennas permit receiving weaker satellites with more reliability. The curved surface of the typical receive dish antenna (there are some flat and even ball shaped antennas, but rare for this purpose) focuses the signal from the satellite to the *focal point* of the antenna. A low-noise amplifier (LNA) or low-noise block converter (LNB) amplifies the signal (and in the most common case; an LNB, converts it to a lower frequency) and feeds the signal down a cable to the IRD or receiver. Whether Ku-band or C-band, the signal is most often down converted to *L-band*. As an MCO, you probably don't need to know about the frequency ranges, or even that C-band frequencies get inverted in L-band, but you do need to know about sun outages and rain fades.

Today, satellites are placed every two or three degrees around the Earth along the Clarke Orbit, named for science fiction writer Arthur C. Clarke who popularized the idea of communications satellites. Domestic satellites (informally called birds) serving the United States extend from 69° to 139° west longitude. *Fixed Satellite Service* (FSS) satellites are lower power and closer together, servicing the program distribution needs. *Broadcast Satellite Service* (BSS) uses higher power satellites that are spaced further apart to serve the DTV need for smaller dish antennas.

There is one other band, Ka-band that is much higher in frequency at 26.5 to 40GHz that is even more susceptible to rain fade but requires even smaller antennas but very accurate pointing. Ka-band is sometimes used for HD distribution and news gathering.

L-Band

Most LNBs output *L-Band* in the 1GHz frequency range, usually 950MHz to 1750MHz. This lower *intermediate frequency* (IF) is easier to transport from the antenna via thin and inexpensive coax that would have too high of a loss at a satellite's operating frequency or inexpensive fiber optic paths.

Sun Outages and Rain Fades

Sun-outages (or *solar transit*) occur during the first two weeks of March and October for the latitudes of the continental United States. Most operators will eventually experience brief interruptions in reception caused when the sun lines up with the satellite and a given ground location. As the Sun appears to pass behind the satellite, the signal will become noisy. Signal level indications on the receiver may actually increase during a Sun-outage as the radio noise of the Sun often buries the weak signal from the satellite. Bigger antennas have a narrower beam and tend to shorten the outage time. Higher-power satellites with lower bit rate, more robust modulation may remain useful during the solar transits. East coast locations are affected first, and the outage band for a given satellite moves west following the Sun.

The program supplier or engineering department can calculate the precise time and length of the Sun-outage. Sun-outages on a given satellite will occur for several minutes at nearly the same time of day over a period of several days. These are very predictable times can be calculated for your location and any given satellite. Most satellite providers' websites include an outage calculator.

This has nothing to do with Sun spots, or solar flares, which are unpredictable and rarely a problem for satellite communications, although a strong solar event can cause significant damage to a satellite, and in extreme cases, satellite operators have shut down satellites and rotated them to minimize damage from an electromagnetic shock wave.

Rain-fades occasionally occur in Ku-band satellite reception, and only the most extreme rain will fade a C-band system, hence the desirability of C-band for high reliability links. Rain absorbs Ku frequencies (Ka frequencies are even more susceptible), and heavy thunderstorms between the dish and the satellite can seriously degrade or completely block the Ku satellite signal. In some stations, an alternate dish located several miles from the primary dish is used so that an operator can route around rain-fades. Uplinks employ uplink power control (UPC) on Ku systems and or alternative sites. It is not uncommon for a Ku uplink to increase power by as much as a factor of 100 to burn through the rain to reach the satellite. A rain fade on an uplink causes the loss of all received signal everywhere, so some Florida, Texas, and East Coast uplinks routinely move their uplink services in preparation for a hurricane.

Snow in the dish will also cause the satellite signal to deteriorate. It is easy for an operator to believe the receiver is slowly failing on a day with light snow or freezing drizzle. Some dishes have heaters that are manually or automatically activated to prevent snow and ice accumulation. An operator may have to use a broom to clear the snow out of the dish or manually activate the heaters.

It is good practice to assure that the dish moved freely to the desired satellite, is free of snow, and is not looking into a thunderstorm or the sun before assuming the satellite equipment has failed.

Some facilities make arrangements to have programming delivered when a predictable sun outage occurs from another site, and even when unpredictable rain fades occur. One popular method is to have a sister station take a feed to record or send over an Internet or fiber connection.

All radio communications have a *link budget*. With satellites, we pay a lot of attention to having a link budget that has enough *headroom* or *fade margin* to survive impairments to the 44,000 mile round trip a satellite circuit makes. Because of the distance, size and expense of the key components in a satellite system, the fade margins are sometimes very thin and the expense of larger dishes and better LNBs is not justified. We expect that satellite circuits and microwave links will fail periodically. The bulk of link budgets range from about 1dB, to a robust 16dB. A 1dB headroom system can fail on an overcast day. A 16dB system, especially on C-band with a low level of modulation might not fail even with solar transits. Link budgets are calculated for *clear sky* conditions. Just to keep this practical, if all we change is the antenna, a 20dB better antenna gain requires an antenna with 100 times the surface area of the original antenna. The cost differential between a 3 meter and a 30 meter antenna is the difference of about thousand dollars versus nearly a million dollars. Heating systems on larger antennas are also expensive, and hence why your station may have the MCO go out with a broom, and accept an occasional satellite problem.

Using Satellites

Unlike fiber feeds or file transfers, satellites can involve steering antennas, dealing with decryption and conversions. Satellite distribution has many advantages, but of all the *wild feeds* (elements that come from anywhere without timing and often with a variety of formats and configurations), satellite is probably the most common and most complex. Most architectures utilize an *edge device*, usually a *frame synchronizer* with channel swapping and conversion capability, to bring a wild feed into the facility, making it conform to the timing and other needs of the facility.

Probably the most common edge device is the Imagine Communications X-75. Edge devices are not always rack hardware with control panels; they may be cards in a card cage controlled via a computer-based user interface that is part of a *monitoring and control (M&C)* system.

IRDs utilize the L-band from the satellite antenna's LNB. To tune an IRD, one needs the L-band

Figure 05-01. A typical frame synchronizer. Courtesy of Imagine Communications.

frequency, but often we have the satellite's transponder frequency. The LNB has both a low noise amplifier and a mixer with a local oscillator (LO). The mixer combines the LO with the satellite's received signal to make the L-band frequency. If you have the transponder frequency, simply subtract the LO frequency to get the L-band frequency to tune the IRD. Most modern IRDs have computer interfaces to input the receive frequency and other parameters such as modulation type (DVB, DVB-S, 8PSK, analog FM, etc). The usual LNB LO frequencies used in broadcast are 10750MHz for Ku-band, and 5150MHz for C-band.

If we have a Ku-band transponder center frequency of 12150MHz, we subtract 10750MHz; the result is an L-band of 1400MHz, which is what the IRD is tuned to.

If we have a C-band transponder frequency of 3850MHz, we subtract it from 5150MHz and the result is 1300MHz, which is what the IRD is tuned to.

Note that the IRD is useful on Ku-band, C-band, Ka-band, and other bands as long as the intermediate frequency is acceptable, which is almost always L-band. LNB LO frequencies can be different than the example to cover different parts of the satellite operating spectrum, so most engineering departments have a means of indicating the LO for each antenna system even if they are identical. Some IRDs have a built in calculator where by entering the transponder frequency it will be translated to the L-band and tune the IRD automatically. This is one good reason to use only LNBs that have the most common 10750 and 5150MHz LOs.

Analog FM (once the mainstay of satellite and microwave video transport, and yes there is analog AM, but it exists only in very special circumstances) is rare and disappearing quickly in favor of digital (DVB-S in particular), but you will likely run into a legacy analog system. In analog systems (digital systems are built so as not to be affected by inversion), the polarity of the video is critical. C-band LOs are high side, meaning above the satellite operating frequency while Ku-band LOs, and most microwave in broadcast use, are low side. The high side mix of frequencies inverts (what was higher frequency and white on an analog receiver's TV screen is now lower frequency and black) the signal, so IRDs and microwave receivers that receive analog FM TV have a video inversion switch that one utilizes to invert the video so that it is not a negative image. Inverting video and using analog links is fast becoming a kind of a poor man's encryption, given that most IRDs won't decode analog signals.

Most systems have an antenna controller where the *azimuth* (left and right), *elevation* (up and down), and *polarity* (where vertical and horizontal planes appear to the LNBs) parameters are stored for each satellite of interest. Telling the antenna controller to move the antenna causes motors to move the antenna to match the three parameters. Occasionally a manual tweak is necessary to peak the signal

Spectrum monitors (a feature- and accuracy-limited version of a spectrum analyzer) are a handy tool as each satellite has a particular look and with some practice, an operator can peak an antenna easily when viewing the monitor's display.

Fixed vs. Agile Satellites

Some satellite dishes are fixed position; others are *agile* (moveable). It's not uncommon to have to point an agile or *ad-hoc* dish to different satellites for different programs. Sometimes, these are automated and the MCO enters times, and coordinates, other times the MCO steers the antenna and *peaks* it to receive the best and most reliable signal. That's an important skill if you are required to do this, as it's easy to miss-point an antenna and sometimes be peaking on a *side lobe* (not the main beam of the antenna but an unintended beam that is generated by the construction of the antenna and far weaker than the main beam). Tuning in to a side lobe might work...for a while.

Satellite Time Conventions

In using satellites, it is important to know two customs: first, times are usually given as Eastern Time Zone times only. Some information sheets from producers might, as a courtesy, list feed times for Eastern, Central, Mountain and Pacific time zones, but if there is only one time listed, a good assumption can be made the time listed is Eastern. Greenwich Mean Time (GMT, or Zulu) is the standard time for international work.

Second, times are normally referred to in *military time*, also known as *twenty-four hour time*. To avoid any confusion, rather than use a.m. and p.m. designations, military time denotes each of the 24-hours in a day distinctly. 9 a.m. is referred to as 0900 (Oh-nine-hundred) hours, Noon is referred to as 1200 (twelve-hundred) hours, 1 p.m. is referred to as 1300 hours. 12 Midnight is 2400 hours (0000 is just after midnight). Incidentally, you'll likely see military time used other places; on air schedules, record schedules, satellite feed times, transmitter data/references, etc. Thirteen-hours-ten-minutes-Zulu is 1310 GMT or UTC (universal coordinated time is for all but the most exacting scientific use equal to GMT) and depending on your time zone and daylight savings time early morning in North America. The Internet has any number of world clocks that make a time translation easy, especially if a day change is involved.

IRD

In most cases, an ***integrated receiver decoder*** (***IRD***) is used to take the satellite L-band signal from the LNB and decode the audio and video. Most services use a DVB format, but there are many different formats for sending programs via satellite. For the most part they are digital and compressed. These IRDs will require that in addition to the right satellite, and right polarity, that the IRD be given the correct frequency, probably channel table information, and often be part of a conditional access (CA) system. An MCO might have to enter several parameters into an IRD to decode the correct program. An MCO might also have to call a provider in order to clear up an authorization (CA) issue.

Figure 05-02. An integrated receiver decoder.

Some CA systems have a shelf life. If the IRD is not kept up to date and misses too many authorization messages (usually because it is not in service) it may need to be flashed at a service center or with special software before it can be used again.

Analog Receiver

There are a very few legacy analog services left on satellite, simply because the cost of using a full ***transponder*** for only one service is most often prohibitive, and the quality of analog is not always good compared to digital, and it is almost a given that it is SD. Nonetheless, the universal means of getting a broadcast out to everyone or anyone is likely to include analog for some time, simply because analog is easy to receive, everyone has receivers, but it cannot be easily or well secured. We're guessing that in any given year, at least once, a broadcaster resorts to an analog satellite feed *in the clear* (not encrypted). Most facilities have a few analog satellite receivers for just this purpose. These require tuning to a transponder frequency, the tuning of audio sub-carriers, and occasionally inversion of the video, decryption, and selection of various filters will be necessary. We doubt that in any following editions of this book, analog satellite will even be mentioned.

Transponder

Transponder corresponds reasonably to channel, where one or more services can be located. Each satellite has several (often 24 on a given band) transponders. Each transponder operates on a different frequency and polarity. Channel numbering schemes vary. Most satellite charts list the frequency and the polarity of each transponder. Ku-Band satellites may have transponders with different channel spacing and bandwidths. In some cases a very wide signal may be encountered, or a transponder may be split to permit two signals to share a single transponder. The receiver must be adjusted for a wide-band (full transponder) or half-transponder signal. Typical transponders for broadcast use are 36MHz wide, but 24MHz and 72MHz are in use and more for other services, bandwidths range from very narrow to very wide. A given satellite may have transponders of various widths and on more than one band.

Polarity

Some satellites place even-numbered transponders on one polarity and odd-numbered transponders on the other polarity. It is often necessary to adjust the polarity to maximize the signal from the desired transponder and, more importantly, to minimize interference from the undesired transponders of the opposite polarity. Polarities are listed as horizontal or vertical for *linearly polarized* satellites. *Circularly polarized* satellites are left and right hand polarized. Circularly polarized birds are popular for DTH because the antenna receive feed assembly need not be mechanically rotated, which makes installation easier and more trouble free. Linear polarization has better performance in terms of separating the horizontal from the vertical.

Azimuth and Elevation

As the dish is steered from East to West to locate different satellites, the ***azimuth*** changes. As the dish is tilted up and down along the horizon, the ***elevation*** is being adjusted. From any given location, each satellite will have a specific ***azimuth*** and ***elevation***. Many satellite receiver systems have controller units that can store the location of several satellites. Some satellite controls allow for the direct entry of azimuth and elevation. If a chart is available with the coordinates for your location, simply enter these and activate the satellite controller to direct it to the proper location.

If a satellite location is not programmed into the controller system, the operator can usually find the satellite by using a satellite chart. The operator must first select the correct polarity and tune the satellite receiver to an active channel known to have programming. The desired satellite can then be located by adjusting the azimuth and elevation to the position indicated in the satellite chart. Some dishes change the elevation automatically as the azimuth is adjusted from East to West.

The operator is often responsible for steering the satellite dish and tuning the receiver. Operators should be familiar with their equipment so they can make the precise adjustments sometimes necessary to receive the best signal.

MCPC and SCPC

Occasionally you will see the *SCPC* (single channel per carrier) designation that denotes that multiple services are coming from various locations but carried on one transponder. Cable and networks often have *MCPC* (multiple channels per carrier) where a single *multiplex* comes from just one location but carries multiple services. A cable multiplex might have a dozen or more services all multiplexed together from one location on one transponder. SCPC is used for SNG (satellite news gathering) as several news services can split up one transponder.

Fiber

Fiber circuits are considerably easier to deal with than satellites, simply because they are largely dedicated circuits that are installed and configured typically once for the life of the service. Fiber circuits are generally point-to-point. Satellite is more economical for *point-to-many-point* distribution, and often the only means of reaching destinations that are not served by fiber.

Encryption and Conditional Access, if they exist at all, are minimal in most of the fiber world.

The edge device is generally an encoder on the source end, and a decoder on the receiving end. Many decoders can be synchronized to the station (making them directly useable for on air) and include conversion processing, making them ideal dedicated edge devices. Occasionally an **IRD** can be used as part of a fiber system, given how similar satellite and fiber delivered compressed video can be. Likewise, systems that send and receive video on fiber may have an encoder and a decoder together, making up a **codec**, similar to the codecs in edit stations and video file server systems.

Internet, WANs and File Transfer

Moving content on the Internet or a private *wide area network* (WAN) is common; however, transferring files of content **non-real time** with lots of time to spare is the sweet spot. ***File Transfer Protocol*** (***FTP***) is a means of moving files of any kind through what can be a hostile environment. FTP sends one piece of a file at a time, and then verifies that it arrived. FTP will slow down when the connection is slow, and the constant verification of delivery followed by a resend of any piece that didn't arrive, make FTP *bulky* compared to a real-time high *quality of service* (QOS) connection. But, if all you want to do is cheaply move a 60-second spot and you have some time to do it, FTP is reliable and economical. Almost any computer can be used to send and receive FTP files. FTP clients are built into all manner of broadcast hardware.

There are also plenty of occasions where the Internet is the way to move real-time content. News content from around the world, backup feeds from anywhere, monitor feeds, are all situations where an Internet connection is the perfect means of moving content. Many companies make hardware that can take in video, send it via the Internet to another piece of their hardware that then output useful (even synchronized to the facility) video. Almost all of these devices can be adjusted to provide either faster, lower delay, or higher quality; some adjust themselves to the best the connectivity can support. Unless the circuit is of very high QOS, there are almost always compromises in latency and quality. Wireless connections are often used by news departments to bring back real-time video, and it can often be very good until lots of stations do the same and the wireless bandwidth becomes restricted. These wireless devices often *bond* several modems on several services to improve reliability and throughput. TVU, Dejero, Comrex and Teradek are common bonded cellular providers.

DVD

DVD, digital video discs, and Blu-ray discs are an inexpensive physical storage medium used for compressed video. Because DVDs have reasonable video quality at low cost, they are popular for home use, and in stations for everything from courtesy copies of spots, to backups, to **archive**. Generally only Blu-rays are considered good enough for air, but that is not a hard-and-fast rule.

DVDs make a good **archive** medium except that they do not last forever (estimates of shelf life range between 20 and 50 years or more), and they are harder to physically handle. Even if they are in a DVD robotic archive, operators will touch the DVD. Carry DVDs with the hole in the middle, clean with a clean non-abrasive cloth using distilled water or alcohol wiping from the middle to the edge (never circular). Keep DVDs in

Figure 05-03. A TVUpack unit used for news gathering. Courtesy of TVU.

protective cases. Scratching is a DVD's biggest enemy. Some label glues and inks over time might degrade the recording layer. Sharpies are okay, as are labels made for the purpose.

DVDs record from the inside to the outside edge, exactly opposite of how a vinyl record was made. The disk spins faster when it is reading or writing to the inside part of the disk, and slows as it moves out to keep the linear speed constant. Formatting and content info is recorded on the inside, the first part to be read after loading, of the disk. This explains the finalizing process when recording.

Tape

There are many videotape formats. In broadcast, Digital Beta, DVC-Pro, DV-CAM, are common, though not unique. ***Archived*** tape can go all the way back to two-inch *quad* tapes recorded in 1956. Very little of the earlier tapes are playable as they have decomposed, and working players are few. Tape has gotten smaller, is almost always carried in a cassette (as opposed to open reel) and is capable of higher video quality, and longer life with each generation. As this is written, tape is fairly economical and very transportable media, so it's likely that tape will be around for some time. Hard drives are the most direct alternative, but costs are more for typical broadcast use (movie houses use drives because they are less expensive for an environment that plays the same piece over and over and then replaces what is on the drive and does it again). Tape lasts longest when stored in a cool, low-humidity environment. Each tape pass (running it through the machine) reduces its life. Dust, and especially mold, damage tape. In any case, tape degrades with time and use.

In data tape storage, LTO-3, LTO-4 is in common use, and LTO-5 tape cartridges are emerging. Placed in a robotic system and manage by a storage management system, data tapes of all formats are common in archive systems. When tapes show wear, the data is moved to fresher tapes and the older tape is removed from the system. Generally this is an automatic function of the tape management system. As better storage becomes available, the tape system's data can be moved forward to the next storage system with little labor, preserving the essence and metadata.

Using Videotape

While many facilities abandoned videotape to use the more trouble free and in most applications more economical video server, some still use tape. It will be our purpose here to give you an overview of videotape and how it can still be a great help to you as an operator.

When we speak of videotape, we mean formats that are specifically designed for video, which usually supports linear video editing, full or very high quality, and recording in a continuous manner. Data tape evolved from video and audio tape technologically, but became a different media designed to store packets of data and what is necessary for error correction; the purpose to be an error-free (down to the bit), high density, storage medium. Videotape has means of error concealment that generally takes advantage of the basic similarity of an errored pixel to those around it. Some videotape can fill in a missing line of video with information from the one before and maybe following. Data tape uses error correction techniques that recreate exactly the lost data from extra *overhead* information contained on the tape. Data tapes can store any kind of data, and that includes audio and video. Digital videotape has the desirable characteristics of both analog videotape and data tape. Among the most common tape machines in use are Sony's Beta machines, and among the most useful and popular are a series of machines that can play analog and digital tapes allowing older archive tapes and maybe lower end legacy camera tapes to be used as well as the later series of digital tapes.

mpex Corporation of Redwood City, CA, introduced videotape in 1956. At the time, videotape was two-inches wide and was stored on open reels (not in cassettes). Dropping a 30-minute show reel on one's foot often resulted in broken bones. Over time, tape width decreased, many features were added including enclosing the tape in a cassette housing. With a few exceptions, most videotape machines are now of the cassette-type and tend to hold a maximum of either 30-minutes or two hours worth of tape.

For our purposes, we will cover only the basics you need to know about videotape. While quite a bit of information can be saved to tape, all videotapes have the capability to record the following four elements:

1. A video band (where video is recorded),
2. An audio band (where audio is recorded, often several tracks),
3. A timecode or address track (where timecode is recorded), and
4. A control track (essentially a recording of your recording – more to follow).

The video and audio bands are self-explanatory. Most decks will have the capability to record at least two discreet audio channels, frequently several more.

The **timecode** *track* or *address track* is where *linear* timecode is recorded. Timecode allows both people and equipment to specifically identify or address each frame on videotape. While you, as an MCO, may not use timecode to a great extent, much of the equipment around you does (notably the automation, if it will control tape decks in MCR).

Then there is the **control track**. Just as the sprocket holes on film guides the film to play at a constant rate, so the videotape control track also keeps the videotape playing at a constant rate. There are other components that stabilize and enhance the signal later in the process, but the foundation of tape speed control is the heartbeat provided by the control track.

Methods of Recording to Videotape

There are three ways to record onto videotape. The simplest is what is called a **crash record.** Once a tape is loaded, you simply press play and record simultaneously, and the deck will begin to record. The crash part of record comes from the fact that when videotape machines are put into record from a stopped position, the point where the recording begins has an uneven or dirty look for a moment (there are almost always corrupted frames of video) and timecode is discontinuous as it jumps to the current time.

The next two methods of videotape recording are actually edit modes: **assemble** and **insert**. These modes first appeared on videotape machines decades ago, but still serve a purpose. Keep in mind that whether you get a brand new videotape, or run

Timecode

Each frame of video has a specific time counted in frames, seconds, minutes, hours, and sometimes days. The format is HH:MM:SS:FF so that 1:23:14:22 is read as one-hour, twenty three minutes, fourteen seconds, twenty-two frames. Because there is a slight difference between the frame rate and clock time, almost all timecode is drop-frame, meaning that following a pattern, the 29th frame is not counted. This keeps timecode and time for all practical purposes, in sync. Linear timecode can be recorded on an audio track, and in some production work the same timecode is placed on one track of a multi-track audio recording as well as video recorders. Most video recording techniques place the timecode either in the vertical interval or in ancillary data. IP video and compressed video may or may not support timecode and there is a multitude of methods in use. Timecode is used almost universally to indicate edit points in an edit decision list (EDL) as well as the start and end of messages (elements).

an existing, pre-used tape through a *degausser* (a very strong eraser that demagnetizes a videotape and thus erases its content), as an operator, you are starting with nothing on the tape.

A blank (bulk erased) tape is different from a *blacked tape* where black and timecode is recorded on the tape similar to how some media is formatted to be ready for use. A blank tape has no timecode or control track, so there are no reference points to command the tape to cue to.

The first edit mode is **assemble editing**: this mode would be used to assemble the elements of a show in order. A characteristic of assemble edits is a fairly clean start point, but an uneven, dirty outpoint of the edit. This necessitates over-recording each edit by a few seconds, then choosing an in-point for the second edit prior to the end of the first edit. All four elements of the tape are edited simultaneously.

As a practical example, if you are to record a 28:30 long public affairs show (no breaks and roughly halfway through the program the guest does or says something you don't wish to put on air; select a natural cut point just before the objectionable occurrence, then perform an assemble edit from there to the end of the show. This mode has its purpose, but also lacks some flexibility. An assemble edit is

Tape Capability Is Often Useful

Consider that one of the authors had the need to put this into practice. A topical talk show discussed a major news event that had tragic consequences. After the show was edited and then distributed, it was discovered a major suspect was, in fact, not a suspect. However, it was mentioned twice in one segment, and a corrected feed wouldn't be received in time for the station's airtime. Legally, the show could not air unless the two references were corrected.

As the show in question was directly recorded into a video server, the bad segment was dubbed to tape (actually two tapes). The edits had to be done in a very short amount of time: double-recording allowed for a backup if an edit turned out badly, and since one of the edits had to be a video edit, the second tape provided the replacement video on the primary dub for the shot to be cut.

The first mention of the suspect was verbal; so the mis-identified suspect's name was edited out (the space was filled with silence). The second reference was visual: a lower-third graphic with the wrong name over news video. As there was no way to just eliminate the lower-third graphic, the shot had to be covered with other appropriate video. From the following segment, a shot was lifted and insert-edited to cover the portion of video with the wrong name. Once completed, the segment was re-ingested into the system using the same house number, but with the letter "A" added to the edited segment. If you need to do this, remember to correct your automation playlist and save the correction!

all or nothing; all four tape elements (video, audio, timecode and control track) must be rerecorded.

As editing became more demanding, the ***insert edit*** was developed. Its only requirement was having unbroken control track throughout the duration of the record session. Also, the tape operator could select what elements to edit; video, audio and timecode, or any combination of these. This was (and still is in some facilities) used to fix a multitude of sins. Mistakes, missed cues, objectionable language or gestures in an audience or crowd shot – the list is endless.

Insert edits give the operator more freedom than assemble mode. Not only can one replace portions of pre-recorded programs with more appropriate audio/video, one can also use assemble edits on a blacked tape to build spot reels, and program elements.

It was common years ago to ***black and code*** videotapes. The operator would route black into the videotape machine and preset a certain timecode number (usually 1:00:00:00) to start recording onto a fresh tape, beginning at the start of the tape and go until the tape ended. Most facilities that use tape keep a supply of blacked tapes on hand.

Digital Delivery

There's not a good, unambiguous term for this piece of television operations, but delivering content via a number of digital (meaning delivering files) methods that have a layer of management and delivery assurance is a big part of how contemporary television works. At one time, tape duplication houses were then norm. Contemporary *digital delivery* systems consist of a *pitcher* and a *catcher*, and use either satellite or Internet to pitch content to the catcher. More content moves on digital delivery systems than its predecessor process: sending commercials and programs on tape and film.

There was a time when syndicated shows were *bicycled* from one station to another to avoid having to make many copies of a show. If the show was mistimed or had other defects, the first station would catch that and adjust the *run sheet* accordingly. In the digital distribution era, everyone gets it at the same time, and some groups have one station do the QA (quality assurance) and let the others know if the content and timing is good.

DG Fast Channel/Pathfire, Media DVX, Pitch Blue and Vyvx/Level-3 are the current widespread players. Tape duplication and distribution, usually sent via overnight mail delivery, has been all but replaced by digital distribution. Each system uses a different combination of transmission means, storage, and file conversion. A syndicator or advertising agency wanting to get content to various facilities will purchase distribution from one (or more) digital delivery service. When the content lands on the ***catch server***, a *receipt of delivery* is generated and sent back to the pitcher and the customer.

Taking the content off the catch server can be performed as:

1. A file transfer
2. A transcode to a format the station can use and transfer
3. Playing out as video and ingested as video

The most efficient process is an automated file transfer. The most universal (and simplest) is the video play back to ingest, but it's easier to lose information about the piece or make mistakes in the data entry. The completeness and uniformity of the *metadata* is often an issue that requires either traffic or master control to intervene and correct. Most facilities then QA the item as mistakes and technical impairments are not uncommon. There is some evidence (taken from equipment logs) that suggests that as this is written, most stations use simple manual playback off the catch server and ingest to file server with manual information entry approach, though one has to think file transfers and transcoding will eventually be the norm. There is comfort too in playing out the video as it allows the operator an additional QA step as the video is viewed. File transfers and transcodes happen out of the view of the operator, so the first time the operator sees what was transferred or transcoded is the QA step that can be forgotten. Transcodes are notorious for unpredictably introducing degradations into the video and audio.

Most commercials arrive this way. Many syndicated programs also use digital delivery, although simple satellite feeds that are taken down and recorded in whatever formats the station uses are not uncommon.

ENG/SNG

Electronic News Gathering, and *Satellite News Gathering live shots* as well as any Internet based program return require some set-up at the facility. It may involve steering antennas, tuning receivers, setting up decoders, inserting frame synchronizers, establishing IFB (*interruptible foldback*; the audio the field talent hear in their earphones with cues and generally, to reduce confusion, none of their own sound) recording pre-feeds, news *packages* and other tasks that are often an MCO responsibility. Many MCOs setup the live shots during news shows as well as rolling in the commercials and keeping time.

Real-Time or Live

Live, linear, *real-time* is a simple concept that is often confusing. Clearly a live shot with a live camera being viewed a few seconds later after all the processing and *compression* is live, and close enough to real-time. Clearly if one records that camera and plays it back a day later, it is no longer live, but we still consider it the linear and real-time product of a live master control. In most common usage, "live" is what is live to the observer, even if elements are pre-recorded. *Live to tape* means that the show was recorded linearly with little if any *post production* (or just "post") editing. Historically, the FCC required radio and TV stations announce that some of their content was mechanically reproduced (an *MRA* or mechanical reproduction announcement, so the audience wouldn't be fooled into thinking a program was being done live).

The term *non-real-time* is generally reserved for stored content that is called for at a later date, often by the viewer as in *video on demand* (VOD). Broadcast stations are inherently live linear environments, except when one comes to Web-based, *on-demand* content.

Time shifting, where the viewer saves a live program to view at a later more convenient time, posses a special problem for ratings. Measuring live viewing is a well-established technology and technique. Measuring the viewing of a show that has been saved and maybe transported to another display or device is more complicated and as this is written, this significant audience may be significantly under reported.

Graphics/Branding (GFX)

Branding and graphics are important master control functions. *Bugs* are branding identifications that can be animated or static, transparent or opaque, on constantly or dropped during commercials and at other points in a program. Generally, these are under automation control, and an instruction to put them in and take them out is entered by traffic. Actually, traffic rarely adjusts these as they are of a *template* for a show that traffic builds on and is repeated over and over. Some portion of the time *MCOs* may have to add, remove, or move a bug.

Moving EAS crawls, bugs, banners and other graphics (where closed captions appear) is often necessary especially if there isn't agreement by all parties about where to place items on the screen. It's rather easy to overlay one graphic on another, sometimes intentionally and other times regrettably.

Lower third graphics (on the bottom of the screen) are often added for *crawls* (moving text) and other data and visuals. MCOs might enter *topical* information (having to do with a news item or the topic of a daily program) or timely data (stay tuned for a delayed show, or weather alerts). Some pieces like time and temperature are constantly updated often from an Internet *RSS* (rich site summary, or less formally really simple syndication) feed.

A *safe title area* might exist in a program that is converted from different aspect ratios (if there is an HD widescreen and an SD feed or mobile or other device feed). There are often areas of the screen reserved for bugs or other graphics for various entities. In analog video, the video is *over-scanned* on displays (the over-scan is the area one doesn't expect the viewer to see as their CRT-based device is designed to lose a small piece of each edge) to allow for the edges of the picture to be covered by a television's decorative bezel. Digital TV displays almost never have this issue, so safe title area is a concern in fewer circumstances. If there is a safe title issue, the monitor for the graphics usually has this marked off electronically (or even masking tape) to help the MCO keep the text in the visible and desirable area. As this is written, there are still CRT televisions with OTA converters and on cable system feeds, so safe title areas are often maintained. Some feel that allowing the use of the full screen, knowing that some older displays will cut off the edges, encourages the purchase of HD displays.

Keying

Graphics are *keyed* into some other video *background*. Graphic elements must go over video that has a *key* literally cut out of it, or at least has the video reduced in level (for a *transparent key*). It's a simple requirement in that if video goes from 0 to 100 units, adding two elements together that add up to more than 100 isn't going to work well. Once maximum brightness is reached, there is no more. Keying a hole with a zero video level and adding in even items with 100 units of bright video works well. A background and a graphic that are both 50 units would combine and lose any detail either had and display simply as a white patch.

Keys can be generated by a graphics unit, or a switcher that looks at luminance levels to create a *luma key* (sometimes referred to as *luminance key*). Luma keys are not as sharp or accurate as the graphics generator, character generator or anything with an alpha key can create, but works in a pinch.

Chroma keys create a keyhole when a particular color *hue* and *saturation* is detected. *Green screen* and occasionally *blue screen* and even *red screen* chroma-keys allow the weather person to stand in front of a background that is keyed out and replace by entirely different video like a weather map. Any color can be used for a chroma key, however primary red, green, or blue are easier for equipment and operator and produce the best results. Of course any accidental use of that color can create strange effects. Wearing a green shirt while on a green screen makes the person's upper body transparent. Blue eyes on blue screens are particularly creepy.

Keyers generate an *alpha* channel, which is simply a black screen with 100% white where the keyhole is to be cut. The alpha channel can be recorded along with the color channels in systems used for production. The alpha channel can be inverted, creating a *super black* signal where the area to be keyed is blacker than black. It can be a useful signal in keying equipment.

Keying can happen at any place in the video path and often occurs a number of times. A *down stream keyer* (DSK) for several derivatives of a program is common and allows different branding for different distribution paths, or just because it is sometimes more convenient to use a DSK as opposed to an integral keyer built into a switcher.

This should be pretty obvious, but an inconvenient fact of life is that once you key in something, including *burned in timecode*, it can't be removed in any rational way. If you want to use a program later, you might want both a ***clean feed*** and a ***branded feed***. The branded feed is used live, and the clean feed has all the elements *conformed (included)* but without the final bugs and graphics. The *clean recording* can be played later and topical and timely branding and graphics added as desired. Sports remotes often record a clean feed that can be used for highlights later without the clutter of potentially outdated graphics.

The term "key" comes from two places. Electrically, a *key signal* is an on-off signal as would be generated by a telegraph key. In graphics, a *keyhole* is something to peer into.

Delay Unit

Over the last few years, wardrobe malfunctions and offensive language have been a greater concern for over-the-air broadcasters. Content has become more risqué and the FCC has pushed back with fines even when a case can be made that the offense was accidental. FCC fines have been quite steep as a result, so many stations utilize delay boxes (this doesn't need to be independent hardware, it can be a software function built into a server or other device) to provide a means of censoring objectionable material.

Most news departments have a policy of avoiding live video where people might suddenly be killed on screen in gunfire or in some cases high-speed accidents or extreme sports. Policies vary, but the MCO may be required to insert a delay into a live feed, or the main station signal path, and may be required to monitor the program and hit the *dump button*.

Call-in shows with obnoxious callers, even a parade where someone might streak, etc.) can be controlled in this manner. Some stations are very careful, others opt for a more live feel.

The delay unit takes audio and video, and digitally delays the output for a pre-determined period (usually five to ten-seconds, with seven-seconds being popular) and then plays it back. During this 5- to 10-second delay, someone (usually several people in the control room or station) can press a *panic button* or *dump button* that will drop the audio and put up a pre-loaded graphic (or animation, etc.) until the button is released so that any program where an unexpected event can happen.

Be aware, however, that if you've preset the box to delay the output for 5 seconds, that means the show must also start 5 seconds early, and then end 5 seconds before the off-time of the show. And when the control room goes to a break, they'll be in black for 5 seconds before MCR rolls the break in real time, and begin the next segment 5 seconds before the break ends in real time. For this to work, the output of the delay unit must show up on the MCR switcher and in the automation as another audio/video source.

6
DRIVING THE STATION

The master control operator drives the station (or stations) or networks. Traffic delivers a *schedule*, which includes the instructions of what to play, how and when. This schedule can be printed for a manual operation, or it can be electronic files that are converted through *traffic translator* software to give to an automation system. Manual switching is rare, often found in small- or part-time operations. If possible (and often it is not possible to operate manually for lack of equipment an operator can access) the loss of an automation system or an unusual event or emergency causes the master control operator to go manual. More often, automation systems are responsive enough that these unusual events are handled by automation systems being given manual updates, instructions and adjustments. In cases where BXF is in use, the traffic department can make many if not all of these adjustments without help from master control.

For many years, stations had paper logs to indicate what ran and when. Especially with multichannel operations becoming more and more common, as well as other business and technologic advances, most stations have migrated to paperless logs, saving reams of paper and allowing for the flexibility of a traffic department to be located anywhere. The biggest challenge here is establishing a workable routine for making log changes.

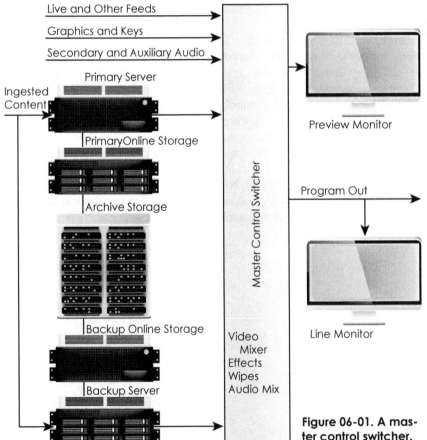

There are other tasks involved, mostly dealing with sources, playing tapes and ingesting material, etc. Chapter 5 discussed the common sources that the MCO will need to drive the station.

Manual Switching

For decades, TV stations were manually switched by MCOs using video switchers (or *video mixers* and *audio mixers*), while tape and film operators loaded content and the MCO called out the countdown to *pre-roll* and take the content. Most of the timing math was done in the MCO's head, and after calculators were developed, a special MCO calculator made time calculations easier.

Figure 06-01. A master control switcher.

Labels in figure: Live and Other Feeds; Graphics and Keys; Secondary and Auxiliary Audio; Primary Server; Ingested Content; PrimaryOnline Storage; Archive Storage; Backup Online Storage; Backup Server; Master Control Switcher; Video Mixer Effects Wipes Audio Mix; Preview Monitor; Program Out; Line Monitor

Today, most MCOs operate the station from the automation system. If there is a master control switcher, it's small, and usually doesn't support the *wipes* (special transitions) and effects of old. Many are *cuts only* switchers and won't perform a fade. Most are *clean and quiet*, meaning there isn't a click or a flash frame caused by the switcher in a transition. An operator control panel might have buttons to quickly set off triggers, recues, and the like in the automation system, and there may be no physical switcher or control panel at all. Touch screens, keyboards, mice and maybe a custom response panel with a few push buttons is the norm. Figure 06-01 shows a typical master control switcher.

Because master control switchers often no longer support anything but the most basic ability, when necessary to support something like a long respectful fade to black or other special effect, a production switcher can be put on line to take the place of the master control for the duration. Some stations basically shut down master control switching with wall-to-wall news events, rolling any spots, or shows, etc., from the news production switcher.

Stations that do have the ability to go manual usually do such to accommodate sports, breaking news or other heavy live production. Automation systems vary greatly in how they deal with manual operations. Some dutifully log every event, others shut down completely and do nothing at all while the station is being operated in manual, and others will still roll ad clusters and log that portion, even if the automation sees nothing else.

Manual switchers usually have both a *preset* and *program* (or *air*) *buses*. Punching *take* transfers the preset to air (and usually what was on air to preset). The concept behind the preset is that the technical director (TD) or master control operator (MCO) can set up the next video (add graphics, effects, etc.) in preset. Alternately hot punching any button on the program bus will immediately take it to air. One can add a *cross-fade* (dissolve) or *V-fade* (fade-to-black then fade up to another video source) to a preset transition, which is easier on the viewer than a hard cut. Rare these days is a *fader bar* (that looked like an airplane throttle) that allows the operator to slowly or quickly, but very manually, control the speed of the transition or effect.

Almost all transitions today are cross fades or V-fades of about 10-frames ($1/3$ second). Here, in five frames the video goes to black, the audio goes silent, and then for five frames, the next source fades up to full video and audio levels.

If master control is a cuts-only switcher, the fades are built into the elements themselves. Each fades up and when done fades to black in a few frames. Putting them back-to-back makes it look like a nice sharp cross fade at each transition. The first and last frames of each element are black, so systems that display a thumbnail of video have to sample some place like the middle of an element or a few frames in if they display beginning and end thumbnails, or all one sees is black.

Master control switchers (and all automation) include clocks: an up-count to tell you how long ago the last event started, and if known, a down count displays the time until the next event.

A very handy option in MCR is a *preview* or *auxiliary* monitor bus. While your playlist is carrying out the day's schedule, you may need to monitor another source – the *auxiliary bus* allows you to do this without tying up the preview bus. Generally, the auxiliary bus monitor is in a location easily visible from the MCR switcher. Your network news operation may contact your station warning of a special report coming up where you need to keep an eye on the network, or if you will need to JIP a show, and would like to join it at a *clean* place in the show.

In centralcast facilities, a single manual switcher or control panel may drive a number of stations running the same live event. They may all have different IDs, bugs, promos and spots, but the breaks all start and stop at the same time. A single operator can run several stations all broadcasting the same game. This is a *gang* function, where essentially the take button of several master control switchers are ganged together into one.

A very few sporting events are distributed with triggers built in, so an operator is required to hear and see the cues to insert the local elements.

Manual switching is the ultimate disaster recovery mode. Some stations keep a master control switcher that can be brought on line if needed. Virtually all stations have an *emergency break-away* or *emergency by-pass* switcher to accommodate some simple form of manual switching if all else fails. This is usually a small independent router that is capable of sending network and maybe a playout channel to the audience even if large pieces of master control fail. This little router is usually not very elegant or clean, given that its job is to be the most bullet-proof and reliable part of the broadcast chain (by its nature, it is a single-point-of-failure. If it fails it will need to be patched or wired around), not the prettiest. For this reason, this simple router is sometimes called a bang box. The bang box term indicates that a switcher, any switcher, doesn't switch cleanly or quietly. Other stations refer to it as "the six-by" or "the ten-by" if it's the only, or at least most special, six- or ten-button stand-alone router in the facility. There are other nicknames, and some are rather creative. Sometimes, the name is derived from the manufacturer of that switcher. Sometimes, the switcher has been replaced but station traditions are hard to change and it may be named after the manufacturer of the long since replaced piece of equipment.

Driving Automation

Chapter 4 describes how automation systems are constructed. Automation systems display a *playlist* that is similar to a spreadsheet. For the most part, driving the automation involves adjusting the playlist much like one would adjust a spreadsheet or document on any computer. The other driving is done on either a hardware panel or software tool that allows instant commands like *take, hold, skip, trim*, etc.

Each automation system is different as to the details and commands; however the basics remain the same. One thing that automation systems facilitate is extensive *secondary events*. In a given spot or program, there can be a series of logos, snipes, voiceovers, squeeze-backs, and other secondary events that are inserted based on a time assigned by traffic that starts when the event starts. If the primary event is *moved* along with its secondary events, the logo that flies in 10-seconds into the spot, still flies in 10-seconds into the spot once the times are recalculated by the automation system.

Figure 06-02. An automation hardware control panel. Courtesy of Imagine Communications.

Sometimes you may need to build a playlist from scratch if the traffic department may not be able to translate its schedule file to a file the automation can read. This would necessitate creating an entire on-air schedule (playlist) by hand, entering the *house number* for each program, commercial, promo and all other elements. As automation systems use computer keyboards, the numeric keypad on the right of the keyboard is especially handy, especially if you become adept at using it (with little practice, it's much easier than touch typing).

Probably the most difficult thing to accomplish in driving the station is the *JIP* (join in progress). Consider a live event that is running long (going over time). We want to *dead roll* the next program with all its breaks, and join it in progress, preferably at some logical place. Because all the elements are moving, it's easy to make a JIP look very ugly. More involved is attempting to save spots from the dead rolled program as same-day make-goods. Each automation system has a means of doing this, some easier and more fool proof than others. Many stations simply go manual.

The typical television viewer probably doesn't realize how many individual events are in a given program, or that there is a need to give them names. The MCO on the other hand has to know what to call such things. Here is a quick overview of some of the most common terms for events. Throughout this book we have referred to many other video and audio events; these are among the more common:

bookends: a break where the same or related spot is placed at the start and end of the break. Some call this "tops and tails," although most reserve this term to refer to trimming spots for time.

bug: a simple, usually transparent logo that remains on during programming to identify the station or network.

built-in/tied-in: a spot that is contained within a program as it is distributed. Some stations *strip* the built-in spots and replace them or rearrange them. Some advertising contracts allow a station to move their built-in spots to other time periods.

bumper (or bump): short little bridge between two elements, usually identifying the main program. Bumpers might be a live tease that breaks up a mega-break.

commercial announcement/spot/ad: usually 30-seconds in length, though 10-, 15-, 20-, 60-, 90-seconds, and 2-minutes are sometimes used to produce revenue for commercial stations.

down-cut: cutting off the end of an element prematurely by starting the next event a bit too early.

fill/filler: a piece that can be exited at any time, used to fill time and avoid up-cutting an element.

flash frame: a few frames of video that doesn't belong there. Usually this is caused by a bad edit or failure to transition to the next source (like a local spot) before the last (network for example) source moves to the next element (resulting is seeing a frame or two of the networks next spot).

interstitial: A package of content between two long-form programs, typically used on movie channels.

logo: Trademark or other graphic element that is inserted.

package: A stand-alone feature, usually in news broadcasts, that tells a story. Unlike a *VO*, where an anchor will *voice-over* video, anchors will introduce a package; the package airs on its own (no anchor involvement), followed by a return to the anchor.

promo: Promotional spot usually assigned by the promotions department.

PSA (public service announcement): a non-revenue message aired in the public interest (e.g.: fire safety, health issues, pet adoptions, etc.).

regional spot (sometimes called breakaway spot): A spot (or series of spots) shown only to a specific audience. An example might be for a cable provider wanting to air generic spots for over-the-air viewers (not on cable), while airing special offers to only those viewers watching your channel on cable. OTA viewers would see the spot in your normal on air playlist, while the regional spot would come from a different video server (and possibly a different playlist) triggered to start by a *secondary event* in the automation playlist and fed to the cable provider by special arrangement.

snipe: Animated graphic, sometimes with audio, promoting programming.

sound on tape (SOT): News packages are usually SOTs. In actuality, most facilities use video servers, not tape, to play news stories in broadcasts. SOT is a carryover from the 1950s-1970s when news film was used and the term was sound on film (SOF).

topical: A promo or spot that is updated to reflect a daily sale price or news topic (or *tease*, where the promo shows just a little of what the viewer can see if they stay tuned).

underwriting announcement: That announcement that helps finance non-commercial broadcasts.

up-cut: Joining an element as its already rolling, most often as a result of the last piece running late and staying on it to avoid a down-cut.

voice-over (VO): A VO is an audio announcement that causes whatever audio is part of the spot or program to duck under the added announcement.

VOSOT: Voice-over, sound on tape (often said as "voh-sot"). Sometimes, a package has *natural sound* (pronounced "nat-sound") that one wishes to keep in background while an announcer introduces the story followed by audio/video from the story only. Sports footage is frequently used as a VOSOT.

Triggers

Most automation systems allow for many different kinds of triggers for starting events. The vast majority of triggers are either automatic, or manual. An *automatic trigger* simply says that when one event is done (usually based on its duration time) the next one starts. A *manual trigger* means that an operator will trigger the next event. For a live event, the MCO will manually trigger the break based on some indication from the event (sometimes on intercom, sometimes after a cue line is spoken like "We will return after these messages").

Other triggers include *fixed time*; where whatever else happens, at a preprogrammed time (or *hard time*), the desired event is fired. This is often used to join networks. MCOs either trigger events or adjust times and enter times to make the programming flow properly.

Manual switching has only manual triggers. The MCO in a manual station has to trigger each and every event, usually with button presses.

Other Tasks

EAS tests are fairly straight forward as this is a scheduled event and may even be entirely under automation control. In some cases the MCO has to manually fire the EAS test message at some point in the EAS test message element being played. A real EAS event isn't going to be on the log, and most stations don't automate this in order to verify that the message is appropriate, and may even delay the message for continuity (so it doesn't up-cut or down-cut another element). If EAS is automated, it's generally for a station that doesn't have news, and when the EAS message is urgent. If the station is unattended, automatic EAS message retransmission is often required in order to be compliant. Like the JIP, there may be make-goods desired, and getting into and out of the EAS message can be clumsy. A great MCO can do a pretty seamless job of this.

Mostly driving the station, once you get through the learning curve, is fairly uneventful, until the unexpected happens.

Audio and (rarely) video level adjustments are part of driving the station, especially for live cut-ins. Audio track shuffling to provide stereo, mono, SAP, and 5.1 surround sound is not an uncommon task.

Likewise, bringing in sources, preparing material, and other tasks not part of driving the station are most often MCO duties. Having excellent organization tools and skills is likely the single most critical aptitude required. Familiarity with the equipment and SOPs are close seconds.

Live and Live News

Stations operate news and live events basically in one of three ways:

1. Master control plays the spots and maybe some other elements, inserting them into the news or live event. In other words, to master control, this looks like any other live program.

2. The live event or newscast plays all of its own elements. To master control this looks like a *sustaining program* (without breaks). Since master control owns the spots, master control might make up a ***spot reel*** in advance, usually using the automation with a separate, small, playlist that assembles the spots, which are then recorded on some transportable media that can be sent out to a live sports remote truck or to a production control room.

3. Something in between. Here the MCO works with the *technical director* (TD), usually communicating with the station or remote intercom system. MCOs will *countdown* the news TD to get him or her into and out of breaks and elements – or vice versa. MCOs might be assigned production duties or might even get a break during the newscast.

Spot reels have other uses. For maintenance, a spot reel that has several hours of programming and/ or breaks can be prerecorded allowing the master control to be taken off line as an MCO with a small router and a playback tape machine (or DVD, etc.) keeps the station on the air.

Intercom

News and sometimes live events require some means for the MCO to speak with various producers, talent, or technical staff. This can be as simple as a phone call, but more often, stations and production facilities (remote trucks or a news control room in the building) have frequently elaborate intercom systems that interface with wireless IFBs, two-way radios, telephone lines, headsets, and *intercom stations*.

Intercoms can be the simple *push to talk* (PTT) variety, usually arranged as a series of *private lines* (PL) that go directly to the person or persons desired. When talent is involved, it is common to have an earpiece that has the program audio along with **interruptible foldback** (IFB). With IFB, the MCO, director, or other staff can *cue* the talent as they listen to program audio. A *mix-minus* can let the talent hear everything except their own voice coming back. This is often necessary as delays in the audio caused by processing and transmission will create a long echo that will confuse the talent and make it hard if not impossible for them to speak naturally or even coherently.

Going Wrong

Every now and again, an entire program may not be available or is unplayable. Most stations have SOPs that address most situations. Many stations have *evergreens* on hand to fill any program hole that might occur. Evergreens are shows or elements that can be used at any time and get old. Some are Paid Inquiry, *program length commercials*; where there is a good chance the station will make some money from viewers contacting the advertiser. Others may be programs sent specifically by syndicators as *backup shows*.

There should be SOPs about recovering lost spots, covering missing spots, and dealing with all manner of issues.

OTA MCOs will almost certainly have to deal with recovering the transmitter after lighting strikes, power hits, and the like. Mostly, these are automatic recoveries; however there is a point where the MCO may need to switch to a back-up transmitter, manually start a generator and transfer to it, change an STL, or any number of emergency activities. Ideally the MCO can hand off anything serious to engineering and the SOPs are clear, detailed, easy to use, and the MCO is familiar with recovering any systems that require it.

Losing your network feed is just as critical. If you cannot *quickly* determine what the issue is your course of action after putting the trouble sequence or its equivalent on air, is to attempt to access your network from another source (an alternate satellite receiver, perhaps you have a microwave/fiber link from another **affiliate**, and for network stations in the West and Mountain time zones, make a habit of recording the East Coast feed and have it *dead rolling* as a standby, especially for major events) and fix the problem later.

For facilities with the financial means, many have planned for unforeseen events potentially impacting their air product. It is not unusual to see duplicate hardware, software and video servers that essentially mirror one another. In essence, you have two identical automation systems running two identical video servers with one system acting as *protection* to the primary system.

In situations where redundancy is not possible, it is then often SOP to back up programming material on tape. Also, for high-revenue periods (such as prime-time and local news, as well as high visibility events like the Super Bowl, Olympics, and major award shows), it may be wise to assemble a *spot reel* (or *dub reel* or *break tape* -- pre-assembled reel of the commercial breaks) as a backup.

Syncing a Backup Videotape to On Air

If a copy of the program is available on tape (and that tape format can be put on air), getting tape synced up with what is currently on the air isn't too difficult. The first goal is getting the tape cued as close to what is on air as possible. Try zeroing the tape counter at first video (of the top of the show, or if in a multi-segment show, the top of that show segment) and shuttling the tape to just past the spot where the server is currently playing on air. Pick a phrase on the tape and then stop the tape.

When you hear that phrase play on air, hit play on the tape machine. Ideally, the audio on air and the audio from the tape will be in close enough sync. If not, determine whether the tape audio is ahead or behind air audio. If tape is ahead, press stop on the tape machine momentarily and quickly press play again. If tape is behind, press fast forward, then quickly press play. If a *jog* control is available, *jog* the media to where you need it to be. The goal is to get both air and tape audio to become time aligned. If you're hearing an echo, try the stop/play or fast forward/play again until you do get the audio to match. This sounds harder than it is, but after a few attempts, you'll feel more comfortable with this technique.

A well-prepared MCO will have plans to deal with potential issues over time: losing a local/syndicated show, losing network, difficulty with or loss of the MCR switcher, and finally what to do if your automation system goes down.

Practicalities

Driving the station can make taking a break difficult. A facility's break rooms and bathrooms often have TV monitors, and every now and then, there is a creative way of keeping control of the station while away from the control room (like a remote take button). Fire alarms are a special issue as evacuating the station for a half-hour waiting for the fire officials to clear the scene can take the station off the air. Some states have legal requirements for work breaks and some have severe penalties for failing to evacuate after a fire alarm sounds. Usually, there is some reasonable and safe accommodation plan.

Food and drink is another matter in that an accidental spill just about anywhere in a technical area can be devastating. Console equipment and to a degree wiring below computer floors are particularly vulnerable. For this reason, most facilities prohibit food, drink and smoking in technical areas. Generally, there are opportunities for an MCO to get adequate relief, but it requires organization and planning.

Coming up to Speed

Depending on the complexity of the station and the skill level of the MCO coming up to speed can take some serious time. Certainly a week or two is normal for experienced MCOs. Expect longer if this is your first MCO gig. It takes time to build up the specific skills for each master control operation. It's a lot harder than learning to drive. The key seems to follow a pattern of observe and then do. An MCO is only ready when the trainer can observe the MCO doing a shift unaided and with confidence.

Invariably, in your first few uncomfortable solo shifts, something rare and impossible to prepare for will happen. Being in tune with your station's systems and policies is what will give you what you need to get out of the mess. Even if it's wrong, it's a learning experience, and every MCO has them.

7
VIDEO

Technical

There are many combinations of aspect ratio, resolutions, digital encoding, audio and ***compression*** that are supported and widely used at various locations in a facility. There are entire books on the subject, but as an MCO there are some basic distinctions that are useful.

Baseband or uncompressed video, either ***HD*** or ***SD*** is the basic commodity in a facility. It runs on SDI (serial digital interface) coaxial cable for about a hundred meters. HD runs at a higher data rate, and some systems require two coaxial cables. The audio may be *embedded* in the same SDI, which makes it difficult to work with (mix, change levels, etc.), but is perfect for transmission and transport where one doesn't want the audio manipulated. If there is need for mixing audio or adjusting levels, the audio needs to be *disembedded*. At some point the audio is re-embedded because it is easier to deal with one combined signal path for transmission.

Analog facilities always have separate audio and video wiring, patch bays, etc.

Digital video can be sampled with various *depths* as in 8-bit or 10-bit. More bits per *pixel* (one dot of video image) results in higher resolution of the video levels (brightness and number of colors) and fewer artifacts. How many video pixels are sampled can also vary. The more pixels used effectively, the higher the resolution of detail will be. The top of the practical pyramid is 4:4:4:4 video, which means that the luminance and both color signals and even an alpha (key) channel is sampled at full resolution. One only sees this in high-end production environments. 4:2:2 encodes the Y (luminance) at full resolution, but the Cb and Cr (chroma or color signals) are encoded at half resolution taking advantage of the human eye's reduced sensitivity to color resolution. 4:2:0, 4:1:1, even 3:1:1 also exist.

Baseband video only travels well for a short distance on coax, and is very bandwidth intensive, so compressed video works better for storage and transport. Compressed video does not manipulate well and the encoding process has delays that make timing difficult.

Automatic Format Description (AFD) is a series of 16-codes (of which four are commonly used) that tells a television how to display video with different aspect ratios. Some few MCOs change or correct AFD information so that the video displays correctly: stretching, letterboxing, etc., as needed. AFD information is included in the video and ideally is passed all the way to the viewers TV. Mixing and switching between different aspect ratios is complicated but for the most part AFD makes it automatic. How a particular TV deals with AFD information may vary, and some displays allow the viewer options for zoom, cinema, normal, and other ways of dealing with aspect ratio variations.

Operator Tasks

MCOs often have to set up cameras and the rare analog tape machine. Cameras need to be *white balanced* (to compensate for even the slight variation in illumination *color temperature*) and their *black levels* (the darkest part to be reproduced) and *white levels* (the brightest part of the picture to be reproduced) set. If there is more than one camera, they need to be adjusted to match each other, or switching from one to another will be jarring. Many cameras are largely automatic, but all cameras have some process to adjust and match them prior to use, adjusting for the scene and the lighting. The usual controls are *pedestal* (or ped for black level), *iris* that controls the amount of light through the lens, and *clip level*, that limits the brightness. Deeper controls for color and *gamma* (the transfer curve that relates light level to electrical level) are things one is best off experiencing if you are required to manually set up a camera to this level.

Analog tape machines and other analog video components often have adjustments for black and white levels, and *color phase* (hue) and intensity (saturation). In the digital domain, there is no drift in the equipment, so color and level corrections are rare.

Video levels are measured in IRE units, where 100 is brightest white and 0 is black (for digital; 7.5 IRE for analog). The test tool is a waveform monitor where the luminance and color levels can be displayed.

The vectorscope displays color content as hue and saturation. See Figure 07-01. As mentioned, **SMPTE** bars is a standard setup and reference signal that displays in a very recognizable pattern on waveform and vector scopes.

A *rasterizer* (there are other rasterizers used for driving other displays) type video and audio monitor has become the standard audio and video operational test tool. Typically a computer-type display screen is segmented into four blocks; a picture monitor, waveform monitor, vector scope, and a multidimensional audio monitor. There are other pieces of equipment used for maintenance and deeper engineering tests.

The actual utility of a WFM and vectorscope in a digital facility is often limited to providing a means of describing a problem from some incoming media or source (low luma, clipped blacks... etc.). Some fully digital facilities have no WFM or vectorscope at all.

Video Monitoring

As you might imagine, there are several components to the video signal; many of the components come in pairs. Let's discuss their differences.

• Analog vs. Digital

Initially, one needs to determine whether a signal is analog or digital. Analog signals are less prevalent. Simply put, analog equipment (and the hardware used to monitor the analog equipment) is susceptible to various errors and distortions inherent in the analog process. Analog systems drift over time and temperature, and need constant adjustment. Successive errors are cumulative, resulting in the possibility of poor quality video if several *generations* of dubs are made.

Each generation of an analog recording is a poorer rendition of the original, where, with the exception of the compression steps and occasional uncorrected bit error or media defect, a properly operating digital system presents each generation as an identical copy of the original.

Digital signals are comprised of zeroes and ones – essentially all video information is represented by very specific (non-variable) data. As a result, digital video is more consistent, more rugged if you will; and is more easily dubbed, transferred, manipulated, and ultimately predictable – it's either there, or it's not. This is sometimes called the *digital cliff*. All is perfect until the digital system approaches the digital cliff, past which the video becomes unusable or nonexistent.

• Standard Definition vs. High Definition

Current systems are generally **standard definition** (**SD**) or high definition (**HD** or **Hi-Def**), although for Web distribution, there may be formats that are less than SD and for projection and high-end homes, there is *4K* or *UHDTV* (Ultra High Definition TV). As technological development moved forward, and the number of scanning lines and pixels was increased, the old **NTSC** format would be referred to as standard definition.

Standard definition has 525 scan lines (of which 480 lines are actually intended to be visible) and is scanned in an *interlaced* (as opposed to progressively scanned) fashion: the odd lines are scanned first, the even lines are scanned. The aspect ratio is always 4:3 (four screen units wide by three units high). You may see the SD signal sometimes abbreviated as 480i (the 'I' standing for interlace.)

High definition video can have either 720 lines or 1080 lines: usually 720p scanned progressively (an entire frame is scanned *progressively,* one line after another) or 1080i scanned in the *interlaced* fashion (odd lines, then even lines). The aspect ratio for the HD signal is 16:9 (16 screen units wide by 9 units high). Perhaps the most notable difference between 720p and 1080i has to do with motion: Video with faster movement (sports, for instance) is better suited to 720p; video that is more static (drama, sitcoms, talk) handles 1080i better.

In any case, 1080p is the best of both and is catching on, but takes more bandwidth and resources. Cinema style *4K* is available but has not become economical enough or efficient enough to be a major force as this is written. Undoubtedly it will soon enough.

Prior to a program (or shorter element) either being recorded or distributed it is sent with a special test signal called *color bars*. This familiar signal serves a very special purpose: it allows the person receiving the video to adjust their equipment so it reasonably matches the levels sent from the sender's end. This means, for example, if a production uses a control room to record or transmit video, the bars (and accompanying audio tone) should come from that control room's switcher and audio board. Alternatively, a video distributor such as a network would use the network bars or house bars from their primary transmission location as the standard to reference video, chroma and audio levels.

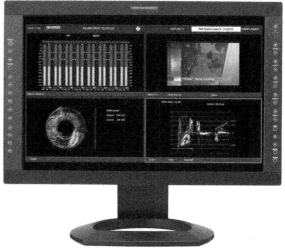

Figure 07-01. A waveform monitor.

Waveform Monitors

This is how it works: To monitor and evaluate the video signal, we use two items: the waveform monitor and the vectorscope. Waveform monitors display the luminance (black and white portion of the video), while vectorscopes display the chrominance or *chroma* (the color information of video). Note the fact that waveform monitors (frequently abbreviated, as *WFM*) in the analog realm register black at 7.5 *IRE* (think of IRE as units of video) and white at 100 IRE, while digital waveform monitors 'see' black at 0. Using color bars to set levels, the white bar gives you something that is 100 IRE, while the black bar gives you something to adjust your black levels (black levels are sometimes referred to as the pedestal).

Vectorscopes

Vectorscopes use a circular display to monitor the color within a video signal. Within the circle, you'll see several small boxes: when you feed color bars to a vectorscope, the vectors representing each color should fall within the little boxes. At the center of the circle is a dot. This represents monochrome (no color). If you were running a black-and-white movie, for instance, a vectorscope would show the colorless movie as a tiny blob of video clustered around that center dot. Conversely, feeding color bars to a vectorscope would reveal a display starting in the center (representing the black bar) and tracing the signal to each of the labeled small boxes (R for red, C for cyan (light blue), M for magenta (medium-purple)). The goal is to adjust the system so the dots representing each color of color bars are inside the small boxes on the vectorscope. That said, digital video systems have few means of adjustment, because once encoded, the values should not change.

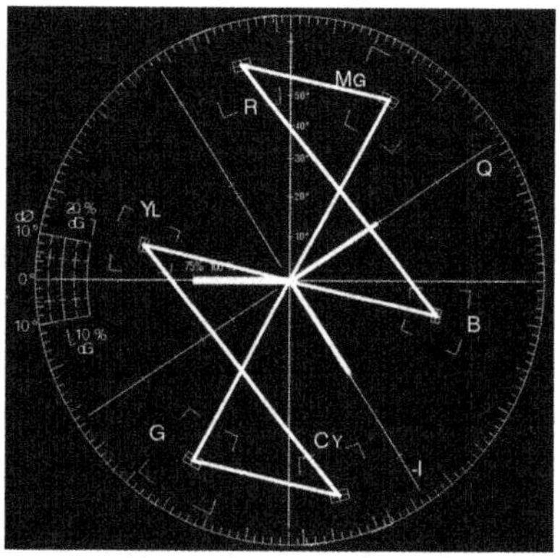

Analog video, on the other hand, can experience nonlinearities and distortion at every step that require adjustments and compensation. You may notice on analog vectorscopes some dots will align perfectly in the boxes, and others will be slightly off-center. In this case, first verify

Figure 07-02. An NTSC vector-scope showing SMPTE color bars.

color burst (about a 1/2 inch line starting at the center of the vectorscope) is at the 9 o'clock position, and then adjust the red vector to fall into the center of the red box. Remember, the most critical color in your picture will be flesh color. Flesh is predominately made up of red, so you want what represents red to be the most accurate.

Test and Setup Signals
• Video Monitors
You probably don't think of a video monitor, a plain old ordinary TV, as a piece of test equipment; yet it is by far the most valuable piece of equipment you have to use and it can do an amazing amount of things. Monitors come in two flavors: confidence monitors and critical monitors (or some name that refers to professional, quality, production, setup, etc.). Confidence monitors can be cheap, ugly, small, and dim. Their task is to confirm that the station is on the air, the source is there, the content is correct, and the camera is pointed and focused. In the old days, confidence monitors were black and white to save money, and these were jammed together to get as many as needed in place. Monitors generate heat at take up space.

Monitors are manufactured, and some allow electrically changing, the color temperature. Ideally, the monitors all have the same color temperature and the room lighting is close. Dimming incandescent lights also lowers their color temperature making the room seem warmer and thus the monitors seem cooler or bluer. Ideally, the control room lighting is dimmable and maintains the decided upon color temperature, although it isn't the end of the world if it does not. Control rooms were traditionally dark to enhance the viewing of dimmer older monitors. While that is no longer necessary and in fact comfortable indoor light levels are practical, tradition often dictates that the control room is darkened. Few monitors are of much use in daylight as it takes an exceptionally bright screen to be visible in bright light.

Multiviewers are more the norm now, where many video sources are pasted into a larger display. Multiviewers often include alarm functions for loss of (or out of range) video or audio, closed caption, etc. Generally, alarms appear on screen as red blinking boxes or the like. Audio levels are often also displayed as VU meters overlaid on or next to the video. Multiviewers often have more than one layout available, typically one for overnights, daytime, news time, etc. where what is needed is displayed and what is not needed is not. Usually, where this feature is used, the MCO has access to buttons to change the monitor configuration to match the task or shift involved.

Most facilities have at least one critical viewing monitor. These range from expensive to very expensive. Much effort is made to display the colors and every pixel of video information as accurately as one can afford. They are used to evaluate picture quality when adjusting cameras, correcting video, etc. If your facility does a lot of critical work, or is in a major market, the critical monitors will be placed in color temperature (the color of the lighting) controlled settings, at an almost precise distance for viewing. Digital media doesn't degrade in the same way as analog video did in storage and transmission, so should require no adjustment, whereas analog material required constant attention and correction. Thus, not every station has a good critical viewing monitor. Many of the test signals we have, have their roots in analog adjustments that don't exist in the same way any longer.

Professional video monitors might allow you to *under scan* the picture to see every last pixel and sometimes things that are in the *HANC* (horizontal ancillary data) and *VANC* (vertical ancillary data), which are not video at all, but audio and other signals embedded into the video. For that increasingly rare analog signal, under scan allows you to look at the sync pulses, and the *cross pulse* setting allows you to look at the intersection of vertical and horizontal sync, timecode and test signals that might be embedded in the vertical sync. You may never see a cross point-capable monitor.

• SMPTE Color Bars
That takes us to the ubiquitous *SMPTE bars*. Found at the head of most tapes, on T-shirts, as filler

when a channel isn't in use, the last thing you see when a remote ***good nights*** a satellite or fiber link, nothing is more TV than SMPTE bars. It's used to setup everything from analog monitors, analog tapes, analog transmissions, to analog color encoders and decoders. In the digital world those adjustments are rarely available, and probably should be left alone if they are, so *bars and tone* simply verify that all is right. The tone part refers to the practice of placing a 1000Hz sine wave of great purity and accuracy on the audio tracks associated with bars at 100% operating level.

There are many fine points to bars and tone, many annotated in the adjacent figure. SMPTE *recommended practice* (SMPTE bars are not a *standard*) 219-2002 is only 15 pages long, so the test and setup signal is not complex. From Figure 07-03 you can see that it's a series of colored and colorless blocks designed to verify the accuracy of the color rendition system. Bars should come from a test signal generator; usually this is built into the facility's master timing and synchronization generator and made available as a source on video routers. Bars should be "fresh" (coming from a test signal generator, usually built into the master clock and sync generator) whenever being laid down at the start of a video project. Copying, encoding or decoding bars might create degradations (what we're trying to minimize) and that makes them unsuitable (and no longer accurate) as the primary source reference for a video project. If the bars do not agree with the video, the odds are good that the video will look bad if the bars are the basis for setup adjustments.

The choice of colors has a basic mathematical relationship to the constituent signals in a video system. On a waveform monitor or vectorscope, both holdovers from the analog era, the patterns formed are easily recognizable. Tektronix and Wikipedia have excellent if not exhaustive material on using these and other pieces of test equipment. Frankly, the best and only way to learn about setup and system test signals

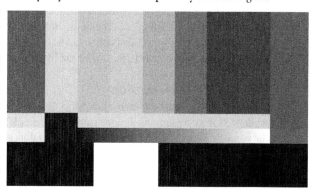

is to use them. Most broadcast maintenance engineers will be pleased to show you how to use test signals on your test equipment.

Setup signals are designed to make setting video and audio levels, and adjusting color easily. Test signals look for impairments mostly in the transmission and storage systems, most often looking at the encoders, decoders, and compression. There are other test signals for the physical wiring, fiber, microwave, and satellite circuits that measure how error free the transmission system is.

SMPTE Bars provide a means of setting up a critical viewing monitor. The black level of the monitor is correct when the black bars of 0% are as dark as they can be, and the small +2% bars are as bright as they can be (which is just barely) without the 0% black being any brighter than the -2%% black (*super black*) bar. In other words, looking at the lower black bars, it should be completely and uniformly black with just one or two slivers of ever so slightly gray.

The color decoders are set correctly when the red and green pixels are shut off (critical monitors usually allow you to, at a minimum, run just the blue guns (in a tube-type cathode ray tube, or CRT) or blue pixels in an LED/LCD/

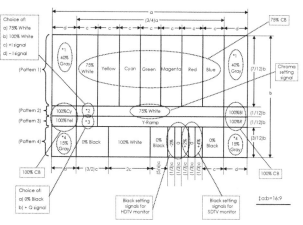

Figure 07-03. SMPTE Bars.

OLD/plasma flat screen. Every other color bar across the set of bars has exactly the same amount of blue in it, so if the monitor is set up correctly, all the bars look exactly the same shade and brightness of blue, separated by black bars.

Parts of SMPTE Bars (and many other test signals) are outside what a monitor can properly display. Super black is blacker than black, which is useful for testing systems and graphics creation, but a monitor cannot display anything blacker than black. Likewise, some analog encoder signals might appear as a strange purple, but actually contain no useful color information. They do have meaning when viewed on waveform or vector scopes. As good as a monitor can be, it cannot reproduce all of the colors in nature or handle anything close to the range from dark to light (*dynamic range*) that the human eye can perceive. Figure 07-03 details on the pieces of the SMPTE Bars.

• Gamma

Gamma is one consideration to be aware of. The relationship between the electrical value of the video and the actual brightness the monitor displays is not a straight line, linear relationship. There is a curve applied to extend the dynamic range displayed. On critical monitors, the gamma may be selectable as different systems have different gammas. Select the wrong gamma and the monitor will not track light levels properly.

Many things can be added to Bars. *Click tracks,* where the audio clicks in time with some movement on screen for lip synch are common. Even more so is some identification of where the bars are generated or what the nature of the content to follow is.

Networks in particular tend to place bars and tone with some sort of lip synch indicator that lends itself to viewing on test equipment on idle transmission paths. Usually there is a timing click at the top of every ten seconds where if one places the audio and video on a WFM one can see and very accurately adjust for lip sync. Network timecode is often displayed and sometimes encoded to make determining the local station's offset from network time. Your facility may compensate for this one or two second offset.

Over-the-Air Transmission

Over-the-air transmission accounts for a significant portion of the North American television audience for many stations. Before cable, satellite (*MVPDs*) and the Internet, *OTA* accounted for all of the viewers. Many MVPDs pick up the OTA signal as their source (some install fiber to the station for a better uncompressed signal). Most recompress the OTA signal. Each time a video signal is compressed, it loses some fidelity. Also, OTA stations often have more bandwidth allocated for their *HDTV* signal than MVPDs do; so the OTA signal is often better, sometimes considerably so, than the MVPD version of the same signal.

The current ATSC OTA system uses MPEG 2 compression, while most MVPDs are a generation ahead and use much more efficient MPEG 4. Ideally one does not *concatenate* the two compressions, so MVPDs prefer having a clean uncompressed signal to work with.

OTA systems can be a series of smallish transmitters with overlapping coverage that creates a *single-frequency network* (SFN), or more commonly a single larger *boomer* of a transmitter with an antenna high above the ground (2000 feet above average terrain in the less populated western states is common, 1,000 feet in eastern states, as going above this height results in decreasing power by regulation, and 2,000 feet is a very tall tower) covering many miles. American systems are rarely SFNs, and mostly each station has its own transmitter. A station may have its own tower, and transmitter building, but many stations share a tower and transmission facility with other stations and services.

OTA systems may have low power (*LPTV*) relays, *translators* or repeaters. These are small transmitters that cover places within the DMA that the main transmitter can't reach because of distance or terrain. These must be identified at least once a day. They most often have different frequencies than the main transmitter and their identification includes the *RF* channel number. A typical translator (this one operating on channel 47) identification is something like K47AB.

OTA stations in rural areas often elect to operate with minimal power that covers the city of license, and no more. The remainder of the DMA is covered by MVPDs. Others have full power *satellite* stations to cover huge areas. Satellite stations have towers and OTA transmitters, and no they don't use orbiting satellites.

Many OTA stations operate on channels other than their original RF (radio frequency) channel. UHF channels being more desirable for digital transmissions than the noisier VHF channels that also require larger receive antennas and do not penetrate buildings as well. On the other hand, VHF channels travel farther, even over the horizon for some distance.

ATSC

On December 24, 1996, the FCC adopted a digital television system based on the A/53 standard of the Advanced Television Systems Committee (ATSC). The United States ATSC standard was adopted after nearly a decade of exhaustive lab and field testing. ATSC transmission standards employ a modulation technique known as 8-VSB.

In a typical station situation, the transmission stream (or path) goes through the MCR/Studio to the transmitter and finally up and out from the antenna or tower to the public. It is beyond the scope of this handbook to go into great detail; however, you should have a basic understanding of what happens from master control through the transmitter to the antenna.

Figure 07-04. A typical TV transmitter. Courtesy of Rohde & Schwarz.

At a certain point, an encoder accepts HD-SDI or SD-SDI video and embedded or separate AES or analog audio and compresses and encodes them into one ASI bitstream that is sent to a multiplexer within the station. The multiplexer accepts several ASI streams and multiplexes them to a single stream.

As we discussed, stations have a ***PSIP (Program and System Information Protocol)*** element that contains critical data about the channel and plays a major role in the DTV signal. If PSIP codes are missing or wrong, most DT receivers won't recognize the presence of an otherwise usable DTV signal. It is the PSIP which identifies an over-the-air signal that may be transmitted from digital channel 45 but appears on a home receiver as *virtual* Channel 2.1, the next channel as 2.2, and so on.

Coupled with this is the ***electronic program guide (EPG)***, which allows program information, length, and other information to be included with the program. Some stations use this to a greater degree than others.

Also, you should be aware of the ***Nielsen Audio Video Encoder (NAVE)***, which essentially puts a *watermark* on your television signal letting "Nielsen boxes" (usually attached to a fixed position TV, and built into the software of a more portable device) know a viewer watched a specific channel, on a specific date, and at a specific time. If the program is viewed later, the watermark remains and the Nielsen equipment then knows when the viewer watched, what and for how long. Most stations monitor their Nielsen data because if it is bad or missing, the result is loss of ratings and thus possible loss of revenue.

Once we have encoded and multiplexed audio/video, PSIP, EPG, closed caption, NAVE, dialnorm and other data it is ready to be sent to the transmitter. It gets there via the *studio-transmitter link* (STL). This link is usually a microwave or fiber-optic connection from MCR to the transmitter. If microwave is used as the STL, there is a microwave receiver at the transmitter site to receive the microwave signal from master control. It is not unusual for stations to have redundant STLs as they play such a critical role in the air chain and present a single point of failure. Some stations have a disaster recovery system at the transmitter that takes over if the STL or even the studio fails.

At the transmitter, the STL receiver receives the ASI signal from MCR and converts it to a *synchronous serial interface* (SSI) following SMPTE 310M standards requirements. An *exciter* converts (*modulates*) the SMPTE 310M data into the ***ATSC 8-VSB*** RF/Transmission standard for broadcast. Up to the exciter the signal is essentially raw. The exciter prepares the signal for broadcast by *modulating* the data onto an RF *carrier*. Finally, the *transmitter* takes the prepared signal and amplifies it and sends it up through filters that remove undesired out of channel RF energy and feed *transmission lines* (the slang is "plumbing") to the antenna high in the air that *radiates* the broadcast to homes.

Multichannel Video Program Distributors

MVPDs account for most of many broadcasters' viewers and all of a cable channels' or a cable netlet. The ***FCC***, too, regulates these. There are two basic relationships with an OTA broadcast station; retransmission rights (*retrans*), or *must carry*.

Stations that have high demand from the ***MVPD's*** customers may negotiate a retransmission fee from the MVPD. Usually this is a few cents per MVPD customer. The major network ***affiliates*** virtually all receive payments from the MVPDs that carry them.

A television station can require any MVPD serving the market to carry at least their primary service. Religious channels, home shopping channels and others that have a lesser demand from the MVPDs customers often exercise *must carry*. With must carry the station simply requires the MVPD serving the DMA to carry the content of its main channel.

MVPDs can receive the signal off-air, or work out a mutually beneficial agreement to install a fiber or other link. Usually the quality is better with a fiber link, and the reliability can increase as a transmitter failure doesn't affect the MVPD fiber feed. Should the fiber fail, the MVPD may be able to take the OTA signal.

As this is written, MVPDs generally carry just the first and primary OTA service. There are relationships where secondary services (sub-channels) are carried, especially when these are second tier networks or other desirable content. Some retrans agreements take carriage of additional services in lieu of cash.

Cable systems can account for hundreds of carriage agreements. Cable also supports two-way communications, so interactive, dynamic and second screen services are being developed. They can also all be different and individual.

Hotels and venues that distribute TV on site are not MVPDs. They do not have to have an agreement with the station to put the station on to their in-house system serving their rooms if they are in the stations coverage area.

Telephone companies (telcos) can also be MVPDs. More telecoms are becoming MVPDs, though their sweet spot is often in rural areas and small communities where they can compete directly with satellite and cable. Telcos have some technical advantages and some limitations. Some are looking to provide a better, more unlimited, ***IPTV*** service; others just see an MVPD business as an add-on, where a less expensive and more limited product than DTH satellite can be an attractive offering. There are hundreds of telcos, ranging from the tier-one massive companies, to tier-three locally owned and operated companies with a few hundred customers.

The other MVPDs are the ***DTH*** satellite services (the US has currently two providers). The *Satellite Home Viewer Act* (SHVA, pronounced "sheeva") sets many of the rules. In general, like any MVPD, they can only allow viewers in the ***DMA*** to see the station. There are some exceptions where a station is allowed to be distributed outside the DMA. Satellite TV on domestic airplanes often carries the major New York or Los Angeles network affiliates and nothing else. In cases where there is no OTA station receivable and nothing local available on the DTH satellite, a station out of market can be designated. As time goes on, these locations become fewer. On the other hand, oil rigs in the Gulf of Mexico get their

TV from somewhere. Outside the United States, there are often creative, if not entirely legal, means of being able to watch domestic TV on foreign soil and on international waters. National boarders don't stop broadcast signals. It's often estimated that some 90% of Canadians can receive US OTA broadcast.

There is a range of relationships the MCO might have with an MVPD. Almost all stations monitor the local cable feed, and the two US domestic **DTH** satellite services. The MCO might have an SOP to call when things aren't right. Avoid calling DTH providers during rainstorms that block the signal reaching the station, as it will cure itself when the rain stops and the satellite service is likely operating well. Other **MVPDs** might receive special feeds, with different commercials or programming. Some MVPDs might receive special data or triggers to insert commercials. All of these tasks probably involve the MCO.

MVPDs have closed caption, descriptive audio, and **CALM** (loudness) regulations to conform to. The MCO oversees all of this, and needs to be vigilant that what leaves master control makes it though all the means of distribution to the limits of the MCOs view.

MCOs in small markets might take calls from viewers experiencing problems. Often the caller wants you to increase power, which of course you can't do and probably wouldn't help in any case. Most viewers with reception problems are not technically savvy, and more often than not, have poor antennas (usually indoor). Usually, one tries to be helpful, but it's hard to be the MCO and troubleshoot viewers' individual issues. Be nice, and if your SOP is to turn the call over to an engineer, get the caller's name, complaint and phone number and pass it on. Whatever you do, don't take these calls too seriously. There are a lot of irrational people who call TV stations.

The general manager and sales staff, etc., usually expect the MCO to be aware of anything affecting the signal distribution. Because of this role, MCOs should learn quickly the basic distribution means and needs of their facility. These are the calls an MCO most often receives on the hotline (perhaps referred to as the red phone): the one with the secret number that only the networks, Federal Aviation Administration, engineers, traffic and executive staff have. Incidentally, the red phone should not be on the same internal phone system as the rest of the facility. It should be a direct line from the outside so that it works when all else fails.

8
SOUND

What is more important: sound or video? Some would say it's a meaningless debate. There is never agreement as to the answer, yet it's not a frivolous question as one debates what to pay most attention to as one prioritizes one's activities. At the very least, both audio and video must be close in importance, but a very good case can be made for the preeminence of audio, despite that video is what makes TV, TV. Far fewer complaints are raised about bad video than bad audio. People will wait through a video failure a lot longer than they will wait through an audio failure. There are even arguments to be made that our minds process audio with precedence over video. The bottom line is that while video may take considerable effort and expense, be a lot easier and more passive to monitor, and some of us focus our careers on the video; at best, video only approaches audio in its importance and the attention that audio demands.

The Technical Basics of TV Sound

TV watchers' investment in their home viewing equipment for both video and sound varies widely. Sound systems can be a simple set of ear-buds or very tiny speakers in a handheld device (cell phone or the like) to rather expensive, sometimes overpowered home theater surround sound systems. A master control operator often has control over what the various viewers' experience will be, and may need to balance that experience. It is entirely possible to have audio that sounds great on a surround sound system, but is useless on a small speaker, and vice versa. All of this is for a number of reasons. Part of your job is identifying when audio is not good for all or some part of the audience, and to understand how to fix it when possible. We will identify many of the typical situations later in this manual.

Like video, all audio starts out as an analog signal. Sound vibrations move a diaphragm in a microphone that then is used to generate a very weak varying voltage that represents the audio. Of course, there are also synthesizers and musical instruments that can directly generate an electronic audio signal. If the analog audio signal is amplified and applied to a larger set of diaphragms (speakers) with some power, we have a simple sound system. That amplification needed between a microphone and speaker is millions of times of gain.

There are a lot of limitations to analog audio. First, the farther you want to send the signal, the more degraded it becomes. Microphone audio levels are so low that they are particularly prone to pick up interference from lighting circuits, power of any kind (creating a low hum or sharp buzz) as well as from *radio frequency* devices. A two-way radio or a cell phone can cause great interference to an analog microphone circuit. Computers, remote controls, motors, all have the potential to introduce noise into the microphone circuit. For this reason, it is best to amplify the microphone-level to something more robust fairly soon in the signal path, or better yet, digitize it. In some cases, a digital microphone can be used, where the analog to digital conversion can happen inside the microphone's container.

Figure 08-01. Male and female XLR connectors. Courtesy of Neutrik.

One way to minimize the problems with analog audio is to use balanced circuits as opposed to single-ended (unbalanced) circuits. If the circuit is balanced, there are two signal wires and probably a ground or shield; hence, the three pins in an *XLR* connector and the tip-ring-sleeve connections in a patch cord. Single-ended circuits have a single signal wire (usually the center conductor in a coaxial cable) and use the shield as the return; hence the center conductor and shield of coaxial cable and the use of *RCA connectors*.

Television Operations

Microphones can sometimes be powered with either a battery in the microphone case or *phantom power,* where dc voltage is fed back to the microphone over the microphone wire to power certain microphones that require power for their basic operation, amplification or digital conversion. Phantom power is used more or less exclusively with microphones. Sometimes, a switch on the audio mixer board turns on and off the power depending on whether you want to feed power to the microphone or not. It usually doesn't matter, but is better not to send phantom power to a microphone that doesn't need it. A microphone that does need phantom power simply won't work without it. Hence as an MCO, you may have plugged in a microphone for a news cut-in, but failed to turn on the phantom power. Most mixers have a small button associated with the fader to which the microphone is attached.

Figure 08-02.
An RCA connector.

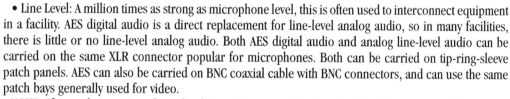

Analog audio comes in basically four varieties:

• Microphone Level: Very low voltage, and very fragile. The only thing this can feed is a microphone-level input. Usually, this is carried to an XLR connector with three pins (Figure 08-01), however, virtually any other connector can be used.

• Line Level: A million times as strong as microphone level, this is often used to interconnect equipment in a facility. AES digital audio is a direct replacement for line-level analog audio, so in many facilities, there is little or no line-level analog audio. Both AES digital audio and analog line-level audio can be carried on the same XLR connector popular for microphones. Both can be carried on tip-ring-sleeve patch panels. AES can also be carried on BNC coaxial cable with BNC connectors, and can use the same patch bays generally used for video.

NOTE: If you plug a microphone-level input into an analog line-level audio input, you likely won't hear anything. A line-level input does not provide enough amplification to boost the mic-level signal. If you plug a mic-level signal into an AES digital input, nothing happens (no sound at all). AES digital and any analog audio signals can't simply be mixed. On the other hand, plugging line-level audio into a microphone input will cause very loud and greatly distorted audio. Sometimes placing line-level audio into a microphone input on a mixer or distribution system produces distortion even in channels and circuits (cross-talk) that seem to be unrelated. Sometimes, you can't even turn down or turn off the sound from a line-level input plugged into a microphone-level input.

• IHF Audio: We said there were four varieties of audio; the third is very similar to line-level audio and is called IHF (Institute of High Fidelity) audio. IHF audio is used in most consumer electronics and usually has an RCA-type connector (Figure 08-03). The voltage level is not as high as balanced line-level audio; however consumer and prosumer equipment often finds its way into use in broadcast facilities. IHF inputs are single-ended or unbalanced, meaning that they use only one signal wire and one return wire (usually a shield). This limits their usefulness in the professional system; however, one can with a little luck, mix IHF and line-level audio with some limitations on matching levels. There are simple amplifiers that convert levels and convert single ended to balanced and vice versa, which, while not always needed, do help.

Figure 08-03.
A BNC connector.

• Digital Audio: Finally, the most common means of moving discrete audio (we'll cover what isn't discrete in a bit) around a facility is AES3 digital. It's also sometimes called AES/EBU audio. This can be balanced (two signal wires and maybe a shield) or unbalanced (on coax, typically using the same cable and *BNC connectors* that video uses). One reason to use coax is that it is available in a broadcast facility, and it allows the same patch bays to be used for audio and video. Besides, BNC connectors are the easiest and fastest of all connectors to install or *terminate* a cable with. As

The AES3 format or protocol is so common that it is jalmost always refered to simply as digital audio. Nonetheless, there are some varieties and options. AES3 is linear pulse coded modulation (PCM) usually sampled at either 48 kilohertz (kHz) or 44.1 kHz. It can operate at any number of sample rates, however 48 kHz (48,000 samples of audio each second) is almost a given within television facilities because it can be easily synchronized with the video timing. Compact Discs (CDs) sample at 44.1 kHz. This isn't a problem except that rate conversion is needed in any system that mixes sample rates, or clicking and popping will occur if it works at all.

mentioned, digital audio works only with digital audio sources and destinations. It does nothing if plugged into digital video circuits or analog audio circuits.

Another option is the resolution or sample size of the AES3 audio. In CDs 16 bits is the standard. Many professional systems take 20-bit samples for better dynamic range and noise performance.

There are any number of articles, books and Web references that go into depth about the workings of how digital audio is expressed in digital form. An operator probably doesn't absolutely need to know the workings of digital audio; however an operator that graduates to regular audio work beyond mixing audio for production or air can benefit from a better understanding. If your job involves setting up a variety of digital audio equipment, do look up how digital audio operates.

Finally, audio can also be carried as an embedded service within digital video. Here, the same coaxial cable (or fiber) that carries the digital video also carries typically four to eight AES3 stereo pairs of audio. Special applications and higher resolution video often has provisions for much more audio.

Most facilities use a mix of both *embedded* and *discrete* audio. Facilities with production, or a need to mix and control the audio, generally employ predominantly discrete audio. In more transmission oriented facilities, where programming is by and large passed through the facility with little adjustment or manipulation, embedded audio is preferred.

Embedding the audio in the video (because it requires only one wire to carry both the audio and video and they can be switched together) is a great convenience from a construction and switching perspective, and ideal for transmission. Tape machines, video servers, transmitters, and more favor the use of embedded audio.

Audio mixers, processors, and even monitors (amps and speakers) require that the audio be discrete. Embedders and disembedders can place the audio into a video stream or pull it out respectively. These are generally located in video processing and distribution frames; electronic equipment frames that contain a series of cards that perform this kind of function. There are also small standalone boxes (about the size of a pack of cigarettes or two) that can be used if only a few devices are needed. Likewise these functions are usually built into frame synchronizers, tape and other storage devices, test equipment and more.

SDI (*Serial Digital Interface*) standard definition video has room for eight stereo pairs. In other words 16-individual channels grouped into eight stereo groups. High definition video has provisions to carry twice that many. There is no universal standard for how these are used: stereo, surround, secondary audio, etc. Audio assignments are often *shuffled* to place the right audio on the right track. Shuffling can take place within certain equipment, or externally.

Stereo and Surround Sound

Most audio for broadcast is either stereo or surround sound. Stereo is the familiar left and right audio that is suited to most devices, headphones, and two speakers on either side of the television. Stereo also mixes down well to a mono (single) speaker.

Surround sound can be discrete (separate channel for each sound channel), or synthetic (matrixed). The matrixed version is based on a decoder that decrypts the surround sound from a stereo pair. Dolby Surround or ProLogic are both surround decoders that reside in many home devices. For the MCO, they are treated as stereo for the most part, although some control rooms have surround sound decoders and speakers so that the MCO can hear what the viewer hears.

Discrete surround sound, true 5.1 (five channels of full spectrum sound, plus a low frequency bass effects channel that may or may not be broadcast) is generally sent using Dolby AC-3 (also called Dolby Digital) or *MPEG-2* audio *compression*. 5.1 is encoded into the audio in such a way that there are six channels with perfect separation. In the facility, each channel of sound is kept on a different audio track of a tape or server. On occasion, an *MCO* might need to assign the correct audio channel from a tape or source to the correct facility channel. Often this is done at ingest or when live, at the edge device (full featured frame sync). In live situations, this may need to be done on the fly.

The process can involve taking a 5.1 feed and converting (*downmixing*) it back into stereo if the facility only supports stereo, or a matrixed surround, if again that is what the facility supports. The process and equipment used will vary from facility to facility. In most cases, some attempt to make the process invisible to the MCO and have it occur in the background automatically is made to reduce errors and effort required. When monitoring audio levels, one must pay attention to the downmix levels first and the other six channels secondarily, because the bulk of problems (and most viewers) can be expected to be in stereo or even mono mode.

Phase reversal is a common MCO challenge. Here, the left and right (or surround channels) are out of phase (when a drum is hit, one speaker moves out, the other in), so that when mixed down the sound largely cancels instead of combining into a solid mono signal. The mono sound will be hollow and thin, but the stereo often seems unaffected. Reversing either stereo channel (usually a push-button function) or the offending surround channels will restore the mono signal to normal. This is why it is more important to listen to the mono program than anything else.

Operator Tools

The primary audio tool for the MCO is a *volume meter, VU meter* or *audio level meter*. It can be a mechanical meter, or more likely an electronic version of essentially the same functions and ballistics (how the needle reacts). Volume, measured in *volume units* (VU) and loudness, measured as loudness, K-weighted, relative to full scale (or LKFS) are vaguely related. Volume is an electrical measurement while loudness is perceptual. What the ear hears is only loosely related to the electrical level of the audio.

Volume is an electrical value and easily measured. More important than that, there is a defined absolute limit to how much volume there can be. In a digital signal, the audio value that represents *full scale digital* (dBfs) is the absolute most volume you can have expressed in decibels. This is where the audio is at its highest value of 1111111111111111. The next step up doesn't exist (as we're out of number space) so either the next step is to remain the same, or in some rare processes, the value inverts to the most opposite value possible, which makes the loudest bang possible. The volume meter helps you set an operating level. Too low and the audio can't be heard well. Too high and the system runs out of *headroom* (the space needed for occasional peaks in loudness) and results in distortion.

Loudness on the other hand is a perception. For the most part, volume, which is easily measured and is the same to everyone; loudness is somewhat arbitrary and individual. There are several devices and algorithms to convert volume measurements into loudness. Loudness has a lot to do with the different sensitivities we have to various frequencies in our hearing and to certain wave shapes, distortion and harmonic content. Depending on your facility, you may have volume, loudness, or most likely predominantly volume and some loudness meters.

Meters all tend to use a logarithmic measure expressed in decibels (Abbreviated dB). The full unit is a bel (abbreviated "B"), which honors Alexander Graham Bell, the inventor of the telephone. Because the bel is a large unit, we indicate the level in $^1/_{10}$ increments and use the prefix "deci." Hearing is largely logarithmic in nature (what sounds ten times as loud takes approximately a hundred times more sound power), so the meter is a fair representation of reality.

The meters all direct you to a standard operating level (ocassionally referred to as SOL). For the most part, -16dB or -18dB below full scale digital (dBfs) is considered the operating point, where the average dialog centers. This leaves 16dB or 18dB of headroom for loud noises. Of the two -18dBfs is the more common (in theatrical work, sometimes it is desirable to reserve even more headroom for loud explosions and the like, so a movie might have an operating level in the neighborhood of -24dBfs).

One interesting meter is the series of displays for surround sound (or stereo) where the values of all channels are represented simultaneously mapped on a grid that represents the space and direction of the sound. This display shows where the center of the *sound field* is, how much spatial information there is and what channels are loudest or quietest.

An MCO can expect to *ride gain* in keeping audio levels within range at the very least, and deal with downmix issues, channel assignment errors, phase reversal, and other audio impairments at the most. In the analog era, the actual level could expect to change as the signal was handed off from one piece of gear to another, and phase reversals and channel losses were common. In the digital world, once set, the levels and all other characteristics will remain unchanged until someone wants to change it. In the digital world, the MCO is adjusting for differences in facilities operating levels, or errors upstream, far more often than to correct for equipment differences.

Given the CALM act, many facilities measure and store loudness levels to offer proof that volume levels are controlled. This book continues the discussion of audio loudness in the regulatory section.

Processing

There can be extreme differences in audio loudness between theatrical audio found in a movie and the audio in a commercial intentionally mixed and processed to be as attention getting as it can be. TV is often viewed (and listened to) in less than quiet conditions. Kitchens, mass transit, the garage, and waiting rooms, among others, all present loud background noise levels that for the TV device to be heard require that the lower, subtle, audio levels found in most production, must be lifted up. This is referred to as *automatic gain control* (AGC).

Further, recall that there is a technical limit to how much volume the audio electronics can handle before distorting. Most microphones (news and talk shows) are *peak limited* before recording or brought into the final mixer or switcher. Peak limiters can be found at many points in the content production and transportation process, and the function is often built into the same device that does the AGC.

Sometimes, there is an attempt to also control loudness, in particular those very loud commercials, in order to make the viewer more comfortable by making the loudness of the program more consistent. There are audio processors that do this.

And finally, there is the concept of a *signature sound,* and compensation for the devices used. Processing for the theater, living room, the small speakers of the kitchen television, and the very small speakers of a mobile device or computer all suggest different approaches to audio processing. This is a science and art form in and of itself. Depending on the content and the intended audience, the audio processing and signature sound of a facility can be quite different. Processing for ear buds, older audiences, and living room theaters should be very different. MTV audio is not processed like HBO.

For the MCO, adjusting or introducing audio processing may or may not appear as a regular task. In any case, audio processing may exist and one might notice that audio meters read differently (usually read higher and don't move as much) after processing than before.

Dialog Normalization

Dialog normalization, or **dialnorm** for short, has wide acceptance in the digital broadcast world. The idea is simple enough: Part of the program stream **metadata** in the Dolby AC-3 signal tells the receiver where the normal dialog level is, and lets the device adjust its gain accordingly. Ideally, the viewing device is equipped to read this information and smart enough to know how to tailor that to the viewing environment.

Dialnorm is complicated in that not all devices deal with dialnorm information well, if at all; and not all programs are properly recorded and distributed. An MCO might need to make adjustments to dialnorm levels in order to make the program a more pleasing experience.

The complexity of dialnorm is a book in its self; however the basic adjustments an MCO might make can be reduced to a simpler station-specific set of instructions. Equipment varies, and the audio flow through the facility might reflect any number of unique requirements that impact where and how this is done.

There is no one way to deal with dialnorm values. Your facility will have a standard practice whether that's written or just passed along. In a new job, do find out early in your training, what, if anything, your facility requires you do with audio levels in general and dialnorm in particular.

DTV Audio

The *FCC* specified a specific audio format for *digital television*: the Dolby AC-3 system. Developed by the Digital Coder group at Dolby Labs, it has been in use since 1991 in the production of Dolby Digital film soundtracks. The digital television version limits the individual audio bitstream to 384kb/s. An ATSC digital TV receiver (and many satellite IRDS) can decode a combination of bitstreams that do not exceed a total of 512kb/s.

The digital television version of Dolby AC-3 allows up to 5.1 audio channels per bitstream. The five full bandwidth channels are *Left, Center, Right, Left-Surround,* and *Right-Surround,* while the 0.1 channel is a fractional bandwidth channel for sub-woofer low frequencies of 3 - 20Hz. The full-bandwidth channels are limited to 20kHz. The Dolby AC-3 system encoder provides digital audio sampled at the rate of 48kHz. This sample rate is derived from the same 27MHz system clock that synchronizes the video. The Main audio service can contain from 1 to 5.1 audio channels. Contained within the stream are dialnorm instructions regarding the average dialog level of the program. The intent of the dialnorm value is to control relative loudness of commercials compared to programming.

Providing high-quality audio with as few digital bits as possible is the primary goal of the audio system. This efficiency is necessary for maximizing the spectrum available for video transmission.

Lip Sync

As mentioned frequently, keeping the audio and video in sync is a seemingly never-ending problem. Viewers find it irritating to hear a sound before or long after the explosion or lip movement would suggest one should hear the sound. The real issue is that if the audio and video are out of alignment enough to notice, it distracts and results in a loss of believability. There is a trigger phenomenon, in that once a viewer perceives an error, it takes more than a few minutes for his or her brain to recover. Everything, even changing channels, seems out of sync and remains to appear that way for some time after the viewer notices a delay.

Facilities where the audio is *embedded* in the same *SDI* signal as the video tend to have fewer problems than where the video and audio are run separately. Where the audio and video run separately, changes in the video path often change the video delay, while the audio fails to adjust.

Technical specifications can be very tight for lip sync (a.k.a., *A/V sync*). As a practical matter, sound arriving 45 milliseconds early, or 120 milliseconds late is just on the edge of detectability. ATSC video frames are about 33 milliseconds, which mean that a frame early or four frames late; the misalignment of the sound to the video will not be noticed. Most people will accept three frames early to about six frames late. Figure 08-04 illustrates this.

Some facilities use a proprietary automatic time alignment system within the facility. Usually, these embed timing marks in or near the audio and video as the content enters the plant, and compensate for the timing along the way or when it leaves the facility.

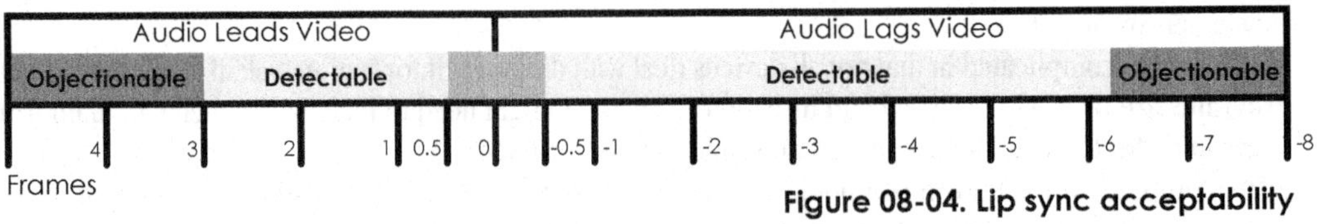

	Audio Leads Video				Audio Lags Video			
Objectionable	Detectable					Detectable		Objectionable

Frames
4 3 2 1 0.5 0 -0.5 -1 -2 -3 -4 -5 -6 -7 -8

Figure 08-04. Lip sync acceptability

Digital processing devices almost all require at least a frame to do their video work. Audio processing generally takes less time. Without adding in audio delay to compensate for the delays of the video, the slip becomes noticeable soon, and can be extreme as many devices take many frames to process.

Worse, this is not always deterministic meaning, not always predictable. Compression and some ambiguity in how standards are implemented also create lip sync issues. Two different receivers or **frame synchronizers** or anything else, often will address lip sync very differently. Editing systems can be particularly prone to errors.

As an operator, you may have any number of adjustable delays to compensate for such issues. There may be a master delay (rarely) to correct for some error.

In-service solutions place a marker (a non-detracting watermark or fingerprint) in the video and the audio early in the process, and devices along the way that are enabled will correct for errors. Generally these are not interoperable between manufacturers, they are expensive, and thus tend to be found in critical applications and within a small community like a given network. As this is written, there has been some ongoing work to craft a common universal method that all manufacturers can use.

Setup solutions are part of many test signals, where there is a *visual clue* and a *sound mark*, often a *click track,* that align. This is far from new as early "talkies" (movies with sound) used the familiar *clapboard*. The current slang for any of these setup test signals is a *"flash and bang."* Aligning the flash with the bang in a test signal is generally an operator adjustment prior to the start of the program. It can be done by eye and ear, but test equipment often makes it easy to see the relationship on a display and the results of your adjustments.

The technical issue is very involved, and much has been said and done about lip sync. Still, contemporary, practical systems almost always constantly drift with only the MCO to keep it in bounds.

Descriptive Audio (or Video Description)

In an effort to assist visually impaired viewers, program suppliers (most notably PBS) began providing a descriptive audio narration of visual activity on screen. This would be similar to "play-by-play" announcing on sports radio. It used to be accessed (if available) by using the NTSC SAP (Second Audio Program) channel; now, this tends to be more a receiver menu option. At this point in time, this service isn't as prevalent as it should be.

Under the 21st Century Communications and Video Accessibility Act of 2010 (CVAA), this updates federal communications laws to increase the access of those with disabilities to modern communications.

9
WEB TRANSMISSION

Over the top (OTT) has become a fast growing means of sending linear, real-time TV over the Internet. As this is written, the **FCC** has not designated OTT providers with MVPD status; however a number of court cases and unresolved rights issues might soon force a re-write of this chapter.

There are many different ways of encoding video and sending it over the Internet. The options are nearly endless, but not uniform. When you buy a TV set, it can pick up any US digital TV station (ATSC/8-VSB), it can almost certainly still view an analog station, and it probably can see *QAM* (quadrature amplitude modulation, a format used by cable services to encode services on digital cable) and it may also work with international standards. As this is written, there is no standardization in Web distributed video, so specific players are built into games, connected TVs, DVD players, and specialized set-top boxes (STBs). The Netflix player appears in many places, as does Hulu's. Many TV stations and others that stream video provide an *application* (app) that loads a given player. As this is written, there is activity to create a common set of players and digital rights management. This is complicated, political, but in the authors' opinion, inevitable; which means as an MCO, what you do and with what technology will be changing constantly for some time. Some of this is reasonably predictable, others not so much. One thing that seems certain is that Web distribution will continue to grow, and seems certain to become the primary means of distribution at some future time.

OTT refers to a special case of Web distribution. The over-the-top piece is a *business model*, more than a technology, where the content is distributed without an MVPD or OTA transmitter. Instead it is delivered to a **content distribution network** (**CDN**) that places the content on the Internet where an Internet Service Provider (ISP) delivers it to the viewer's home. CDNs typically place content as close to the viewer as practical in order to reduce traffic on the *backbone. Multicast* protocols and local servers are the CDNs key tools.

Any barrier an ISP puts up to prevent outside video **streaming** is defeated as the OTT content goes up and over the fire wall, into the walled garden. There are some technical tricks here. As this is written, OTT usually uses HTTP as a transmission protocol, breaking video into approximately 5 to10-second chunks (HTTP chunking), which look like content destined for a Web browser. Shutting down HTTP would also stop all Web functions, so an ISP would have to be more creative to stop the OTT traffic.

The constant battle is that video content is bandwidth intensive, some incredibly so. Video is the largest user of bandwidth on the Internet, and it is just beginning. ISPs generally want to defend their systems from being swamped by this traffic, and of course to profit from it. Some ISPs *throttle* video traffic or charge a premium for video delivery. Some providers pay some ISPs fees to allow for their higher bandwidth services.

OTT usually uses adaptive bit rate (ABR) streaming from the CDN to the viewer. Generally there are about 4 or 5 different encodes of the same content ranging from a low quality, low **bit-rate** version to a high quality, high bit-rate version. The CDN in some systems, and the player in others, constantly monitor the state of the network and when congested, will select lower bit rate feeds until the connection improves. This reduces the odds of freezing and stuttering video and may avoid buffering all together.

Generally some buffering is used. A period of content is stored before playing so the player can tolerate an occasional low bandwidth period. The price is that the player generally won't play until some, or all, of the buffer is first filled. If the buffer isn't big enough, the player will pause if it runs out of content and refill, resulting in the familiar "buffering" message.

How and where the rate is controlled varies, sometimes it is the player that requests the proper stream, others are controlled at the CDN, some require both. There are benefits and limitations to both approaches.

Over time, we can expect that the business of OTT will employ other technologies. Certainly HEVC (High Efficiency Video Codec, or H.265) and 4K display technologies will be employed to give OTT providers more efficient encoding and their displays much more detail than broadcast **_HD_**.

While there are many challenges, there are also many advantages to OTT. Unlike cable, satellite and OTA, there is no inherent limit to the number of services that can be carried via the Web. The limits of bandwidth and connectivity are pushed back with every day as more and faster connectivity is installed. OTT is inherently *connection based* which is great for second screens and interactive features. There is no natural limit to where or one what one can view OTT, including personal wireless devices and internationally. How fast the Internet can grow its bandwidth seems the only challenge.

Cable systems are with very rare exception a primary ISP (providing Internet to customers), but they are also all **_MVPDs_**. OTT impacts their ability to aggregate content rights and profit from their sale to their subscribers. Satellite presents even more difficulties. OTT is an upsetting technology.

Without MVPD status or other regulatory controls, it is unclear who can distribute what where. It seems reasonable that OTT providers will continue to grow and some stations may take the initiative to distribute their own content. Many do now. PBS, religious, foreign language, and shopping channels all want to reach as many people as they can and they own their content, so can determine where and how it is distributed. Local stations have the same situation with their owned content, generally local news. Many radio stations have streamed their content for some time to reach places where their OTA signal doesn't go, like office buildings and home kitchens. TV stations continue to increase the amount of content and viewers that stream their content.

Web distribution is hugely powerful. It allows **_non-real-time_** catch up TV where **_MVPDs_** can, at best, under the current rules provide a customer with similar delay capabilities using a digital video recorder function.

The Web also has no natural physical boundaries. An OTA station only goes so far, cable only goes where the wires go, and satellite only reaches where the satellite coverage goes (usually a continent, or country). Web content can be viewed wherever the bandwidth supports the connection, and that is growing quickly. Methods of limiting viewers to a DMA or country are in development, but generally easy to defeat or so cumbersome as to be nearly useless.

While cable can have a return connection, Web streaming always does. As we mentioned, there is a connection to each and every viewer, and that allows all sorts of targeted advertising and interactive functions. What this allows and what it becomes will certainly fundamentally change broadcasting and affect the way MCOs work.

The immediate impact is that most MCOs are involved with turning on and off Web feeds for newscasts, or repurposing material for use with Web distribution. Currently, most stations operate their Web services and their OTA services largely separated, except that the content and some data is shared. Over time, one can expect that the OTA and Web distributions become tighter with staff working in tasks that serve both. Ingesting content is often done twice, once for OTA and once for Web. Better tools will eliminate that. Repurposing; the process of taking content in one form and making useful for another, is likely to come more and more under the control and care of the MCO.

Fortunately, most of the tools and processes you have learned are also useful in Web distribution. There are just more tools and processes.

10
REGULATIONS and RESPONSIBILITIES

The Federal Communications Commission (FCC)

All OTA broadcast stations in the United States and its territories are licensed by the *Federal Communications Commission*. The FCC also regulates satellite cable and other services. The FCC was created by Congress to implement the Communications Act of 1934, which regulates the private use of the *radio frequency* spectrum. In the United States, the military controls its allocated spectrum. The complete set of rules and regulations for OTA broadcasters is contained in several parts of *The Code of Federal Regulations* (CFR, Title 47). Part 73 contains most of the rules pertaining to OTA television. Other sections regulate other services.

While some FCC rules are technical or legal in nature and may not come up in the day-to-day operation of the television station, compliance should be a daily and on-going activity. Rules dealing with the operation of the transmitter, monitoring the tower lights, keeping the station log and the Emergency Alert System (EAS) are important to the television operator. This book covers many of the FCC rules and technical information necessary to a television operator.

The most recent version of the FCC Rules and Regulations should be used to answer any additional questions you may have. The *chief operator* or *chief engineer* will likely maintain the latest version of the relevant FCC Rules and Regulations in a loose-leaf binder or computer file provided by a rules subscription service. Alternately, all of CFR, title 47 is available on the Web.

Each OTA television station is issued a television broadcast station license. The station license authorizes the technical parameters for a television station. When the license is renewed, the FCC issues a license renewal document showing a new expiration date. These documents in combination constitute the station authorization.

This station authorization must be posted at the *control point*. Posting may be by affixing the license to a wall, or enclosing it in a binder or folder at the control point location (typically, the master control room).

Chief Operator

As mentioned earlier, there is a special role that exists parallel to the normal station structure in *OTA* facilities. Pursuant to the FCC Rules and Regulations, each television station must designate a chief operator. The chief operator is responsible for the station's compliance with FCC Rules and Regulations. An acting chief operator should also be designated in the event of the absence of the designated chief operator.

A copy of the chief operator designation (usually in the form of a single page letter or notice) must be posted at the control point of the transmitter along with the station license. Posting may mean the documents are actually posted on the wall or placed in a binder.

The chief operator is not required to hold any FCC permit or license. The chief operator and the chief engineer are often the same person but that is not always the case. The chief operator may be the production manager, operations manager, crew chief, general manager or any operator who is employed by the station. The person designated as chief operator is expected to be technically competent for the task and aware of the rules and regulations.

On a weekly basis, the chief operator will review and initial the station log. He will initiate any necessary corrective action to ensure compliance with FCC Rules. He will inform the station management of any action that may require further attention.

Even though a chief operator must be designated, the station licensee is ultimately responsible for proper station operation.

Station Identification

Every television station must transmit **station identification (ID)** on a regular basis. A legal ID must include the call letters and city of license. The only material permitted between the call letters and city of license is the TV channel number. For instance: "WHMB-TV, Indianapolis" or "WHMB, Channel 40, Indianapolis", are both legal IDs. Note that call signs for the primary station can be three, four, five or six letters: for example, KGO, KGO-TV, KRON, KRON-TV, KNBC-DT (**digital television**). It is important that legally required IDs use the correct call sign. This is because some stations have AM, FM and TV licenses with the same parent call; for example, KZXT for the AM station, KZXT-FM for the FM station, and KZXT-TV for the TV station. The station's official call sign will be indicated on the station license. While some may feel it unnecessary to include the -AM, -FM, and -TV designations, it is required. If one were to refer to KCBS, which entity would this be referring to? KCBS is an AM station licensed to San Francisco, KCBS-TV and KCBS-FM are a television station and an FM radio station licensed to Los Angeles.

A visual or aural ID must be made hourly, at the top of the hour. This identification can be made by a live announcer, a character generator, or a pre-produced program element. An aural ID would be the spoken phrase "KMGH, Denver." Other items may be added, such as the channel number, other cities covered, or a promotional phrase, but a legal ID requires the call sign and city of license to be announced together.

There is a difference between a legal ID and an ID. If the key elements of call sign and city of license are missing, interrupted or unclear, the ID is not a legal ID. It may be aired, but it does not qualify as a legal ID. For example, "Denver's News Channel KMGH" or "KMGH, Channel 7" are not legal IDs. In practice, many promotional items contain IDs but they are often not legal IDs. Promotional IDs may be given at any time and are not required to be legal IDs. However, this does not relieve the operator from the responsibility for airing timely and legal IDs. Most stations label any item that contains a legal ID as a legal ID, so they can be dropped in as needed by the MCO. A variation of the station ID is the **shared ID.** This is when station identification is shared with a promotional message ("Watch *Hollywood Today* at 3 p.m."), or a brief public affairs message ("Go to your local Humane Society.").

IDs are run at sign-on, sign-off and once each hour at the top of the hour at a convenient break in programming (typically within two minutes of the top of the hour). One rare exception is if the ID would unduly interrupt programming. If this is the case, then the ID must air at the first opportunity. Emergency information coverage or a similar event could be cause for a delayed ID.

TV translators must be identified twice each day. **LPTV stations** (low-power TV stations) can be identified in the same manner as full-power TV stations, or, if analog (soon these will all be gone), may be identified by use of Morse Code on a hidden audio program channel. These IDs are continuous and automatic and cannot be heard by the viewers without special equipment. Satellite uplink transmitters are also identified in this manner, though new methods are in the works. Most digital modes on satellite allow placing a static ID in the bit stream. One often sees this displayed on an IRD's status display when decoding a satellite or remote vehicle transmission.

FCC Inspections

FCC inspections are a fact of life. The Field Operations Bureau (FOB) of the FCC has field offices throughout the country, and the FCC inspects each station on an average of once every seven years. The selection of stations for inspection is primarily a random process, though there are times when enforcement is stepped up for a targeted service, and there are times when budget considerations reduce enforcement efforts.

The purpose of the inspection is to assure that the station is operating properly. An inspection often involves examination of the logs, asking the operators specific questions on transmitter operation (how to adjust power, take readings, calculate power, turn off the transmitter, check tower lighting), EAS, station policies and practices, Public File, and other information.

Ideally, the **chief operator** will be available at the time of the inspection to show the FCC inspector the logs, explain procedures and answer other questions. If the chief operator cannot be present, any operator is expected to fill in. Even with the chief operator present, the FCC will often ask the operator on duty to demonstrate some task or locate a document.

The FCC may issue an official Notice of Violation to a station that fails to comply with FCC Rules and Regulations. Three very common offenses resulting in a Notice of Violation are associated with EAS, tower lighting and the Public File. An operator, who is unable to demonstrate knowledge of EAS and transmitter control, will likely result in a Notice of Violation and possibly a fine for the station licensee. The value of having a binder with less-frequent tasks outlined handy is hopefully becoming clearer to you as an MCO.

Transmitters

Over time, transmitters have become more stable and less of a concern for the operator and the station. At one time, the FCC required that transmitters be checked for proper operation and the key operating parameters every half-hour. Today, you may not even have a transmitter as such or it may be under automatic transmitter control (ATC) or some other control arrangement. There are specific requirements and rules for ATC/ATS operation that must be met as described below. Management and engineering generally deal with ATS issues, relieving the MCO from most responsibilities.

The FCC requires two things: First, if the transmitter is causing interference, or for any other reason the FCC determines that it needs to be shut down, they can call upon you to stop transmission. At the very least you need to know how to shut off the transmitter, generally even if under ATC.

Secondly, the FCC requires that the transmitter be operating within its licensed parameters. Some stations maintain manual or automatic logs in order to prove to the FCC that reasonable efforts were made to keep the transmitter operating properly.

One operating parameter is of particular importance: the power output. The FCC allows a station to operate between *80% and 110%* of its licensed power. The FCC requires notification under certain circumstances if continued operation at reduced power is anticipated. You simply can't operate over power, and must either reduce power, or shut the transmitter off if you can't. Unless there are other issues or emergencies, getting the chief engineer involved under these circumstances is good practice.

As a practical concern, most transmitters will occasionally require a *reset* or *restart*. Most often this is caused by power problems, but occasionally there is a serious problem such as a damaged antenna system where the reset won't take for more than a few seconds or minutes. To avoid additional damage (in some high power systems each reset can vaporize several feet of transmission line several hundreds of feet up a tower) *do not repeatedly keep restarting the system*. This is a time to call in the transmitter engineer or *chief engineer*.

Automatic Transmitter Systems

An *automatic transmission system* (*ATS*) can remove the operator's need to directly control a transmitter. The ATS will do all of the logging and transmitter adjustment. Under the ATS rules, the ATS will operate the transmitter automatically. One of the requirements of the ATS is that if readings drift outside certain parameters that cannot be corrected by the ATS, the ATS must then shut down the transmitter. The ATS may notify an operator of a problem prior to the shutdown. The operators can then take over, and make manual corrections that are beyond the ability of the ATS.

Manual operation may be difficult for operators if the ATS has been reliable. It is easy to forget basic transmitter controls. The operator should know the procedures to follow if the ATS or transmitter fails. If certain commands/functions are not regularly carried out, it is highly recommended a concise, how-to manual be kept close by.

A properly operating ATS system may relieve a master control operator of most routine transmitter duties. It does *not* relieve the operator from overall responsibility. The operator must be familiar with accessing the ATS logs in the event of an FCC inspection.

Do not confuse an *automatic transmission system* with an *automatic logging system*. An automatic logging system by itself has no ability to make an adjustment to the transmitter; it only logs what has happened. An automatic logging system is just a part of a complete automatic transmission system.

One consideration is that an automatic transmission system requires that the transmitter automatically shut down within three-hours of any technical malfunction that might cause interference under FCC rules.

Tower Lights

The *Federal Aviation Administration* (*FAA*) regulates tall structures that could pose a hazard to aeronautical navigation. In cooperation with the FAA, the FCC exercises *primary authority* over towers used for broadcasting. In general, towers that are 200 ft. (61 meters) or taller require certain markings and lighting. The station license sets forth the markings that were originally required for your station. These markings may have been modified during the FCC tower registration effort of the late 1990's. The current *Antenna Structure Registration* (ASR) for your tower outlines the latest painting and lighting requirements for your station's tower. The ASR also contains other important information about the height of your tower and the precise geographical coordinates. Most stations post the ASR at the *control point* along with the *station license* and the *license renewal authorization card*. Posting shall be by affixing the document to the wall or enclosing it in a binder or folder at the control point location.

Flashing red beacons and red obstruction lights are the most common form of nighttime tower obstruction lighting. These lights are installed at several levels for visibility. There will usually be a flashing red beacon at the top of the tower and depending on the tower height, flashing red beacons at different levels of the tower. These towers have alternate bands of aviation orange and white paint, which enhance tower visibility during the daylight hours. These towers must be re-painted when the colors fade. Almost all towers have either 7 or 11 stripes, with orange on top and bottom, taller towers having the 11 strips. You can't tell how tall the tower is by counting stripes.

Medium- and high-intensity strobe lighting is often used on unpainted towers. The strobe lights will flash very brightly for daytime visibility and with reduced brightness for nighttime visibility. Occasionally the daytime lighting levels, which can be annoyingly bright, will be stuck on at night. This often results in complaints to the station.

Dual lighting systems use a combination of both strobes and red lamps. The tower might be unpainted using strobe lights for daytime visibility. Flashing red beacons and red obstruction lighting might be used for nighttime visibility. Again, if the system doesn't shift to the nighttime lighting mode, expect complaints from those near the tower. Dual mode systems usually report back to master control via the remote control system as to their state. On some systems the MCO can force the lighting to a mode. It is standard practice to not only report a night lighting outage to the FAA, but to activate the day time system at night if it can be.

If any flashing beacon lamp or strobe light should fail for more than 30-minutes, the nearest *FAA* Flight Service Station (FSS) *must be notified immediately*. While most flashing beacons contain two lamps in each fixture, the failure of a single bulb still requires FAA notification. The FAA must be informed day or night if a strobe light fails.

The FAA local phone number should be posted at the control point of any station with a lighted tower. In many states, the toll free number, 1-800-WXBRIEF (1-800-992-7433), will connect you with the FSS serving your area. It is good practice to make an entry in the station log regarding the details of the outage, including the date and time of FAA notification and the name of the person spoken with at the FSS. *Be prepared to give the FAA detailed location information (latitude & longitude coordinates of the tower)*.

The failure of obstruction lights does not require FAA notification. These are the constantly burning red sidelights that assist pilots in identifying the obstruction to air navigation. They should be repaired or replaced as soon as practical. Tower lights are normally operated by a photocell mounted on the tower that detects the amount of sunlight and then turns the lights on and off automatically. Some systems follow a schedule maintained by a control computer.

Proper tower lighting is essential for aircraft safety. The proper operation of tower lights must be confirmed at least once each night, although there is no longer an FCC requirement to log this observation. If the tower is visible from the control point, the operator may make a direct observation of the lights. If necessary, a means of verifying proper tower lighting must be provided via remote control.

Remote control systems must be able to indicate the failure of any single beacon lamp or strobe light and verify that flashing lights are in fact flashing. A remote control system may report back a go/no-go indication for the entire lighting system. The remote control system may report the status of groups of lamps, or individual lamps or a numerical value that indicates the amount of current drawn by the lighting system. If a numerical value is reported, the number and or size of the failed obstruction lights can be determined. Many station engineers prepare a chart for the operator to make this determination easier.

If the tower is located out of sight of the station, often the station has an arrangement with a nearby resident or two with a clear view of the tower that an MCO can call to confirm or clarify a fault.

Proper tower lighting is a serious requirement and the FCC has severely fined television stations for allowing their towers to go dark. Having an airplane collide with an unlit tower would be a major incident.

The Children's Television Act

The FCC adopted the ***Children's Television Act*** (***CTA***) in 1990 to limit commercialization inside Children's programming. Further expansions in 1996 encouraged educational or informational (E/I) children's programming, and expanded the focus from 12-year olds up to 16-year olds. As the eyes and ears of the station, it is important for MCOs to understand CTA guidelines because the FCC closely monitors station compliance, and fines and penalties can be stiff. These are sometimes referred to as the *kid-vid rules*.

Programming that is geared to general audiences falls outside of the CTA jurisdiction. Two examples are The Flintstones and The Simpsons. They are not affected by CTA rules because both shows were originally broadcast in prime time for general audiences. As an operator, you need to know specifically which programs on your shift, (if any), are affected by CTA.

Further, there is a strong suggestion that an ***OTA*** station carry some core children's programming. As this is written, the guideline is that a minimum of three hours of such is carried in each week and meets the following:

- Airs between 7 a.m. and 10 p.m.
- Regularly scheduled
- At least 30-minutes in length
- Described in the station's children's television report
- Listed in published program guides
- Broadcast with the ***E/I*** logo or bug

The E/I bug or logo is definitely something the MCO needs to be aware of and execute (if not burned into the program already), and in general being aware of the subtle issues that might violate the CTA and need to be brought to the attention of programming or traffic.

There are three key areas to monitor for CTA compliance; commercial time limits, host selling, and program length commercialization.

Commercial Time Limits

The Children's Television Act restricts total commercial content to 12-minutes per clock hour on weekdays, and 10.5 minutes per clock hour on Saturday and Sunday. A clock hour starts at the top of each hour during children's programming. Each clock hour is measured separately. Commercial time cannot be averaged over a block of several hours.

Since the time limit is measured over the entire clock hour, the commercial load does not have to be evenly split per half-hour. The first 30-minutes of a weekday CTA clock hour could have eight minutes of commercial content, provided that the second half of the same clock hour does not exceed four minutes of total commercial time. A CTA violation would only occur if the total of both half-hours exceeded 12-minutes.

If a clock hour only contains 30-minutes of CTA programming, the commercial time limit is exactly half. Commercial inventory inside a stand-alone, half-hour CTA program is limited to six minutes on weekdays and five minutes fifteen seconds on weekends.

The most frequent problem for the operator is a traffic error that may overbook a given hour. Violations are often difficult to detect and are usually unintentional. A built-in commercial may not have been reported to traffic, or an operator may attempt to **make-good** a blown spot. In these cases, a violation of the CTA occurs. Fines start at $8,000 and can exceed $20,000. Most stations follow a policy of prohibiting make-goods in children's blocks simply to avoid the possibility of a violation.

Host Selling

In the early days of television, Captain Kangaroo (a historic and long-running kids show with a unique host) routinely endorsed breakfast cereal and children's toys during his daily show. The Children's Television Act forbids host selling because it is felt that kids are unable to separate program content from advertising. Under the current rules, Captain Kangaroo could appear in commercials any time of the day, except during his own program. If a children's show lacks an obvious host, the host-selling concept extends to the primary character(s).

Program Length Commercialization

Program length commercialization occurs when a spot airs inside a program that advertises products directly related to the program. For example, if a spot for a miniaturized Batmobile appeared inside a Batman cartoon, the entire program is considered to be a half-hour commercial for a Batman toy. (A 30-minute commercial obviously exceeds the commercial time limits for a CTA clock hour). If Batman appeared in the same spot, there would also be a host selling violation.

Program length commercialization applies to any spot that advertises related merchandise and/or characters associated with a program. Some examples include action figure toys, theatrical movies, videos, DVDs, computer games, merchandise with logos, fast food promotions, and breakfast cereal giveaways. Even theme park rides can be included. A spot featuring the Six-Flags roller coaster Joker's Revenge cannot be placed inside the animated adventures of Batman.

A CTA violation occurs if any of the characters appear in any of the commercials during the same children's show. It does not have to be a significant character or major part in the commercial. If the same character is recognizable in both the program and the spot, the occurrence is considered a CTA violation.

Stations can avoid host selling and program length commercialization by screening all spots in advance searching character appearances and/or related merchandising. Spots with CTA sensitive content are usually time restricted to prevent a placement inside the related program or the adjacent breaks.

Operators need to be on high alert for program length commercialization anytime there is a program schedule change. If the commercial time restrictions are not simultaneously revised, a taboo spot could appear inside of the rescheduled program. One-time-only schedule changes are a high risk for CTA problems.

Remember that it is perfectly acceptable to run spots for Sponge Bob merchandise during any children's programming except during Sponge Bob the show. Even if a restaurant chain were to advertise free give-away Sponge Bob items at its stores, it cannot run in the Sponge Bob show. CTA rules do not apply to any Sponge Bob theatrical movies that might come along as films are produced for mass audiences.

If station procedures do not prevent an erroneous spot placement, most operators are instructed to delete the spot in advance or to abort the spot if it is already on the air. When in doubt, it is better to error on the side of caution than allow a potential violation.

Even though most procedures to prevent CTA problems occur upstream from master control, it is important for operators to understand the concepts and rules. An alert operator can prevent a simple oversight from becoming a costly CTA violation.

Talk Shows

Television talk shows are a challenge for the OTA operator as they are often live and therefore unpredictable. Live sporting events and feeds from outside the station may require the station operator to exercise control over an occurrence of poor taste, immoral or profane behavior. The operator is required to monitor the show for unacceptable language and respond by muting the audio or cutting to black until the offense has passed. Other remedies include disconnecting callers, or invoking a *content delay*. The operator's talk show duties should be clearly understood by all operators. Each station should have a clearly defined policy.

Currently, the FCC does not look with tolerance on profanity and explicit content even if accidental. For this reason, many stations and networks employ a content delay system, where an operator can at the touch of a button remove the last few (usually 7-15) seconds of a program and replace it with some filler content for as long as the dump button is pushed. It's not unusual to have several delays employed at various places in the path of live distribution, in particular when the risk of a wardrobe malfunction or accidental expletive is high.

An MCO may have as part of his or her duties setting up a content delay. Sometimes these are standalone and others are a software routine that runs on a video file server taking up a record and play port that would otherwise have other duties. It's a bit of a trick to insert and remove the delay cleanly, especially if it's at the output of master control. While radio stations frequently leave the delay inline constantly, TV stations generally do not as the delay makes live news shots using the station as a time reference impossible. Also, 15-seonds might not seem like much, but if the competition can get into a show 15-seconds before you do, and viewers are surfing, there can be a negative ratings impact as they find something to watch and never come back to see what you are airing.

Disclaimers

Television stations frequently opt to disclaim violent or questionable programs. In some stations it is the operator's duty to run a ***disclaimer*** just before or after a program. The traffic department will normally schedule this announcement.

There are legal ramifications for failure to air a disclaimer. For example, many stations choose to disclaim any paid show or infomercials to avoid potential legal problems or negative viewer reaction.

The operator is the last line of defense when a disclaimer is needed, whether it is scheduled or not. Frequently there is a well-known SOP regarding disclaimers.

Contests

Many broadcast stations run contests. There is a basic prohibition against advertising or running lotteries on OTA television, with the exception of state-sanctioned lotteries and gambling. This can be subtle. A lottery has three elements: prize, chance, and consideration. If any of these elements is missing, it is not a lottery.

A *prize* is something of value. Usually this is fairly obvious, but whether something is of value (information or a secret for example) is sometimes, but rarely, debatable.

Chance is also generally obvious. However if skill is involved, shooting a basket for example; it is a game of skill and not chance. Many games are a combination of skill and chance, so again this may not be as obvious as one might wish.

Consideration is the most nebulous. If the contestant is required to buy a ticket, merchandise, or deliver anything of value in trade for a chance of winning; it is a lottery. Generally, if one can enter the contest without surrendering anything of value, even if most contestants enter by buying a product or making a donation, it is not a lottery. What is of value is also nebulous. Having to go to a store to enter, even if the entry is free, or mail or email a free entry may or may not be consideration. Broadcasters have lawyers to determine where such lines are drawn.

The MCO is likely responsible to bring a potential lottery to the station management's attention especially if the potential lottery arrives on a new commercial to ingest and may have been missed up to this point. Small market advertisers may not be aware of the broadcast rules that address contests, and most lottery violations are innocent, minor, subtle, unintentional and often hidden in content. The most common violation is a contest where a store must indicate that a purchase is not necessary to win, and that element or message is lost in production. Most SOPs simply call for any staff to notify management or traffic anytime a contest might appear to be an unsanctioned lottery. Lottery rules are particularly hard to justify to the local volunteer fire department whose PSA includes a contest with a donated prize. In a small market, an MCO can become involved when the fire chief cuts the PSA and the MCO sets up a flash cam and records it. Management may elect to use the test of reasonability and allow what would otherwise be a lottery on the air, which, as the license holder is their prerogative. In such cases, the MCO is best advised to remove him- or herself from the discussion.

Closed Captioning (CC)

Nearly everyone is familiar with **closed captioning (CC)** and to a far lesser extent, teletext. CC is a visual text service for the hearing-impaired. CC decoding is a required feature on television receivers above a certain size. Teletext supports text for other purposes such as presenting stock quotations or school closings. For the most part, CC is inserted sometime in the program production process. For sports and news, this may be done live. For news, the CC is either done live or it is automated and generated as part of the news automation system that also provides text to the teleprompters for the talent to read. With some exceptions, the master control operator's role is to verify that CC is present, and perhaps, verify its content. Most stations keep a standard TV in the master control area that displays CC.

Third party, captioning services are ubiquitous. For the most part, they dial into the stations audio on an answer-only telephone coupler dedicated to the off-air audio. Somewhere in the world, a captioner using a stenographer's keypad, or some combination of speech to text software and keyboard, creates the text that is sent back to the station for insertion. Captioning services must be scheduled in advance, or in the case of a sudden change in programming like breaking news, an MCO might have to call and book time. An MCO might also have to route the caption text from the desired source. Most stations have a telephone coupler dedicated to captioning, but others might simply assign an IFB phone coupler. Likewise when IFBs are in short supply, some will call and steal the captioning coupler. An MCO generally needs to manage these resources and occasionally dump someone or a coupler that has locked up in an off-hook condition based on priorities. CC is a high priority, but live, life saving news is higher. Live captioning involves a number of delays. By time the CC message is on screen, it

CC messages are encoded into the digital transmission stream (the VANC for EIA-708 is the standard for captioning) and out of view in analog video (EIA-608). Analog video CC data follows CEA-608/EIA-608 (Extended Data Service or XDS) and is inserted on line 21 (a line generally not seen in the vertical blanking interval or VBI), so a DTV video, whether SD or HD will not display CC on an analog monitor unless the converter either burns in (adds a small window to display the text in or just places text over video, generally an option that can be turned on or off as desired) the CC message into the video output, or converts it to ATSC CC. In some cases legacy closed captioning from CEA-608 (analog) data will be transformed from SD to HD upconverted programming to CEA-708 closed captioning. Burned in means that if one records the video with CC or timecode in the video, it remains burned into the video and cannot be removed or turned off once burned in.

is the text for something that happened as much as 15-seconds in the past. Up-cutting and down-cutting the live CC text is almost universal. Prerecorded CC is likely to be more closely time aligned.

In ATSC systems, CC information is inserted into the DTV bit stream following the CEA-708/EIA-708 specification. Analog video CC data follows CEA-608/EIA-608 and is inserted on line 21. Given that there is legacy content with EIA-608 CC and some distribution reaches analog EIA-608 displays, the translation of analog EIA-608 to and from EIA-708 is likely to fade away only slowly.

There are any number of reasons why CC may fail. It may not have been supplied with the program, it may have been stripped (removing the data from the video) at some point, or it may not have been translated or stored at some juncture. For the MCO, the most notable effect is how easy it is to mess up the CC, in particular if playbacks are sped up or slowed down, or format converted without consideration of the CC.

CC text files can be sent separately from the video, especially when the CC is done in a different location some time after the show is completed. In this common case, the CC data needs to be married to the video before or as it is aired. Some video file servers facilitate this as a standard workflow that has the added benefit of allowing a Media Asset Management system to search the CC.

One other common complication is that local news often has an interface between the newsroom computer and the CC inserter to display to the CC audience what the news talent sees on their teleprompter (a device that shows the talent text from a script to be read, generally placed in front of a camera so the talent can make eye contact with the camera while reading). MCOs often have some duties associated with setting this up.

For the most part, the MCO needs to monitor the CC in most circumstances, and seek engineering help when it fails. The FCC has CC requirements for OTA stations, MVPDs and some Web-based delivery.

A possibly unintended side effect of CC requirements is that carrying a special event on a streaming service or a sub-channel probably requires closed captioning. While it might cost nothing more than a switch of programming to cover an extended press conference, funeral service, or minor sporting event; it might cost several hundreds of dollars to have that program captioned. Usually the event has some interest to a particular audience but the audience is too small to justify broadcast on the main channel. Often there is no revenue from these special events to offset the closed caption costs, and there is an exemption for CC if the cost exceeds 2% of the revenues of the program, however, this is sometimes complicated to establish, document, and defend; given some complicated revenue situations.

Positioning or repositioning the CC can be an MCO task. This is rare and generally considered a fancy touch to the broadcast product. The basic issue is that many stations brand their product with graphics, and CCs are placed when encoded; unaware of what graphics might be layered over video. Generally the CC messages will obscure the graphics, and some stations wish to move them apart.

It is rare to see a master control without CC monitoring; local cable channels and some limited Web based broadcasting being below the line where CC is required or practical might not have a CC monitor. MCOs almost always have CC messages displayed on a confidence monitor tuned to the off-air signal, so that they can verify that the CC messages are complete and made it home. It's rare to have automated CC monitoring as some pieces of programming (especially commercials, which are not required to have CC) would result in many false alarms.

The rest of the world makes little distinction between closed captioning and subtitles. The English might call it "subtitles for the hard of hearing."

There are other data feeds that can occur in EIA-608 and even more in EIA-708, but are generally outside the MCOs area of concern. Many messages are static; station identification, location, network, etc. Other messaging can be dynamic tickers and weather, but this is rare. Secondary languages are also possible, and operate similarly to the primary CC. Facilities vary widely in their use these data services.

Note that CC rules tend to change or be modified; your facility should stay up-to-date with this topic. Also, stations with Spanish language programming have modified rules compared to English language programming. Most especially, as this is written, Internet delivered content seems to becoming part of the CC world. OTT players are being upgraded to include CC, and some Web broadcasters are supporting CC in a variety of way, including a separate feed with CC burned in, in some special cases.

Exceptions to FCC Closed Caption Rules

*Certain elements are **not** required to be captioned (current as of July 2014):*

- PSAs shorter than 10 minutes and not paid for with federal dollars,
- Promotions and interstitials,
- EAS programming,
- Primarily non-vocal musical programming,
- Where captioning expense would exceed 2% of gross revenues,
- Channels producing revenues of under $3,000,000/year,
- Locally produced educational programs for K-12 & post-secondary schools,
- Programs shown in early morning hours (2am to 6am, local time),
- Programming other than English or Spanish languages,
- Programs primarily "textual" in nature,
- Non-news programming with no repeat value, locally produced by the video programming distributor (generally, local public affairs programs).

PSIP

Program and System Information Protocol (*PSIP, pronounced "pee-sip"*) is a core part of the *OTA* digital television signal. PSIP is an essential set of broadcast *metadata* that allows DTV to operate. One of the main goals of PSIP is to make DTV viewing simple and intuitive, hiding the complex interrelationships between the digital components. PSIP provides capabilities to enable familiar channel numbering, familiar methods of tuning (up-down surfing and direct tuning) as well as an on-screen program guide.

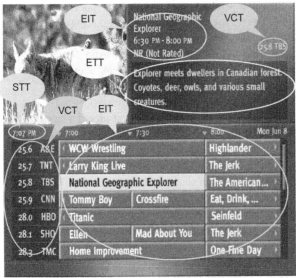

Figure 10-01. The electronic program guide

When the broadcast industry made the switch from NTSC to the ATSC standard in 2009, many stations also used this transition to switch from the VHF band to the UHF band of frequencies to broadcast because UHF works better for DTV. That meant a channel that had been broadcasting on channel 2 for many years could, in fact, now actually be broadcasting on channel 43. This would be both confusing to viewers and a promotional nightmare, so another solution was sought. PSIP's primary function is to take a digital signal (in our example, channel 43) and place the signal on its *virtual channel number* (in our example, channel 2) with the inclusion of metadata relaying this to home receivers. Additionally, PSIP can also add elements such as content ratings and electronic program guides (brief synopsis/cast of a program).

PSIP is the thing that allows a station to retain its old channel number (e.g., "We're News 4") even if the old channel-4 elected to move to RF (radio frequency) channel 38, or any other channel. A viewer never sees that TV 4 isn't really on RF channel 4 anymore. In the DTV transition, this allowed stations to retain their identity while moving to different spectrum, and virtually all stations spent at least some time with

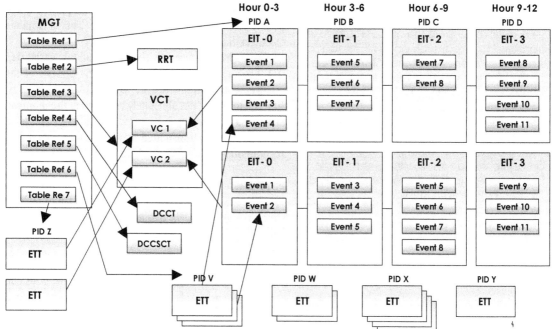

Figure 10-02. PSIP table interrelationships

a DTV transmitter operating on some other channel. Cable and satellite MVPDs have similar technology that allows the virtual channel to be different from any physical channel. The physical RF spectrum assignment remains fixed, but the payload (the actual construction of the data bandwidth transmitted) can be (and often is on some stations) changed on the fly to accommodate different program lineups and bandwidth needs, while all the time appearing with the same *virtual channel number* to the viewers.

Non-over the air services (cable, satellite, etc.) often have functions that perform the purposes of PSIP. Often the piece that sets up the technical parameters of the digital multiplex is very similar to that used in broadcast; however it is typical to have an ***electronic program guide*** (***EPG***) in a multichannel system which in most cases is tied to access control. There are many EPG systems available, the primary difference with PSIP is that the EPG carries the entire MVPD's program information for all services, and PSIP carries only the data for a single OTA station or a service on that station. In PSIP, we can only see the information for the station we are viewing. Currently, there is no means for cooperation between stations to support a common program guide, nor do DTV receivers scan all of the OTA stations to present a common guide. DTV receivers also tend to make searching guide data clumsy and lack the search features common in most stet top boxes (STBs).

EPGs allow us to see all of the relevant information from all of the services available, usually several hundred channels. EPGs that have OTA stations listed often get their information from the OTA stations' PSIP data. This is ideal, as an OTA station may change its lineup of programming at the last minute, and if the EPG gets its information from the PSIP, it too will be updated quickly. In general, there are more similarities between the PSIP's program information (EIT, ETT) and EPG than differences when it comes to the part the viewer and the MCO sees… the program information.

PSIP provides the information necessary to tune and decode DTV signals, as well as providing branding and promotional information. Recall that a DTV OTA broadcast may carry a number of program streams with video and audio. At its simplest, PSIP provides signaling information (information about what is playing now) telling the receiver how to extract, reassemble and decode the pieces that make up the television program. This basic metadata is often static in that it does not change.

PSIP data is one of the components (required) making up the output multiplexed transmission stream of an OTA broadcast station. Once encoded, the PSIP data needs to be injected or inserted (added) into the transport stream by the multiplexer. The simplest method for doing this is to utilize an ASI connection from the PSIP generator into one of the input ports of the multiplexer, in the same manner as the connection from an audio or video encoder. The multiplexer is provisioned to allow sufficient bandwidth for the PSIP stream (typically far less than 250kb/s is appropriate). The PSIP generator creates an MPEG-2 packetized stream with all of the PSIP tables encoded and scheduled to meet the required (or desired) cycle times.

Some muxes have the capability of storing encapsulated PSIP tables in internal memory and playing them out according to a predetermined schedule. This PSIP carouseling is especially useful for that rare, static PSIP that never changes.

A mux is a device that collects data from several input sources and packetizes these data into packets and releases them one after another. This transmission stream is then recovered at the receiving end. The recipient may be an OTA receiver, converter box, satellite or cable IRD, and includes a demux (usually built in, but an external, separate, demux is useful if the demuxing is complex, or multiple streams are needed). For carouseling, the connection between the PSIP generator and the mux usually utilizes Ethernet. The PSIP generator loads the encapsulated (packaged) PSIP tables into the mux over an IP connection, along with instructions on how to schedule the playout. The tables only need to be refreshed when there is a change, typically at the 3 hour EIT boundaries or when the events change (if there are differences in the descriptors). Carouseling can offer a form of resiliency in the case of communication problems between the PSIP generator and mux, since the PSIP tables can be configured to constantly play out from the multiplexers memory in the event of loss of real-time PSIP information.

Announcement information (what will be playing later) is used to construct the program guide. This is dynamic metadata that is constantly updated.

Accurate PSIP is currently required in all terrestrial OTA DTV broadcasts by the FCC. This means that all of the requirements in the ATSC PSIP standard (A/65) must be adhered to. While not absolutely required at the moment, there is a growing trend towards mandating complete accuracy in the transmitted PSIP schedule, including accommodating last minute changes.

PSIP Basics

PSIP consists of a number of MPEG-2 tables, whose structure and usage is defined in ATSC standard A/65. The following is a list and brief description of the most important tables:

• **Master Guide Table (MGT)**: The MGT serves as a directory of all PSIP tables. It lists the locations, sizes and versions of each table so the receiver can extract them from the stream.

• **Virtual Channel Table (VCT)**: The VCT defines each of the virtual channels within the DTV stream, defining major and minor channel numbers as well as which program elements to assemble to reconstruct the television program.

• **System Time Table (STT)**: The STT carries the current time information from the broadcaster to the receiver.

• **Event Information Table (EIT)**: The EITs carry the main program guide information (event titles, times and information about captioning, ratings, audio and broadcast flag). Each EIT covers a 3-hour time span – at a minimum, 4 EITs must be sent (up to 12 hours of schedule information)

• **Extended Text Table (ETT)**: ETTs carry extended text descriptions of individual events within the EITs.

• **Rating Region Table (RRT)**: The RRT defines the rating parameters used for the region. For the US (Rating Region 1), transmission of the RRT is optional.

The PSIP tables can be thought of as a database with a dozen or so interlocking pieces. Index pointers within the tables enable the PSIP data to be used in various ways.

All the dynamic information in the EPG comes from the various PSIP tables, as shown in Figure 10-02 below.

PSIP Sources

PSIP data can be entered manually via a keyboard or transferred as files from anything and anywhere including the traffic systems, program management systems and/or automation system. Each of these systems can be characterized as having different depths of information about the current scheduling, as well as different degrees of accuracy concerning event details (such as start time, duration, and rating for parental control). The PSIP generator may accept schedule information from one or more of these sources (in the latter case, it is helpful to be able to prioritize the information sources). Information may be obtained by polling the source at periodic intervals (*pull*) or by having the information source send updates when available (*push*).

Manual or internally generated information gathering is uncommon as most stations, cable networks, and anyone doing real-time live broadcasting is likely to use a Web based *listing service* (Tribune Media Services is popular) to upload their schedule data which is in turn downloaded into PSIP and EPG systems by subscribers that include OTA television services and MVPDs.

If the programming is part of a continuous DTV stream from a network or syndication source, then this source may include in the stream properly formatted PSIP tables at reasonable intervals. The PSIP generator (or some ancillary input device to it) should then extract from this stream the PSIP data that is relevant.

Note that a station may be fed by more than one of these DTV sources, and they don't have to be MPEG-2, Almost any compression and distribution system can carry PSIP or PSIP-like information. It should be noted that while there is a standardized protocol for exchange of PSIP information (PMCP - ATSC A/76), there are also other interfaces and protocols in use today.

PSIP Insertion into the Program Stream

Many stations undergo changes in the virtual channel configuration during the broadcast day, known as day-part changes. Day-part changes are typically transitions from multiple standard definition virtual channels to a single high definition channel and back or some combination of SD and HD channels. If you are running an important sporting event, you might not want to have any of the bandwidth diverted to other services. Because the virtual channel configuration is signaled by PSIP, the PSIP data must be modified to match the actual configuration. Some PSIP generators can synchronize directly with the encoder/multiplexer systems to automatically deal with day-part changes. The Virtual Channel Table (VCT) contains flags. The hidden flag and the hide-guide flag control tuning access to virtual channels and whether a non-active virtual channel will be represented in the EPG.

The MCO's PSIP (or other EPG and control data) responsibility varies from facility to facility. In some facilities, the MCO may be required to update EPG information when programming changes, even last minute.

Commercial Advertisement Loudness Mitigation Act

The ***Commercial Advertisement Loudness Mitigation Act*** (***CALM Act***) requires MVPDs (multichannel video program distributors: broadcast, cable, satellite and some others) to keep the loudness of commercial advertising (including promos, PSAs and political ads) at a loudness consistent with regular TV programming, per the recommendations in ATSC Recommended Practice A/85. Enforcement became effective on December 13, 2012. As this is written, no known fine has been levied, but consumer complaints have also reduced dramatically, indicating that loud commercials are not the problem they were before the CALM act.

Loud commercials had been a top consumer complaint to the FCC for decades and were listed as such in 21 of the FCC's 25 quarterly reports between 2002 and 2009. According to a 2009 Harris poll, almost 90-percent of TV viewers were bothered by loud commercials, prompting 41-percent of viewers to turn down the volume, 22-percent to mute the TV, and 17-percent to change the channel altogether.

The CALM Act mandates that the FCC write rules enforcing the "ATSC *Recommended Practice: Techniques for Establishing and Maintaining Audio Loudness for Digital Television* (A/85), *and any successor thereto*, approved by the Advanced Television Systems Committee (ATSC), only insofar as such recommended practice concerns the transmission of commercial advertisements by a television broadcast station, cable operator, or other multichannel video programming distributor." The law applies to virtually everyone that delivers commercial content to a viewer that doesn't travel on a physical media such as DVD.

In brief:

- TV stations and *MVPDs* are responsible for any commercial content that they insert.
- TV stations and MVPDs are *not* responsible for any commercial content inserted by upstream providers when the TV Station or MVPD holds a certification of compliance by the upstream supplier and the station or MVPD guarantees a *pass through* of the upstream content.

Compliance with the FCC Rules relating to the CALM act requires that station policies must be determined and implemented. These rules impact multiple departments and must be station-wide. Some of the policy topics are listed as the bullet items that follow. Others may be added by your legal counsel or your *affiliate* network. Once policies and workflows are put in place, the MCO's responsibilities are straightforward.

The *ATSC* A/85 document is a recommended practice, not a standard per se. However, within reason, the legislation in effect elevates it to a level on a par to a standard. As such, it is important for the MCO to understand what it recommends:

Each TV station needs to select its loudness target for operations. This loudness is measured by loudness meters compliant with ITU-R BS.1770. This measurement reports in units of loudness, K-weighted, relative to full scale (LKFS), which is a different scale than VU (volume) meters (see Chapter 8 for an explanation of the differences). LKFS is a system; it is not an instantaneous measurement but a measurement averaged over time. Units of LKFS are measured in dB but acquired with a filtering system that better aligns with perceived loudness.

LKFS numbers are reported as a negative number. The more negative the quieter. Zero dB LFKS is as loud as anything can get. Zero dB is full-scale digital meaning there simply is no way that anything can ever be louder than the loudest value the system can support. The ATSC has specified a recommended average loudness level of -24 LKFS, which most domestic networks and operators have adopted. This means that the average program should be 24dB below the full scale digital value that cannot be exceeded.

- If your station is a network affiliate it will most likely follow that network's CALM-related recommendations, especially as it relates to their target loudness.
- Ingest of content, especially commercials and promos, should include verification that their loudness matches the target loudness of your station or an adjustment will be required to match the target loudness. Many transcoders provide such mechanisms.
- Loudness should be measured according to the technique specified in ITU BS.1770 with guidance provided by ATSC A/85. BS.1770 (LKFS) is a long-term, time-averaged measurement, very suitable to the wide dynamic range of DTV and different than the VU and PPM meters. In addition to the long-term, time-averaged measurement value, the meter will also report a true peak value, which MUST be kept below -1dBfs. A/85 recommends maintaining true peak below -2dBfs. Failure to observe this may result in digital clipping, which yields harsh audible artifacts
- The AC-3 metadata dialnorm value broadcast with each content item must match the average measured loudness within ±2dB.
- A/85 contains two Quick Reference Guide annexes, one aimed at station engineering (annex H) and the other at audio engineers and editors (annex I). Annex H is of particular value in that it is only five pages long and designed to give the reader the most vital information without the need to cover the rest of A/85. Given the timeliness, this is included in this guide as Appendix D. It contains more information than most operators will need or want.

- A/85 recommends that dialnorm be set to -24dBfs but any value may be used as long as it matches the average loudness of the content. Operating with a variable dialnorm value which tracks the loudness of individual pieces of content presents operational and station architecture challenges so most facilities elect to operate in a fixed dialnorm mode.

More recently, the industry is using a newer term: *LUFS* (Loudness Units Full Scale). For all practical purposes, LUFS is interchangeable with LKFS. LKFS tends to be used here in the U.S.; the European Broadcast Union prefers LUFS.

Most critical for master control operations:

A/85 specifies that the loudness of the *complete mix* of short form content (ads, promos, PSAs and political ads) is measured and reported in units of LKFS.

A/85 specifies the average *dialog loudness*, not whispered or shouted, of long form content (programs and infomercials) is measured and reported in units of LKFS.

The MCO will likely oversee or monitor the equipment that does measure the loudness of all content from all workflows and sources in units of LKFS as above and correct or report significant instances when the loudness does not match the dialnorm value. The really important loudness value is of course what is broadcast. More than likely there is some means of monitoring and logging those loudness values.

There are many ways that loudness can become a problem, but the two most likely are mistakes or lack of detail on the part of content suppliers or ingest operators, which can cause CALM act violations, and incorrectly set Dialnorm *metadata*. Any seasoned MCO knows that content suppliers and their distributors often make a mess of audio levels, and seemingly anything else that can be messed up.

Some facilities employ automatic loudness control equipment, a form of dynamic range control processing. This equipment controls the range of the audio in an effort to automatically bring content with loudness variation into compliance. Generally these devices are not something an MCO has control over (in fact most are locked to prevent MCOs, program directors, and other from adjusting the station sound). Because there are so many options in loudness control processing, the SOPs for a given facility will vary widely and the manufacturer of the processor is often be involved in the unit's set up.

Emergency Alert System (EAS)

All TV broadcast stations (except low power) are required to participate in the Emergency Alert System (EAS). Cable systems also participate but generally they have a scheme where an alert is sent to customers either by interrupting or at least adding a crawl to most channels (high value channels, pay per view, etc., sometimes are excluded) by sending the alert out of band as a data message to the set-top box (STB) or satellite receiver. The STB may have the capability of alerting the household even when TV is not being viewed.

While we won't cover much of this here, alerting is often carried to the vision and audio impaired, non-ambulatory, and to devices from cell phones to special alert radios, sirens and public address systems (weather, some systems near nuclear facilities and military) and Internet-based warning systems. Ideally and usually, all of this works together, and OTA broadcasters and MVPDs are just a part of the alerting fabric.

Emergency Alert System Basics

The primary purpose of the EAS is to enable the president of the United States to address the people even when normal and conventional means to do so are no longer functioning properly. The EAS system takes advantage of digital technology, including the Internet, to create a fairly sophisticated communication system capable of alerting the public of national, state, local and weather emergencies. The Emergency

Alert System has the ability to target a specific geographic area for emergency notification. The EAS system is able to interface with computers and other digital devices and includes provisions for the hearing and visually impaired.

The central piece of equipment is the EAS encoder/decoder (Figure 10-03), which is a small computer capable of receiving and transmitting messages in the proper format. The EAS decoder has at least two inputs for audio messages and an input for data messages. Alternatively, data messages may be handled

in a separate device then routed to the EAS decoder. All data messages must conform to the *Common Alerting Protocol* (CAP) standard. When an emergency message is received, the unit may activate a speaker, display a message, or print a brief explanation of the EAS activation, or any or all of the above.

Figure 10-03. An EAS encoder/decoder. Courtesy of TFT.

EAS transmissions adhere to a standard four-part message format referred to as the *EAS protocol*. The transmissions include EAS header codes, an 8 to 25 second two-tone EAS attention signal, the emergency message in the form of audio or text (preferably both) and finally the end of message (EOM). The EAS digital header codes and two-tone attention signal must modulate any audio stream at no less than 50% modulation, which makes them reasonably loud. All EAS digital codes and audio tones must be produced directly by the encoder, never prerecorded and played back from a storage device. Because all EAS digital messages contain a time stamp, it is not useful or legal to reproduce the digital alert message or alert tones from a storage device. It won't work in any case as the time stamp will not match current time. An EAS decoder is capable of storing at least two minutes of audio or text. The EAS header codes are a stream of digital information contained at the beginning of an EAS message. There are four important pieces of information embedded in the EAS header: the *originator* of the message, the type of *event* triggering the activation, the geographic *area* affected by the event, and the *expiration time* of the situation.

The attention signal is a leftover from the EBS (Emergency Broadcast System) that *EAS* replaced. The thought is that people had been trained to recognize that set of tones (853 and 960Hz) transmitted together as reason to stay tuned and listen for important information. There are legacy EBS receivers that remain powered but silent until they decode the EBS tones and *un-mute*. These legacy EAS receivers are old and rare, and there are very few compared with the number of EAS receivers, however some stations and states included the EBS tones in order to accommodate any that might remain in service. Only the national level activations *require* the attention signal (sometimes called the dinosaur tones, given that they are fairly archaic at this point and most people recognize the EAS duck quack); so most tests, state and local alerts (including weather) simply save time by not sending the legacy EBS alert tones. The thought here is that the duck quack (there is a more colloquial term that is common, that rhymes with duck arts) that is the data being sent to activate and direct the information is enough (if not too much) of an alerting sound. There is some concern that repeated testing of EAS might be teaching viewers and listeners to tune-out, so tests are usually done in the least obtrusive manner allowed.

Station management determines the station's EAS decoder programming. Based on information contained in the header code, the programming of the decoder may cause the EAS message to be automatically re-broadcast, to be ignored, or to be brought to the operator's attention in the form of an aural or visible indicator.

It's important to realize that *EAS decoders can only store one message at a time*. When a message is received, a station may delay forwarding that message until a later time, perhaps due to programming considerations. The message will be held by the EAS unit. However, if another message is received before the first one is forwarded; the new message will replace the first one. This process could deny citizens access to important information. Messages may arrive close together in times of emergency, so most station SOPs call for each message that is to be broadcast to be forwarded as soon as possible.

In the case of a state or local EAS activation, broadcasters must follow the *state* and *local plan*. If the station is a *State Relay* (SR) it must monitor the *State Primary* (SP) or follow the state plan for instructions. *Local Primary* stations (LP) must monitor the *State Relay* (SR) station for instructions or follow the state plan. *National Participating* (NP) stations are required to monitor their *Local Primary* (LP) for instructions. In some cases, where a broadcast station is near a state line or serves more than one local area, there may be more than one EAS plan involved. Your station should have a copy of all applicable state and local plans for your reference. You, as the on-duty operator, are responsible for knowing your station's state and local EAS type (SR, LP or NP) and must proceed accordingly when a state or local EAS message is received during your shift. TV stations are only occasionally given responsible roles in EAS distribution, which favors radio stations and non-broadcast communications systems for distribution.

Broadcast stations must monitor at least two EAS audio sources and one data source as assigned in the State EAS Plan. The audio sources are typically either two local radio stations or one radio station and the local *National Weather Service's All Hazards Weather Radio*. The data source is specified by the EAS State Plan but could be the Federal Emergency Management Agency's (FEMA) Integrated Public Alert and Warning System (IPAWS) server or another data source. The FCC EAS TV Handbook, the State EAS Plan and any Local EAS Plan *must* be available at the station EAS control point when an operator is required to be on duty in attended operation.

Operation During Emergencies

When the *EAS* is activated for a national emergency, a National Participating (NP) EAS station is required to retransmit it immediately and for its entire duration on all program streams. This activation is called an *Emergency Action Notification* (EAN) and *must take priority over all other EAS messages pre-empting any in progress*. An EAN is the only EAS message that may continue beyond a two-minute maximum limit to which all other EAS messages must adhere. The goal of the EAN is to have *all* broadcast and cable systems transmitting the same information at the same time (a media roadblock so wherever a viewer tunes, he gets the same message, hence this cannot be delayed or ignored). When the national emergency has ended, an Emergency Action Termination (EAT) message will be sent. Like the EAN, an EAT message must also be transmitted immediately upon receipt.

A non-participating station must leave the air during a national activation. Stations that do this are called Non-Participating National, or NN stations. NN stations must have a letter of authorization from the FCC to operate in this manner.

When the EAS is activated for a state or local emergency, a participating EAS station is required to retransmit it immediately. *National level emergency messages with an Emergency Action Notification (EAN) have priority over all other messages including state and local messages.*

When broadcasting an EAS message, in addition to the EAS audio, television stations must transmit a visual message containing the originator, event, location and valid time period of the EAS message. If the visual message is a video crawl, it shall be displayed across the top of the screen or other location to reduce interference or clutter with other visual messages.

The *EAS TV Handbook*, published by the FCC, summarizes the actions to be taken by television station operating personnel, establishes monitoring guidelines, and gives examples of EAS message scripts.

Tests

The EAS system is tested in several ways on a schedule defined in the FCC rules. All participating stations are required to carry a National Test. There is a *Required Monthly Test (RMT)* originated from local or state sources as assigned in the EAS State Plan. The RMT must be re-transmitted within 60 minutes of reception. An RMT, in an odd-numbered month, must occur during the day between 8:30 a.m. and local sunset. In even-numbered months, the RMT must occur overnight between local sunset and 8:30 a.m. The RMT consists of the EAS header codes, two-tone attention signal, a test message script and the EOM. This test is designed to last 30 seconds or less. All stations required to install EAS equipment must carry the RMT, including non-participating stations.

All television stations (except low power) must originate their own EAS test once a week at random days and times. This is the *Required Weekly Test (RWT)* and is not required during the week that a RMT is conducted. The RWT is brief and consists of only the EAS header codes and EOM codes. No attention signal, aural message, or visual message is required for the RWT, though stations usually precede it with an informational announcement or accompany it with a visual graphic so that viewers understand what is happening.

The Required Weekly Test (RWT) serves to insure that station's EAS equipment is able to receive and generate an EAS message properly. It is also good practice to check the EAS equipment daily for normal appearance of the display and other indicators and even to quickly listen for the monitored stations. As the station operator, you should notify your chief operator in the event of an EAS equipment failure noticed during your daily check or when you are attempting to use it. The station may operate for 60 days pending repair or replacement of EAS equipment, if appropriate entries are made in the station log showing the date and time the equipment was removed and restored to service. During equipment repair and for personnel training purposes, the monthly test script must still be transmitted for the RMT.

FCC rules require that the date and time EAS messages are sent and received must be entered into the station log. Some EAS units may automatically log EAS messages and provide a printout that can be attached to and become a part of the station log. Station policy may require manual logging of each EAS message sent or received. As the on-duty operator, you are required to know and adhere to your station's EAS logging procedures.

Because an EAS message transmission will interrupt programming, you, as the station operator, may be required to notify the traffic department of a programming interruption caused by the EAS message. In some cases, the station SOP directs the MCO to attempt to **make-good** any missed spots. Additionally, most stations will require the nature of the EAS message to be entered in the station log by the operator. In many cases, you will see and hear the EAS message at the same time your audience does. One of your primary responsibilities will be to recover and rejoin programming smoothly as practical after the EAS activation.

Amber Alerts

Your station may also choose to participate in the Amber Alert program. This is a message (sometimes distributed via EAS) that aids law enforcement in the recovery of abducted children. The program may operate differently from area to area. Because of the nature of child abductions, the sometimes horrific outcomes, and that fast, mass response is often successful. Amber alerts are usually given much support and special care by broadcasters, so much so that of all the alert codes, the Amber alert is special, and may trigger on air coverage, special crawls, and other station action that other alerts don't.

Compliance

EAS compliance is a high-priority with the FCC and therefore should be a high-priority with the station. The FCC is known to make unannounced inspections to check on various compliance issues. You can be sure that EAS compliance will be near the top of its inspection list. Some stations are involved with the voluntary inspection program called the Alternative Broadcast Inspection Program (ABIP) offered by a state broadcasters association. In these cases, the station inspection may be performed by non-FCC personnel.

Logging of EAS activity is highly recommended, and in some cases, required. How a station elects to log EAS activity is up to management. It is recommended that the following items, dates and times be logged:
- Receipt of RWTs. The station should receive two each calendar week. (At least one RWT from each monitored EAS source.)
- Receipt and retransmission of RMTs.
- Receipt of other tests.
- Receipt and retransmission of actual EAS messages and Amber Alerts.

In some stations, the EAS activity log printed by the EAS decoder is attached to the station log to reinforce logging compliance. One of the first things an inspector will look for is installed and operational EAS equipment.

Stations can be ready for inspections by having the following on hand:
- The current FCC EAS TV Handbook.
- A copy of your applicable State and Local EAS Plans.
- Clear and easy-to-understand instructions for handling EANs, RMTs, RWTs, and local EAS alerts.
- A log of EAS activity.

Questions that you may be asked during an inspection may include:
- Is your EAS decoder monitoring the correct frequency assignments in accordance with your local or state EAS plans?
- Does your log show that your station is:
    a. Transmitting RMTs and RWTs and logging them properly?
    b. Receiving at least two RWTs weekly? (one from each monitor assignment)
    c. Logging failures to receive or send the monthly or weekly tests?
    d. Logging any EAS equipment failures?

You may also be asked to demonstrate your ability to transmit an EAS test.

Your *chief operator* should keep you advised of the latest changes in your responsibilities regarding the EAS and your station's policy. As the station operator, it is your obligation to remain current on your station's written EAS policies each time you operate the station.

Weather Alerts

Many *OTA* stations have a weather alert policy, outside of the EAS requirements. Stations with active news departments may frequently break in to update weather when important. Many stations with active, often live, weather coverage elect to selectively carry what might be redundant weather alerts. Many stations will continuously run a *weather bug* and crawl with important weather data in times of a threat.

Weather and EAS

There is no required or specified response to weather alerts and tornado warnings unless EAS activation is requested. Most stations have a policy that may include activation of the EAS, rebroadcast of the live weather statement, text crawls, alert beeps, closed captions, newsroom cutaways, program interruptions, or other responses. Messages of the National Weather Service must be rebroadcast within one hour of receipt. In the case of tornado and flash floods, delaying rebroadcast is simply irresponsible, so virtually all broadcast stations that rely on EAS for such coverage and alerting will rebroadcast immediately. Credit must be given to indicate that the rebroadcast message originates with the National Weather Service. The operator should know from the *SOP* what to do during any emergency involving an area inside the coverage of the station.

Stations with an active weather reporting function may actually be covering a weather emergency live as EAS activation is received. The station's SOP may be to hold or even not to transmit the EAS activation given that live coverage is probably better information. Information from the received EAS messages becomes input to the news and weather departments. Important here is that no other stations depend on your station for their EAS messaging, which would be normal and part of the state plan. These stations might use EAS as a source of additional weather information more than an alert trigger. Overnights might be a different operating practice; if the weather reporters are not at the station, the EAS system might be set to respond automatically to weather alerts.

EAS and Commercials

While ingesting commercials (particularly movie commercials), be aware of any commercials that have EAS or EAS-like elements within them. Airing these spots is forbidden, and stations can be fined severely for airing EAS-like elements in non-EAS venues. The FCC takes EAS compliance on this matter very seriously.

Program Logs and Discreps

Television stations also have a *program log* that reports all the elements, commercials and programs that are aired. The program log is no longer required by the FCC, but it is a practical necessity. The FCC does require a means of demonstrating compliance with programming rules and the program log can be used to verify compliance.

There is a subtle difference between the air schedule and the as-aired log, or more appropriately *as-run log*. The term "log" is often used inaccurately to describe the air schedule. The air schedule is prepared by the traffic department and describes what is scheduled to air. The as-run log is prepared by the on air operator (MCO), or by automation performing the MCO function, and indicates what commercials and programs actually did air. Part of the confusion between the air schedule and the log is, that in manual operations, the pre-printed air schedule is annotated (check off what ran, ink in any changes, erasures are not allowed, strike outs with initials of the editor are) to produce the as-run log.

The differences between the air *schedule* and the as-run log are known as *discrepancies* (or discreps for short). Some discrepancies don't indicate real problems, but note slight changes in scheduled timing. Normally a separate report with the meaningful discreps is prepared to help engineering and traffic determine when equipment is not operating properly and to correct future errors or inconsistencies.

It's generally bad form for an MCO to editorialize, vent or make unnecessary comments on a discrepancy report or log. Just state the facts. A clear concise report will assist traffic, sales, production and engineering in their task of correcting future problems. Pointed comments often backfire as whoever is targeted becomes defensive. Often the cause of a discrep is not so much human error as broken process or some nearly unfixable condition.

The on air operator is the last human in a chain of people and equipment. As an MCO you are the one who has the final opportunity to prevent mistakes that have been overlooked by everyone else. The MCO should learn to think and look ahead. Confirm that the correct programming material is loaded, that the labels and **slates** on the programming agree with the air schedule and shipping containers. At the beginning of your shift, review the air schedule and make sure all the programming materials and information are available. In automated operations, the computer may alert you if a scheduled item in the playlist cannot be found in the library. You are the last person that can prevent (for instance) the Christmas special from airing in June.

During the period of station license renewal or change of ownership there are certain announcements that must be run within specific time periods. It is very important that these announcements be aired properly.

The television operator will often make entries into the program log confirming that the programs and commercials aired as scheduled. It can be a serious mistake to make an error on the program log. Most stations will invoice clients based upon your indication that the programming and commercial material was properly aired. If a mistake occurs, write it up on the discrepancy report so that it can be corrected and billed properly. It is embarrassing to the station when a client learns that their commercial material did not air properly. A mistake can cause lost station revenue and may reduce good will when **make-goods** have to be aired. In some cases it may even expose your station to legal action or FCC fines.

Station Log

The FCC Rules require every broadcast station to keep a written record of station operation. It may be called the *transmitter log* or the *operating log*, but officially it is the *station log*. The station log contains entries to show that the station is operating in compliance with FCC rules. The FCC Rules require that some means should be provided to measure the transmitter parameters as often as necessary to ensure proper station operation.

The station licensee must establish monitoring procedures and schedules to determine compliance with operating power, EAS and antenna tower lighting. A large portion of the station log may be generated by the transmitter remote control system as it automatically records periodic *readings* and prints them, or more likely, saves them in a file. This function might be performed by a third party transmitter monitoring service or at the hub in centralcast operations.

Automatic logging systems should be checked frequently. Stations equipped with an automatic logging system often have an alarm system that signals the operator if certain readings are out of tolerance. In the event of failure, the television operator must manually make the required readings. These manual readings should be taken at intervals no greater than three hours (this is the interval the FCC last required when it made such specific requirements) in order to ensure that the transmitter has not operated out-of-tolerance longer than FCC rules allow.

When you make a mistake on a written log entry, do not scratch it out, erase it, or use correction fluid or tape; the FCC Rules specify that a single line be drawn through the mistaken entry and the correction entered

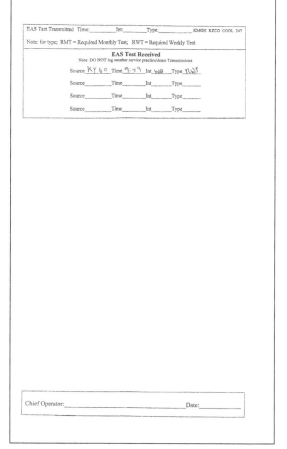

Figure 10-04. A sample manual station log.

near the original entry. If the mistake is discovered after the operator has signed off the log, the correction may be made by that operator at a later time, however the time and date of the correction is required with the operator's initials. If this is electronic, the logging systems will generally keep track of any edits, and who made them when.

Corrections to the log may also be made by the *chief operator*, the station manager, or an officer of the licensee. A written explanation of the mistake must be included with date and signature of the person making the correction.

While virtually anything can be included on the station log, the FCC has the following requirements regarding station log entries:

1. Date
2. Daylight saving or standard time
3. Details of any tower light failures
4. Details of EAS equipment out of service
5. Time EAS tests are sent or received
6. Operator's signature when making entries to the log (It is accepted practice to sign on when the operator begins the shift and sign off at the end.)
7. Any special entries as specified on the station license
8. Details of any out of tolerance readings (power, frequency) and the action taken to correct them
9. Weekly review by the designated chief operator with signature and date

If the EAS log (or any other) is physically separate, it is still considered part of the station log.

In addition, stations may place many of the following entries in the station log or in the maintenance log:

1. Plate voltage, collector voltage, or beam voltage for each transmitter cabinet
2. Plate current, collector current, or beam current for each transmitter cabinet
3. Total power output for each transmitter and/or any combiner
4. Forward and reflected power to the antenna system
5. Notations of adjustments or transmitter operational changes
6. Daily check of tower lights
7. Meter calibration details
8. Maintenance notes
9. Building conditions (temperature, power line voltages, etc.)
10. Cooling system status (flow, temperature, etc., if cooling systems are involved)
11. Frequency (this may be kept on the maintenance log)
12. Quarterly lighting system inspections (the actual inspection is mandatory; logging the inspection is a good practice)
13. Nature and details of EAS messages sent or received
14. Check of proper *PSIP* information.
15. *SNR (signal-to-noise ratio)* of digital transmitter or *EVM (error vector magnitude)* or similar
16. Closed Caption status
17. Nielsen Data status

Manual logs like the one above are reasonably rare, and if they exist, they are often fairly brief. Many stations utilize a *monitoring and control* system that combines the transmitter control with the automatic record keeping of parameters, usually far more than the required FCC records. This is useful in troubleshooting and maintaining the transmitters.

The monitoring and control systems most often monitor additional support systems beyond than the transmitter.

Public File

All *over-the-air* (OTA) broadcast stations are required by the FCC to have a *Public File*. This must be kept on the station's website.

The purpose of the file is to allow the public, during regular business hours, to come to the station and inspect the stations performance. In smaller stations, you might be the only person available during the designated business hours and be expected to take an inquiring member of the public to the file and allow them access. In any case, it is a fair question on the part of an FCC inspector to ask to see the file, and as an MCO you should know where it is kept, how your station manages it, and what kinds of things are in it.

Plate (for a tube), collector (for a transistor), or beam (for the klystron family of power devices) voltages and currents refer to the amount of voltage and current applied to the final amplifier of a transmitter. These are a good indication of health and an indirect measure of the power output of the transmitter. Cooling and the antenna system (where we might look to see how much power is reflected back from the antenna, which is to be minimized) are the other key systems to monitor. The building too is important, it needs monitors to indicate if there is a break-in, flood, fire, loss of temperature control, etc. Many have a technician on site (TOS) indicator that tells you when an engineer is in the transmitter building. You can keep an eye on the technician for his or her safety, and of course if something changes at the site, it is probably caused by the technician, frequently inadvertently as repairing or adjusting one system may cause a problem elsewhere not obvious to the technician.

You probably should ask a new employer about the Public File when you are being trained. While the public file must be kept on the station's website, almost everyone keeps the originals and base copies in a file drawer and offers to make copies of certain documents. Somehow, one must protect the file from theft, intentional or inadvertent. When a visitor comes in, if the Web is the only place that the public file is kept, the online public file must be accessible, meaning the station must provide a means for an interested party to view the files.

Requests from the public to see the Public File are surprisingly rare. The process might be to refer the requester to an available person or the Web first. There must always be a means for the public to get to the Public File during business hours. There are significant fines and penalties for not having a public file, for having an incomplete public file, and for not making the Public File accessible.

What is in the Public File? First and foremost, a copy of the FCC's manual "The Public and Broadcasting," which is a guide for the public wishing to communicate with the broadcaster.

Next, and very important, is a copy of the station license and all related applications and letters that speak to the technical operation of the over-the-air broadcast part of the station are part of the file. Any authorization from the FCC must be copied in the file, as well as any application filed with the FCC (including renewal applications).

Maps of the station's OTA coverage area, usually called *contour maps*, are part of the file. A contour map lays out city grade coverage, grade A and grade B coverage, so appears as two or three circles of increasing size centered on the transmitter site.

Any *citizen agreements* that deal with employment or programming are also part of the public file. Likewise, copies of any local public notice announcements that may be required of the station. Usually any FCC required notices that require publication in the local newspapers of record or other media concerning changes in ownership, status, or construction are included.

A *political file* contains any request for broadcast time made by candidates, and how the station responded to the requests. All political free and paid time records, political spot or programming records, must be retained for two years.

An *annual employment report* and related material supporting the stations equal opportunity employment (EEO) compliance is required.

The *issues/programs list* details how the station has addressed community issues in their broadcasts. Time brokerage agreements and similar agreements where the station allows others to sell or program the station must be included.

Class A television stations have additional requirements. Class A stations are low-power stations that were protected from displacement during the digital transition process to serve particular communities.

Most public files include other items that the station feels in *good faith* the public should have access to. Most stations have rules and processes surrounding how public files are made available, and these vary widely. You should know what those conditions are. You do not have to provide a Public File outside of business hours. The Public File must be at the *station's operating point* (studio) unless the station is located outside the city limits of the city of license, then there must be a Public File maintained within the city limits. Most often this will be at a library, the city clerk's office or a local attorney's office. Stations that fail to have a public file, or have one that is incomplete or out of date, routinely are fined by the FCC.

While the public inspection files must also be maintained on the station's website, the completeness and ease of finding what one is seeking varies greatly from station group to station group (the ownership is likely to handle this requirement with the same software and policies market to market). In some cases, a serious inquiry does require coming to the station to see the hard copies, or to get help navigating the Web site. In some small stations, it may be an MCO that deals with the public looking for access to the Public File.

The Public File contents might also be distributed to libraries in the station's broadcast area for the sake of convenience. In these cases, there is no FCC requirement, so public correspondence from viewers, political reports, and other more sensitive or bulky items can be left out to reduce cost and lessen the odds of misuse of the information provided.

11
TRANSMITTER OPERATION

All **OTA** television stations are required to operate in accordance with Part 73 of the *Code of Federal Regulations*, (*CFR*, Title 47). The FCC Rules and Regulations contained in Part 73 establish modulation levels, power tolerances and other technical parameters that apply to all television stations.

Each television station is issued a television broadcast station license. The station license authorizes the specific details of operation for a television station. Call letters, channel assignment, city of license and transmitter location are all set forth in the station license. The frequency and operating power of the station and type of antenna will also be listed.

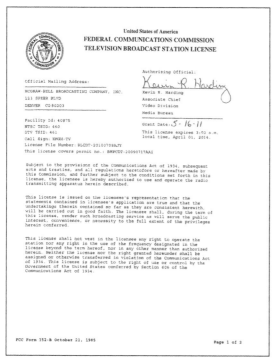

Figure 11-01. A station license. Courtesy KMGH-TV.

The height of the antenna, type of tower markings and tower lighting will be specified. Any special conditions that apply to the operation of the station will appear on the station license. In most cases, the original station license was issued many years ago and will display an expiration date that has passed. When the license is renewed, the FCC issues a License Renewal Authorization in postcard form with a new expiration date.

The station license, the license renewal authorization card and any other instrument of station authorization must be posted at the ***control point***. Posting shall be by affixing the license to the wall or enclosing it in a binder or folder at the control point location.

The television operator, usually the MCO, is responsible for operating the station in accordance with FCC Rules and Regulations and the terms specified in the station license. You will see that the specifications called out in the license are incorporated in the transmitter control system. The license might specify a TPO (transmitter power output) of 13kW, and the control system might simply normalize this to 100%, or it may actually read 13kW or both.

Local Control

In a few OTA stations, the transmitter is located at the station. This is rare simply because the operations of the station are most often best performed in the city and transmission (in countries that favor one or a few high power transmission facilities rather than many low-power transmitters) is often best

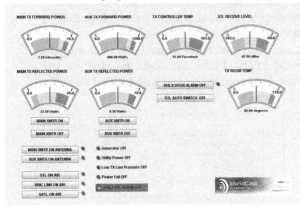

Figure 11-02. A screen shot of an M&C system. Courtesy WorldCast Systems.

done outside the city on tall towers, mountain tops or on top of tall buildings. Further, modern transmitters aren't really built with local control in mind, the cost of remote control is low, and the benefits of automatic and accurate logging found in remote control are worthwhile; hence, even when one could operate with local control, most facilities don't.

The primary purpose of transmitter control is to minimize interference to other services. A misbehaving transmitter could interfere with other broadcasters, or far worse, air and safety communications. For this reason, the FCC emphasizes the quick and capable means and knowledge to shut off any offending transmitter, which is the primary function of a transmitter control system. Know the location of your transmitter (both street address, as well as geographic location; necessary info if you need to contact the FAA about tower light outages).

Part of preventing interference is that the transmitter must maintain power levels and frequency. Very early transmitters needed constant manual adjustment. Modern transmitters adjust themselves automatically. Transmitter control generally considers a few critical parameters necessary for the minute-to-minute operations and dozens or hundreds of more detailed parameters that are largely recorded to assist in the maintenance and repair of the transmitter. For most transmitters the key parameters are:

Forward power (or just power): The output power of the transmitter. It should always be at its licensed value, which is usually converted to read 100% when correct on meters and remote control *dashboards.* Broadcast transmitters are required to operate between 80% and 110% of the licensed value. The station must have a means of dealing with a transmitter that is operating outside of parameters. Usually the SOP is to call a maintenance engineer, specifically, the transmitter engineer. In some stations, the operator manually adjusts the power, but most transmitters automatically adjust their own power, so a variation in power is generally an indication of more serious problems than a manual adjustment can correct.

Reverse power (or reflected power): A measure of the power *rejected* by the antenna system. The energy that isn't transmitted into the air is *reflected* back to the transmitter. This reflected or *rejected* power is not good and must be a low value, usually 3% or less of the transmitter's power output (TPO) range. If the antenna system is in trouble, the reflected power will increase causing a reduction of the transmitter power in an effort to reduce damage to the transmitter and antenna system. Antenna icing can cause the reflected power to increase until the ice melts away. Other damage, e.g., lightning or corrosion, generally gets nothing but worse, often quickly as the transmitter's power stresses damaged components and may cause an *arc over* in some component, literally melting and burning components. Increasing reflected power and decreasing forward power is one event that requires contacting a maintenance engineer day or night. In the worst cases, antennas and or transmitters may be damaged to the point where days of expensive work are required to repair and bring the station back on air. Repeatedly trying to bring up a transmitter into a damaged antenna can result in arcs that remove more and more metal with each attempt to restart the transmitter. *The repetition of trying to turn on a transmitter that will not stay on usually causes serious damage.*

Mains power/generator: Making sure that there is power, and if necessary, fuel for the generator and transmitter. Stable power is a necessity. Power that experiences voltage fluctuations is a problem. Most stations have a procedure for dealing with this situation. When power is unstable or might become unstable (a storm moving in), some stations preemptively manually *transfer* to generator power.

Almost all transmitter sites have at least a small uninterruptible power supply (UPS) that keeps the necessary communications and control equipment functional long enough to see that the main power is out and control the generator if there is on. If there isn't a generator, or the generator fails, the UPS will discharge and the operator will lose visibility into the transmitter site, generally in 10 to 30 minutes. When power returns, many sites have difficulty starting up again, so it may be SOP to send an engineer to the site.

Calling the power company might also be in the SOP. If the outage is widespread, one can expect that the power company will be working on it. If the outage only affects the transmitter, the power company probably doesn't know to fix it. Many stations have run out of fuel waiting for power to return. Many engineers have arrived at the transmitter to see the transformers that feed their building have burned up or blown line fuses.

Cooling: There can be several parameters monitored for a transmitter and its building, but keeping the facility and transmitter cool (removing the waste heat) is critical. Cooling failures are definitely a reason to call in maintenance engineering. Equipment can overheat quickly, and ideally it will shut down before permanent damage is done. *Delta-T* (delta being the mathematical symbol for change, and T representing temperature), the difference in temperature between the cooling fluid (air or water) entering the transmitter and that leaving, is a parameter that stays fairly constant despite the outside temperature, and thus is often used to monitor the health of the cooling system. If the delta-T is rising, the cooling system is failing.

Some sites have fire control systems, while others have none at all. Most all have fire and smoke alarms. Most stations have an SOP to shut down the cooling and transmitters in the hope of minimizing damage. When to shut down is a difficult decision. It may be that smoke from a small melting wall-wart or blown dust in a windstorm sets off the alarms. Or, it may be that there is a major fire and the cooling system is madly feeding air into the fire.

Heating is a rare problem for transmitter sites as all transmitters are essentially furnaces heating the transmitter room. If there is alternative heat at the site, it probably hasn't been on for years. Transmitters that used distilled water (as opposed to water and glycol solutions, or air) as cooling fluids can freeze with loss of heat and cause extensive damage, bursting pipes and heat exchangers. Again, getting an engineer to the site is probably your SOP.

Tower Lights: If there is a lighted tower, validating that the lights are operating properly is critical to air safety. The SOP might have you call in help to deal with a lighting failure, and probably direct you to notify the FAA.

Security: Most transmitter sites, or individual transmitter rooms in shared sites, have some level of security. Transmitter sites tend to have desirable quantities of copper in particular. Being isolated, thieves can often remove thousands of dollars worth of copper from a transmitter site faster than anyone from the station can reach the site. This is a dangerous situation for station staff to walk into, so most SOPs call for alerting local law enforcement. Many sites have cameras, and the MCO can see that vandalism is occurring from the safety of the control room. In the case of shared sites, not all tenants are good tenants. Sometimes, security is just knowing when another tenant might have borrowed something. Some sites include an intercom function to the control room. Many have a technician on site (TOS) indicator so you know when an authorized person is on site.

In general, any other readings (there are special circumstances) are not critical.

Security blends into safety, in particular in the case of medical emergency. Engineers often go to sites alone. There are plenty of opportunities to be hurt or killed on the drive or at the site. Occasionally the MCO and the security system prove the saving factor in a safety situation.

OSHA and Safety

The *Occupational Safety and Health Administration* (*OSHA*) is a federal agency that regulates safety in the work place. Many states also have state and local agencies concerned with worker safety.

You should be aware of federal, state and local regulations governing your actions in the workplace. These regulations exist to protect you, your co-workers and the general public from injury. You should be aware of the location of fire extinguishers, first aid kits and emergency telephone numbers.

Your station may have a *safety lockout/tagout* program that sets forth detailed procedures associated with electrical equipment and mechanical machinery. You must receive training in these safety lockout/tagout procedures before attempting them.

You should be aware of the *lockout/tagout* procedures used widely around high-power equipment, including heating and air conditioning and transmitters. Appendix 19C has the complete procedure, but the key idea is that a person can lockout the power feeding some device under maintenance, and only that person can unlock it when all is clear. Tagout means that a tag secures a power or other control in the off position and only the person applying the tag should remove it. This simply prevents someone from turning on the power while a piece of equipment is being worked on, and informs others of whom and maybe why power has been shut down. Before lockout/tagout procedures, accidents (often fatal) were too common.

Locking out power to movable satellite antennas, on site transmitters, generators and HVAC equipment to allow safe maintenance is often under-emphasized. The MCO is charged with keeping things on, steering antennas, etc. Without a lockout/tagout policy put into practice, it's easy for an MCO (especially during a shift change) to inadvertently steer an antenna or activate a system while it is being worked on.

Your station may have a hazardous materials handbook that outlines the chemical composition and safety measures to be used in the handling of these materials found at the station.

If you work at the transmitter site, you should be aware of American National Standards Institute (*ANSI*) guidelines that govern the limits of human exposure to the *non-ionizing radiation* emitted by the OTA television transmitting antenna. The FCC and the *Environmental Protection Agency* (*EPA*) have adopted these ANSI guidelines to protect workers at broadcast stations. These guidelines establish areas near transmitting antennas where access by humans is not permitted unless protective clothing is worn or the station is operating at reduced power. In some cases, the station must temporarily cease operation. These ANSI guidelines also set forth specific time limits for exposure to humans who are not wearing protective clothing.

In the case of television antennas located on tall towers, these areas rarely extend to the ground. You may be called upon to reduce transmitter power or sign-off the transmitter during the period a tower worker is performing maintenance on the tower. In such cases, it is imperative that you confirm that workers have cleared the critical areas before resuming normal operation.

Shared antenna systems usually have maintenance periods where all users must stop transmitting. In some cases, there is an auxiliary transmitter site or system that can be operated without *Radio Frequency Radiation* (RFR) issues. Usually MCOs are nowhere near RFR hazards, and if they are, there will almost certainly be SOPs and protections in place. You cannot sense or feel most levels of RFR considered dangerous. An exposure monitor is required to alarm when dangerous RF levels are present.

Remote Monitoring and Control

If one doesn't control the transmitter locally, there is a remote control system and a means of allowing the remote control to control the transmitter. There are times when you do not want the remote control to operate. It is common when the transmitter is being maintained for the transmitter to be placed in *local control,* which prevents an operator from accidentally turning a transmitter on or making any other adjustment or change in operation while being unaware that a maintenance engineer is working on it. This of course can be dangerous.

All remote control systems organize their functions into three categories:

Status: These are on or off functions. The transmitter is on or off. The antenna heater is on or off. Either *exciter* A or B is on line. Status is most often displayed with *buttons* or *lamps* (either physical or virtual on a computer's screen) that change color and words appropriately.

Command: For the most part these are also on or off functions, but they may also be raise and lower commands to adjust a power level or temperature setting. They can also be in the form of a *go to* (some value) direct entry command. You might be able to type in "78" and press "enter" in the appropriate way to set a room temperature. Commands all go back to the transmitter from the remote control location. Status lights (and/or a change in some measured and displayed value, like power output) validate that the command was executed. Command buttons and status indicators are often combined into a lighted button, or placed close together for that reason.

Values: These are numerical values, often *normalized* for the operator's convenience to 100%. These are used for *metering* parameters. Transmitter power, mains power, temperature, and all manner of data are expressed in a numerical value. It is not uncommon to for a system to be able to display hundreds of values, although only a dozen or so will appear on the remote control panel or computer *dashboard*.

Any newer or more than completely simple remote controls are almost always accomplished with the use of a computer application. A simple remote control (typically 16 channels of command, status, and metering) might be used for a translator or remote ENG receive site. Most of what goes into a transmitter facility is networkable, and what isn't can be adapted to a computer network with a small amount of intervening interface hardware. The transmitter, transmission line air dryers (transmission lines might be pressurized with dry air or nitrogen), heating and ventilation systems, generators, tower lights, security, and all manner of receivers, antenna controls, heaters, coolers and the like can all interface to the transmitter site network. Extending this network to the control room is typical.

In the studio, a computer (generally dedicated, but not necessarily) runs a remote control application or a monitoring and control application that allows the operator to see the transmitter systems operating parameters and allows the operator to turn the transmitter on and off.

Remote controls do not have to be built around computers or use IP connectivity. In particular, small transmitters located in hard to connect locations (e.g., translators and low-power transmitters serving mountain communities) are often controlled with dedicated devices that operate via telephone lines, cell phone connections, or radio circuits. Some can be controlled with touch-tones from a telephone, and others can give and/or listen to voice commands and information.

Serial data protocols (such as *MODBUS*) have been used for many years between equipment to be controlled and the control system within a building. Likewise, analog voltages and simple contact closures can form the interface between equipment and control, but only for a short distance.

Simple Network Management Protocol (SNMP) is an IP-based, best effort (meaning message receipt is not verified) means of using a computer network to create a command and control system with few limitations. Many pieces of equipment, including transmitters, are *SNMP enabled*. The vast majority of microprocessor based, network connected hardware supports this protocol: storage servers, firewalls, environmental and security systems and more. A *facility control system* that supports SNMP can communicate with and control equipment anywhere on the network, often garnering much more detailed information than is available through any other means. Recently designed broadcast equipment (video switchers, media servers, transmitters, microwave links, etc.) also support this protocol, and newer facility control systems can easily integrate data and control functions obtained through SNMP communications alongside other data and control functions supported by serial or hard-wired connections.

SNMP, in particular, allows broadcasters to communicate with and control a much larger variety of equipment, over any geographical area.

In general, many readings are not considered critical, but many stations monitor a large number of performance indicators, particularly in the transmitter, to help with planning and maintenance efforts, in particular, good data can make *Root Cause Analysis* (RCA) to determine what started the problem easier.

Another common human interface on many facility control systems is a *voice response system* connected to an ordinary telephone line. The system can call engineers to alert them to problems, and engineers can obtain information about the site, and control site functions using the *Touch-Tone* (officially known as DTMF) buttons on their phones. Though somewhat less common as network connectivity expands through satellite, 3G/4G and other networks, the voice response telephone link is still a good backup for when normal communications with the site have failed.

Larger systems often employ an enterprise level *network management system (NMS)*, where many monitor and control (M&C) system alarms and status feed a *mother of monitors (MOM)* giving a single *dashboard* view of the entire facilities status.

Resiliency

The control network is generally separate from the studio-transmitter link (STL) and sometimes the transmitter-studio link (TSL) simply because one doesn't want to lose visibility of the transmitter systems if the STL (or TSL) should fail. You can't give a command to reroute the signal around a bad STL if the STL has failed. Likewise the M&C system is usually on its own uninterruptible power supply (UPS). Likewise, there is usually some back up communication path, sometimes a dial-up circuit, cellular connection, etc. Ideally, the M&C system is the most resilient of the transmission systems.

The FCC has two rules that apply in the case of loss of transmitter control:

Unattended operation using an automatic transmission system (ATS) requires the transmitter to automatically shut down within three-hours of any technical malfunction that might cause interference (73.1400(b)). The numerical notation is a citation of the rule found in Part 73.

Remote control operation requires that within three minutes of the loss of the ability to shut the transmitter off via the remote control or any alternative means, the transmitter must automatically shut down (73.1350(b)(2)).

Station Log

We covered station logs earlier. We come back to that for a moment because facility monitoring and control systems also help meet that vital regulatory requirement and can prove that the station made good faith efforts to maintain the facility. The FCC Rules mandate that every broadcast station keep a written record of station operation. It may be called the transmitter log or the operating log, but officially it is the station log. The station log containing entries to show that the station is operating in compliance with FCC rules. While less stringent than earlier iterations, the FCC Rules still require that some means should be provided to measure the transmitter parameters as often as necessary to ensure proper station operation.

All personnel at a station have an obligation to ensure that all operations of the station fall within the legal guidelines and limits established by the license and FCC regulations, and the MCOs assume that responsibility in a direct and daily way. The facility monitoring and control system is a critical tool in meeting those responsibilities.

12
SBE and CERTIFICATION

The SBE Program of Certification was launched in 1975 as a service to its members and for the advancement of broadcast engineering. The objectives of the SBE Certification program are threefold:

1. To raise the status of broadcast engineers by providing standards of professional competence in the practice of broadcast engineering and related technologies.

2. To recognize those individuals who, by fulfilling the requirements of knowledge, experience, responsibility and conduct, meet those standards of professional conduct.

3. To encourage broadcast engineers to continue their professional development.

Currently, there are eight certification levels, plus three specialist certifications. To be eligible for certification, you must have a strong interest in the design, operation, maintenance or administration of the day-to-day problems and achievements associated with the operation of a broadcast facility or related technology. You must also meet the specific eligibility requirements of the desired certification level.

SBE certification is not a license; it is a document that recognizes professional competence by peers in a professional, independent organization. Certification is for individuals only and may not be used to imply that an organization or firm is certified. SBE membership is not required for SBE certification, but is certainly encouraged.

The *Television Operator's Certification Exam* covers much of the fundamental knowledge necessary for the proper operation of a digital television transmitter in particular and complying with FCC rules in general. It covers many of the practical topics necessary for the proper operation of a typical television master control room. Each television station has its own policies and procedures that are unique to its operation and cannot be covered in this handbook. However, all master control operations have the same basic procedures and the same FCC Rules apply at all stations.

SBE Certification is not an FCC requirement, however it is industry recognized evidence of your qualification to serve as an operator at a television station and will be useful when seeking employment or advancement. Many stations have made the SBE television operator certification a requirement for employment.

The SBE website (sbe.org) has everything you need, and you can call the office with questions.

13
ADVICE AND OBSERVATIONS ABOUT A MASTER CONTROL CAREER

If you feel overwhelmed by what you need to learn to be a master control operator, don't worry. There are lots of things to know, but it all works together. Also know that you will be constantly learning throughout your career. Following this section, we've provided a recommended list of books primarily chosen for the broadcast operations newcomer. We'll also note that you must also become proficient with basic computer technology if you aren't already.

Master control jobs are frequently multitask-intensive and sometimes highly stressful. To that end, it is wise to develop a routine for completing your duties. For instance, think of your work area as a clock face; start at a 12 o'clock position and work your way around the room completing your tasks. Or divide your shift into hour blocks and note what needs to be done during each hour. It is not unusual to be interrupted or distracted. Having a routine or system will help you complete all your tasks in an orderly fashion.

Training periods are always too short (if one gets them at all). Taking notes during any training/ orientation session and keeping a personal cheat sheet can be very helpful. Very few people will remember all the details, logins and passwords, and note taking indicates you are serious about succeeding in your new position.

Often operators work with another person on their shifts. It is important to clearly understand what is expected from each position. When duties aren't clear-cut, you can quickly fall into the I-thought-you-did-that-already trap. It is in the best interest of all concerned to know what, for example, the switcher on duty is responsible for doing, and what the second on duty is expected to do. There *cannot* be ambiguity here.

Earlier, we encouraged you to begin your career in a smaller market. Again, while this isn't an absolute, by starting in a smaller market you will gain much more experience in the long run, so when you do (if you wish) make it to a larger market, you'll be a much better operator. The bigger the market is, the bigger the fallout from mistakes and the greater the opportunity to make big mistakes.

If you're new to the media business, it's possible a good deal of your self-image will be tied to your job. Try to wean yourself away from this. Know that your media work is but one of your talents. You are not (and should not be) defined by your job. Seeing jobs shift and layoffs happening throughout the industry, it's insane to tie your values and worth only to those things that are your job.

Finally, what makes a great master control operator? Several factors: diligence, maturity, quick thinking, professionalism, not easily being panicked and being detail-oriented, memory, creativity, intellect, and the list goes on. Perhaps the best praise I heard was, "I know I have a great MCO when a crisis happens and he makes the right decisions." A successful master control operator considers what is in the best interest of both the company and the public. If he or she can't immediately get hold of a supervisor on the phone, and as a manager, I can trust his or her good judgment and maturity to make the right decision on his or her own; I then have a truly accomplished operator.

- *Nick*

I'm not sure if good MCOs are made or born, but I do know there is a certain temperament and a way of thinking and reacting that makes a good MCO. I am also certain that there are very capable people who will never become a great MCO. I like to think of myself in that manner because I can design a facility and build it, but I do a very poor job of driving one. The last time I did, I finished the short shift sweaty and it took an hour to recover enough to be useful. Not everyone can do this well and with acceptable stress levels. If you are lucky, you get to do the things you love to do, and of course you will do those well. I can name 10,000 jobs that are nowhere near as much fun.

Mistakes will happen. Things will go wrong. It's the ability to calmly and with confidence recover that separates the good from the great. Covering up mistakes generally backfires in this business. Yet, especially at the higher end of this career, there is intense pressure for perfection. Losing a job in this business is just an opportunity to start fresh. There is an MCO nightmare that many if not most MCOs experience on occasion: an anxiety dream where nothing works right and you move from one disaster to another. Believe it or not, this does seem to be part of getting good at this. Ask around and you'll be amazed at how many people have experienced this. Not all jobs are this intense. The hours are normally strange, and if you're good, you get to work evenings while the rest of the world relaxes. Wages vary by market and station size. Some want to work at the networks, others in small towns. In broadcasting, you will work with people moving up and then back down market. In a while, you will know a broadcast gypsy you worked with in just about every part of the country.

There is a lot to be said for this as either a career or a job. No heavy lifting. It *is* show business, and you can meet interesting and often famous people. It is highly stimulating. If it's not your career, it is a good day job when working remotes and other TV production, and it keeps you in touch with opportunities. MCOs can wind up in engineering, sales, news, on air, or even management. But most of all, if it's in your blood, it's in your blood.

- Fred

Suggested Reading

1. Lee, Dana M. Television Technical Theory. Dubuque: Kendall Hunt Publishing Company, 2010.
2. Weise, Marcus, and Weynand, Diana. How Video Works: From Analog to High Definition. 2nd ed. Burlington: Focal Press, 2007.
3. Pizzi, Skip & Jones, Graham A. A Broadcast Engineering Tutorial for Non-Engineers. 4th ed. Burlington: Focal Press, 2014.
4. Whitaker, Jerry C. Standard Handbook of Video and Television Engineering. 4th ed. New York: McGraw-Hill Professional, 2003.
5. Whitaker, Jerry C. Standard Handbook of Broadcast Engineering. 1st ed. New York: McGraw-Hill Professional, 2005.
6. Whitaker, Jerry C. Mastering Digital Television: The Complete Guide to the DTV Conversion. 1st ed. New York: McGraw-Hill Video/Audio Professional, 2006.
7. Baumgartner, Fred. SBE Guide to Writing Broadcast Station Operations Manuals. Society of Broadcast Engineers, 1998.
8. Schneider A.C.E., Arthur. My Fifty Years of Television History: Been There, Done That. PublishAmerica, 2005. (optional)
9. Abramson, Albert and Sterling, Christopher H. The History of Television, 1942 to 2000. McFarland & Company, 2003. (optional)
10. Federal Communications Commission. TV Broadcast Station Self-Inspection Checklist. Information Bulletin: EB18TV080. www.fcc.org. August 2006. (optional)

The first two texts are both good texts to learn basic video principles. The first book looks at the essentials of basic video theory. Great detail is given in the second book to both analog and high-definition theory.

Our third text provides a great foundation for general TV engineering theory. It's a comprehensive text that assumes you do not have a deep background in television. Highly recommended, and has the most recent publication date: 2014.

Then, for advanced texts, we recommend any of the Whitaker books; these texts go into great detail on many topics at several levels. While Mastering Digital Television: The Complete Guide to the DTV Conversion is the most current, any of Whitaker's texts are highly regarded and worth your time.

Should you need to compile a station operations manual, we highly recommend the coauthor's 105-page book on this subject. It includes all sorts of information, suggestions, contracts, and letters. In short, anything necessary for easily compiling a station operations manual.

We've included Art Schneider's My Fifty Years of Television History as an optional text. In this autobiographic work, Schneider talks about his time at NBC Burbank, working various broadcast operation network jobs including videotape operator and editor. For those with an interest in network on air operations and technology used from the 1950s through 2000, this is an especially intriguing text. (An earlier version is entitled Jump Cut, Memoirs of a Pioneer Television Editor. McFarland & Co. Inc., 1997).

Another optional text included is the reference book: The History of Television, 1942 to 2000. Note this is actually a heavily illustrated reference book on the technical and equipment developments, inventions, and processes of broadcast operations during this period, and does not cover general broadcast history. If you have an interest in television equipment and engineering practices, you'll find this a unique reference. (Note: This is Part 2 of a two-book set. Abramson's first book, The History of Television, 1880 to 1941, is very worthwhile, but is not as relevant to broadcast operations.)

For those tasked with keeping the station legal and running smoothly, the FCC has compiled the TV Broadcast Station Self-Inspection Checklist available online. This provides a concise, easy-to-read source to determine how compliant your station is, as well as providing helpful information regarding contact data for the FCC, getting questions answered and is a great resource to look up FCC Rules.

Finally, if you have a specific area of interest, please check the SBE Bookstore online at sbe.org.

14A
APPENDIX: Broadcast General Business Function Chart

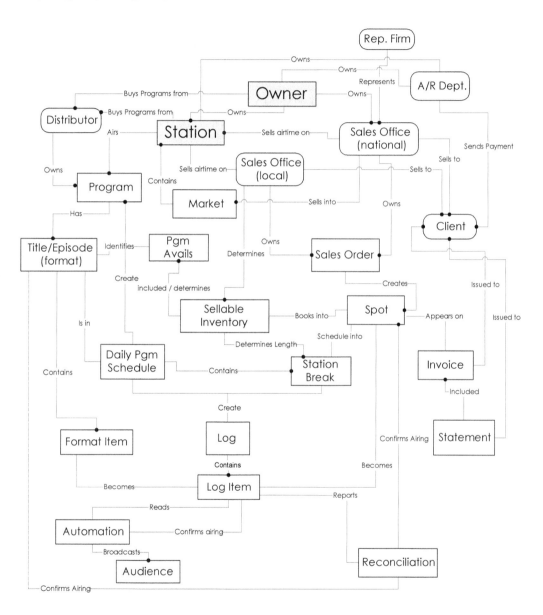

Figure 14-01. Flowchart of the broadcast general business functions.

14B
APPENDIX: Broadcast Business Flow Chart

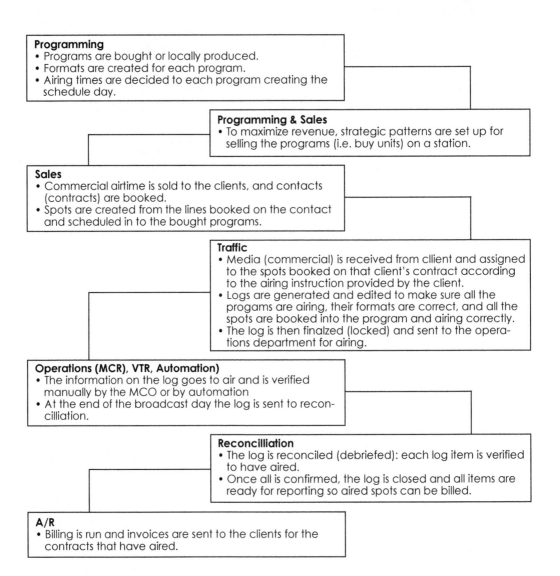

Programming
- Programs are bought or locally produced.
- Formats are created for each program.
- Airing times are decided to each program creating the schedule day.

Programming & Sales
- To maximize revenue, strategic patterns are set up for selling the programs (i.e. buy units) on a station.

Sales
- Commercial airtime is sold to the clients, and contacts (contracts) are booked.
- Spots are created from the lines booked on the contact and scheduled in to the bought programs.

Traffic
- Media (commercial) is received from cllient and assigned to the spots booked on that client's contract according to the airing instruction provided by the client.
- Logs are generated and edited to make sure all the progams are airing, their formats are correct, and all the spots are booked into the program and airing correctly.
- The log is then finalzed (locked) and sent to the operations department for airing.

Operations (MCR), VTR, Automation)
- The information on the log goes to air and is verified manually by the MCO or by automation
- At the end of the broadcast day the log is sent to reconcilliation.

Reconcilliation
- The log is reconciled (debriefed): each log item is verified to have aired.
- Once all is confirmed, the log is closed and all items are ready for reporting so aired spots can be billed.

A/R
- Billing is run and invoices are sent to the clients for the contracts that have aired.

Figure 14-02. Flowchart showing the general order of business activity at a broadcast station.

14C
APPENDIX: Control of Hazardous Energy (Lockout/Tagout)

In most MCO situations, a transmitter, generator, HVAC equipment, and other dangerous equipment are located at the facility or remote location. Because the MCO often has control of such things, and unintentional activation or adjustment can cause injury or death to a technician working on the equipment, we need to cover this topic in depth.

Introduction

On September 1, 1990, OSHA issued a final rule on the *Control of Hazardous Energy (Lockout/ Tagout) of Title 29 of the Code of Federal Regulations* (29 CFR) Part 1910.147. This standard, which went into effect on January 2, 1990, helps safeguard employees from the unexpected activation of equipment or release of electromagnetic radiation while they are performing servicing or maintenance. The standard identifies the practices and procedures necessary to shut down and lock out or tag out equipment, requires that employees receive training in their role in the lockout/tagout program, and mandates that periodic inspections be conducted to maintain or enhance the energy program. OSHA has determined that lockout is a more reliable means of de-energizing equipment than the tagout and that it should always be the preferred method used by employees. OSHA believes that, except for limited situations, the use of lockout devices will provide a more secure and more effective means of protecting employees from the unexpected activation, release of hazardous radiation or startup of equipment.

Scope and Application

The lockout/tagout standard applies to all telecommunications employees and covers the servicing and maintenance of electronic equipment in which the unexpected activation or the release of electromagnetic radiation could cause injury to employees. All employees are required to comply with the restrictions and limitations imposed upon them during the use of lockout. The authorized employees are required to perform the lockout in accordance with this procedure. All employees, upon observing a piece of equipment, which is locked out to perform servicing, or maintenance, shall not attempt to start, energize, or use that equipment.

Energy Control Program

The lockout/tagout rule requires that the employer establish an energy control program that includes (1) documented energy control procedures, (2) an employee training program, and (3) periodic inspections of the use of the procedures. The standard requires employers to establish a program to ensure that equipment is isolated and inoperative before any employee performs servicing or maintenance when the unexpected energizing, start up, or release of electromagnetic radiation could occur and cause injury.

The purpose of the energy control program is to ensure that, whenever the possibility of unexpected equipment activation or energizing exists or when the unexpected release of electromagnetic radiation could occur and cause injury during servicing and maintenance, the equipment is isolated from its energy source(s) and rendered inoperative prior to servicing or maintenance.

Employers have the flexibility to develop programs and procedures that meet the needs of their particular workplace and the particular types of equipment being maintained or serviced.

Energy Control Procedure

Preplanning for Lockout (Preparation for Shutdown)

1. An initial survey shall be made to determine which switches or other energy-isolating devices apply to the equipment being locked out. Any questionable identification of sources shall be cleared by the employees with their supervisors. Before lockout commences, job authorization should be obtained from the supervisor.

2. Only supervisors or authorized individuals shall prescribe the appropriate duties and responsibilities relating to the actual details of affecting the lockout/tagout. Energy isolating devices shall be operated only by authorized individuals or under the direct supervision of authorized individuals.

3. All energy isolating devices shall be adequately labeled or marked to indicate their function. The identification shall include the following:

a. equipment supplied

b. energy type and magnitude

4. Where system complexity requires, a written sequence in checklist form should be prepared for equipment access, lockout/tagout, clearance, release, and start-up.

Lockout/Tagout Procedures

1. Preparation. Notify all affected employees that a lockout is required and the reason therefore.

2. Equipment shutdown. If the equipment is operating, place the equipment in standby or off by the normal procedure. Personnel knowledgeable of equipment operation should be involved with shut down or standby procedures.

3. Equipment isolation. Operate the switch, or other energy-isolating device so that the energy source (electrical, electromagnetic radiation) is (are) disconnected or isolated from the antenna. Pulling fuses is not a substitute for locking out. A yanked fuse is no guarantee the circuit is dead, and even if it was dead, there's nothing to stop someone from unthinkingly replacing the fuse.

4. Application of lockout/tagout. Lockout and tag the energy isolating device with an assigned individual lock, even though someone may have locked the control before you. You will not be protected unless you put your own padlock on it. For some equipment it may be necessary to construct attachments to which locks can be applied. An example is a common hasp to cover an operating button. Tags shall be attached to the energy isolating device(s) and to the normal operating control and shall be attached in such a manner as to preclude operation.

5. Verification of isolation. After ensuring that no personnel can be exposed and as a check on having disconnected the energy sources, operate the push button or other normal operating controls to make certain the equipment will not operate.

6. If there is a possibility of re-accumulation of stored energy to a hazardous level, verification of isolation shall be continued until the maintenance or repair is completed, or until the possibility of such accumulation no longer exists. Filet capacitors in high voltage power supplies may re-accumulate charge.

7. CAUTION: Return operating controls to neutral position after the test. A check of system activation (e.g. use of voltmeter for electrical circuits) should be performed to assure isolation.

8. The equipment is now locked out.

Sequence of Lockout

1. Notify all affected employees that servicing or maintenance is required on a piece of equipment and that the equipment must be shut down and locked out to perform the servicing or maintenance.

2. The authorized employee shall refer to the company procedure to identify the type and magnitude of the energy that the equipment utilizes, shall understand the hazards of the energy, and shall know the methods to control the energy.

3. If the equipment is operating shut it down by the normal shutdown or standby procedure.

4. De-activate the energy-isolating device (Beam P/S Circuit Breaker) so that the equipment is isolated from the energy source.

5. Lock out the energy-isolating device (beam power supply circuit breaker) with assigned individual lockout plate and tagout sign.

6. Ensure that the equipment is disconnected from the energy source by first checking that the transmitter is in standby, then verify the isolation of the equipment by operating the beam power supply circuit breaker by testing to make certain the equipment will not operate.

7. The equipment is now locked out.

8. Restore the equipment to service. When the servicing or maintenance is completed and the transmitter is ready to return to normal operating condition, the following steps shall be taken.

9. Check the equipment and the immediate area around the transmitter to ensure that nonessential items have been removed and that the equipment components are operationally intact.

10. Check the work area to ensure that all employees have been safely positioned or removed from the area.

11. Verify that the transmitter is in standby.

12. Remove the lockout devices and reenergize the transmitter.

13. Notify affected employees that the servicing or maintenance is completed and the transmitter is ready for use.

Additional Safety Requirements

Special circumstances exist when (1) transmitters need to be tested during servicing, (2) outside (contractor) personnel are at the worksite, (3) servicing or maintenance is performed by a group (rather than one specific person), and (4) shifts or personnel changes occur during servicing or maintenance.

Testing or Positioning of Transmitters and Antennas

OSHA allows the temporary removal of locks or tags and the re-energizing of the equipment only when necessary under special conditions. For example, when power is needed for the testing of equipment or components. Re-energizing must be conducted in accordance with the sequence of the following steps:

1. Clear the transmitter and antenna of tools and materials

2. Move employees away from the antenna if a dummy load is not used,

3. Remove the lockout or tagout devices as specified,

4. Energize and proceed with testing or positioning, and

5. De-energize all systems, isolate the transmitter from the energy source, and reapply lockout or tagout devices as specified.

Shift Change Coordination

Supervisors shall ensure the continuity of lockout/tagout protection during shift or personnel changes. Each worker shall be responsible for removing his own padlock and tag at the completion of his shift. If work is to cease until the following day the supervisor shall place his personal padlock and tag on the equipment and the workers shall remove their padlocks and tags. When work resumes the workers shall affix their personal lock and tag to the equipment and the supervisor shall remove his lock and tag.

Conditions for Padlock Removal by the Supervisor

Only the owner of the device except in exceptional situations where the owner cannot be contacted shall a supervisor with all caution and precautions remove lockout/tagout devices.

14D
APPENDIX: Audio Loudness Quick Reference for MVPD and Station Engineers

With the CALM act enacted, and the focus the industry has on the topic, facilities have invested heavily in equipment and training. For now, it's important that we provide in depth support. This is the recommended practice:

A/85, Annex H: (Captured 3-2013 courtesy ATSC)
Quick Reference Guide for Station and MVPD Engineers – Audio Loudness Management

H.1 Introduction
Note: The Quick Reference Guide is based on the ATSC Recommended Practice A/85, "Techniques for Establishing and Maintaining Audio Loudness for Digital Television," (the "RP") and its full text is found as Annex H of the RP.

The Quick Reference Guide summarizes the recommendations in the RP and provides guidance to broadcasters and other video program distributors on controlling and maintaining consistent audio loudness of their TV stations and channels.

H.2 Scope
The Quick Reference Guide is not intended to replace the complete RP. Its scope is limited to a how-to guide for television station operators and MVPDs. Readers of this document are encouraged to review the complete RP for more detailed information and the background to this Guide. In the event of a conflict between the Guide and the RP, the RP takes priority over this Quick Reference Guide. This Quick Reference Guide is based on the use of a fixed metadata system (see Section 7.3 of the RP).

H.3 Definitions
anchor element – The perceptual loudness reference point or element around which other elements are balanced in producing the final mix of the content, or that a reasonable viewer would focus on when setting the volume control.

BS.1770 – Formally ITU-R BS.1770 [3]. This specifies an algorithm that provides a numerical value indicative of the perceived loudness of the content that is measured. Loudness meters and measurement tools that have implemented the BS.1770 algorithm will report loudness in units of LKFS.

dialog level – The loudness, in LKFS units, of the anchor element.

dialnorm – An AC-3 metadata parameter, numerically equal to the absolute value of the dialog level, carried in the AC-3 bit stream. This unsigned 5-bit code indicates how far the average dialog level is below 0 LKFS. Valid values are 1 - 31. The value of 0 is reserved. Agile metadata is an alternative to using the fixed metadata system approach. See Section 7.5 of the RP for details concerning the agile metadata approach. The term "Dialog Level" is based on dialog's widespread use as the anchor for mixing of content and historically it was felt that for most programs dialog would be the Anchor Element. Advanced Television Systems Committee Document A/85:2011; 1 to 31 are interpreted as –1 to –31. The decoder applies an amount of gain reduction equal to the difference between –31 and the dialnorm value.

LKFS – loudness, K-weighted, relative to full scale, measured with equipment that implements the algorithm specified by ITU-R BS.1770 [3]. A unit of LKFS is equivalent to a decibel.

target loudness – A specified value for the anchor element (i.e., dialog level), established to facilitate content exchange from a supplier to an operator.

H.4 Loudness Management

Key Idea: The goal is to present to the viewer consistent audio loudness across commercials, programs, and channel changes.

H.5 FCC Requirement

ATSC document A/53 Part 5:2010 [1] mandates the carriage of dialnorm and correctly set dialnorm values.

Key Idea: Set the station AC-3 encoder's dialnorm to match the loudness of average dialog level of the content.

H.6 Measurement of Content as Delivered

See Section 5 of the RP.

H.6.1 Long-Form Content

A representative section of the content that is dominated by typical dialog (i.e., not shouting or whispering) should be isolated and measured. In the absence of dialog, the loudness of the element of the content that a reasonable viewer would focus on when setting the volume control, should be measured. If neither technique is possible or practical, the loudness of the entire duration of the content should be measured. If the content has significant periods of quiet, see Section 5.2 of the RP.

Key Idea: Measure the long form content loudness when dialog is present. This value is the Dialog Level of the content. The Dialog Level (in units of LKFS) should match the dialnorm value of the AC-3 encoder.

H.6.2 Short-Form Content

See Section 5.2.4 of the RP. Techniques for Establishing and Maintaining Audio Loudness for DTV, Annex H 25 July 2011 65

Key Idea: Measure the loudness of all audio channels and all elements of the soundtrack integrated over the duration of the short form content. The value of the loudness measurement (in units of LKFS) should match the dialnorm value of the AC-3 encoder.

H.6.3 Newscasts or Other Live Programming

The principle of measuring the loudness of the dialog of the content applies to live productions done in real time as the production progresses. The intent of loudness measurements made during a live event is to guide the mixer to produce the content at a Loudness that matches the dialnorm setting of the station's AC-3 encoder. A BS.1770 loudness meter may be helpful when mixing in noisy environments, or when a consistent monitor level cannot be maintained. See Section 5.2.2 of the RP.

Key Idea: Use a BS.1770 meter to help ensure that real-time content loudness matches the dialnorm setting of the AC-3 encoder.

H.6.4 File-Based Content

File-based storage makes it practical to automate the loudness measurement and to adjust the content loudness and/or the dialnorm value (if any) that may have been assigned to the content. See Section 5.2.5 of the RP.

Key Idea: Ensure file based content agrees with the station's dialnorm setting in the AC-3 encoder.

H.7 Target Loudness to Facilitate Program Exchange

See Section 6 of the RP.

Target loudness is a specified value for the dialog level established to facilitate content exchange from a supplier to an operator. For delivery or exchange of content without metadata (and where there is no prior arrangement between the parties regarding loudness), the ATSC specifies a Target Loudness value of -24 LKFS, which serves to establish a common operating level for use with that fixed value of dialnorm. Minor measurement variations of up to approximately ±2dB about this value are anticipated, due to measurement uncertainty, and are acceptable. Content loudness should not be targeted to the high or low side of this range.

Key Idea: For content without metadata, use the target loudness value of -24 LKFS.

H.8 Methods to Effectively Control Program-to-Interstitial Loudness

Large loudness variation during transitions can be effectively managed by adhering to the following practices:

For operators using a fixed dialnorm system, see Section 7.3 of the RP:

a) Ensure that all content meets the target loudness and that the dialnorm value matches this value.

b) Employ a file-based scaling device to match dialog level of non-conformant content to the target value.

c) Employ a real-time loudness processing device to match the Dialog Level of non-conformant content to the target value.

Key Idea: Ensure that all program and commercial audio content matches the dialnorm value of the AC-3 encoder. Use a BS.1770 meter to verify the dialog level of the audio context.

H.9 Affiliate Dialnorm Setting

See Section 7.3.5 of the RP.

An operator (affiliate, station, MVPD, etc.) receiving content that is delivered at a fixed loudness, where there is no gain adjustment or processing after the receiver, should set the value of dialnorm in the operator's AC-3 encoder to match the network originator's specified dialog level. If a fixed gain or loss is applied in the signal chain, the AC-3 encoder dialnorm value needs to be offset accordingly from the originator's dialog level.

If loudness processing is applied to the originator's audio, the processor's target loudness value should match the operator's AC-3 encoder's dialnorm value. See Section 9.3 for additional background on audio processing.

Key Idea: Set the AC-3 encoder's dialnorm value to the originator's dialog level (as adjusted).

H.10 TV Station or MVPD Content Insertion

In the case of TV station or MVPD insertion of local commercials or segments, the operator should ensure that the Dialog Level of the local insertion matches the dialnorm setting of the inserted audio stream. Techniques for Establishing and Maintaining Audio Loudness for DTV, Annex H 25 July 2011 67.

Key Idea: Ensure that the dialog level of inserted content matches the dialnorm setting of the inserted audio stream. If the network originator's feed is decoded to baseband, the loudness of the decoded audio is to be measured and the value of the re-encoder's AC-3 dialnorm value is set to match the measured loudness for the next stage of encoding. In this case either the operator needs to modify the network originator's loudness to match the target value of the operator's system, or the originator's loudness value (as measured) will be used as the dialnorm value in the next stage of AC-3 encoding. At this re-encoding stage the operator needs to also ensure that the other audio metadata parameters are set appropriately.

Key Idea: If the network originator's feed is decoded to baseband, ensure that the measured Dialog Level of the content matches the dialnorm setting of the next stage of AC-3 encoding.

H.11 AC-3 Dynamic Range Control (DRC)

The AC-3 system includes DRC profiles for Line mode and RF mode. While choosing these parameters may be useful to the operator and viewer for limiting the overall loudness range, DRC should not be relied upon to correct loudness variations between programs, programs and commercials or between TV stations or cable channels and during channel changes. See Section 8.3 and Annex F of the RP.

Key Idea: AC-3 Dynamic Range Control should not be relied upon to mitigate program to commercial or station-to-station loudness variations.

14E
APPENDIX: Master Control Training Checklist

Training MCOs completely as possible, as quickly as practical is beneficial. To aid in the process, here is a quick outline of hands on, facility specific training needed. Each facility is different, they may not have some of these pieces, and there are other pieces that likely are important to your facility that require hands on experience to operate.

1. WFM (waveform monitor), vectorscopes, audio
2. Server/VTR setup/record
3. Satellites (setup, adjustments)
4. Router (what's where?)
5. News updates: procedures
6. News updates: equipment, staff
7. Transmitter/STL controls
8. MCR switcher crosspoints
9. EAS procedures, manual
10. Automation
    a) Basic functions/procedures
    b) File loading
    c) Recording & special functions
11. Flashcam: lights, phone, mics
12. Bypass switcher
13. PL/Intercom system
14. MCR switcher operations
    a) Keys
    b) Audio over/under
    c) Audio/video-only switches
    d) Switcher (including "squeeze-back") options
    e) Switcher reset procedure
15. Still store & graphic system
16. Special scopes/meters & calibration
17. MCR dubbing capabilities
18. Automation device server
19. MCR character generator/crawl system
    a) Crawls (news/programming)
    b) Snipes/captions
20. Network communications
21. MCR paperwork
    a) Official program schedule & as-run log
    b) Transmitter log (sometimes referred to as station log)
    c) Discrepancy reports

22. Automation ingest
    a) Spots (Single Elements)
    b) Programs (Multi-segments)
    c) Dub lists
    d) Purge lists
23. Video file transfer systems
24. Network fiber/satellite system
25. FCC & related Issues
    a) EAS activation
    b) Frequency of transmitter readings
    c) Children's TV Act
    d) FAA tower light outage
    e) SBE Certification
26. Unique program requirements
27. Fill programs/Evergreens
28. Awareness: program/traffic operations
29. Special reports
    a) NET (warnings, DR's)
    b) Local (who can authorize?)
30. Monitor air (switcher-output vs. off-air)
31. STL/transmitter failure procedures
32. News computer system Ops
33. Program spot-check process
34. Preview switcher: use & sources
35. Program formats (Local & Net)
36. Routine for early AM shift
37. Routine for midday shift
38. Routine for swing/overnight shift
39. Special needs of studio & crew?
40. Emergency procedures
41. Microwave ingest procedures
42. Phone lists (station/home numbers)
43. Office supplies, extra forms

14F
APPENDIX: Centralcasting Notes

The current trend in master control operations is centralization or hubbing. This is combining resources to share personnel, equipment or both among a group of stations. The control point is considered the hub, and the facilities at the end of the hub are referred to as the spokes. While the concept is easy enough to understand, the execution presents challenges.

Because this seems to be a constant conversation in the industry, whether to hub or to change the configuration, we thought it might be good to publish as an appendix at least one conversation along these lines to give some perspective.

Shawn Maynard, vice president and general manager of Florical Systems of Gainesville, FL, presented this at the 2009 National Association of Broadcasters Convention. Florical Systems was among the first to successfully implement centralcasting on a large scale. It is with Florical Systems permission we present a synopsis of that presentation, *The Top Ten Considerations for Centralization*. Whatever approach and vendors are involved, the conversation runs along these lines:

1. Choosing the Proper Model

Once the decision is made to centralize, senior management must determine what model or scenario would be the most advantageous to the group. What are the current and future needs of the group?

There are three basic models to choose from:
a) Central control with remote storage
b) Central control with central storage
c) Shared control with shared storage

Central control with remote storage takes the operations out of the local facility, thus saving on operator expense. However, much of the hardware is left at the local facility. While this may have some logistical advantages, it also means maintenance of those systems is the responsibility of the local facility, not the hub.

Central control with central storage takes virtually everything from the local facility and moves it to a hub. As we've discussed, the business of broadcasting is going through many changes: takeovers and mergers, cost-effective measures, not to mention the consolidation of physical plants. It is infinitely easier to move a facility's infrastructure (MCR, storage, playout, etc.) to a newer, already established hub, rather than maintaining a current MCR, while also building a new version within the same building. And for many, their existing MCRs were first built perhaps in the 1940s, 1950s or 1960s. If a facility is in the midst of a sale, or there's a possibility of a move to a new facility, this model may be a more efficient way to proceed.

Shared control with shared storage is simply a hybrid of the two previous models. The biggest advantage in this model is having the capability to share both control and storage with more than one location for disaster recovery.

With each of these systems, there is a balance within each of these 3 models: if more is spent in capital expenses, operational expenses tend to be lower. Conversely, the less spent on capital, the more operational expense is required.

2. Politics: Getting Local Buy-in

To begin, the process must be corporate driven, and locally executed. It is at this point that all parties must come to an agreement regarding what is the local goal for facilities, the levels of acceptable error, and in short, honestly discuss the benefits, risks and costs for an endeavor such as this. Because you are essentially combining operations for multiple facilities, each party must be on the same page for this to work successfully.

3. Gathering and Measuring Data

It is at this juncture everyone must roll up his sleeves and begin to examine the details of each facility's infrastructure.

Discrepancy Database: How does each station track, monitor, and correct discrepancies? Is a database kept of discrepancies? How will this impact multi-channel facilities? Also, is there a desire to go from paper discrepancy reports to an online (paperless) system?

Sales processes: While this may impact MCOs the least, it is important within the buy-in that sales' processes be discussed and how they will dovetail into traffic's infrastructure.

Traffic processes: This may be the most complex element in this data gathering process. Traffic is dependent on sales for much of its work, then traffic must compile daily on air schedules for (often) multiple channels and have them distributed by a certain time (generally late afternoon/early evening).

News processes: If the traffic process is the most complex, news may be the most straightforward process. Obviously, you may have regularly scheduled news programs. Are there local pre-shows/teases before the program begins? Who rolls breaks within the show? Is the end of the show hard-timed, or is the terminal break of the news simply rolled whenever news is done?

Alternately, what are the exceptions for news? News crawls, weather alerts and school closings, Amber Alerts and, to some degree, EAS alerts & tests: How are they handled procedurally and technically? Also, how are local news cut-ins and special reports handled? What would be the worst case scenario for an extended special report? If news is a major element of your facility's brand, you may need to examine how to execute a special report with no traditional technical support (utilizing only newsroom personnel, no MCR or control room staff).

Acquisition processes: How does the facility acquire programming and commercials? How many different vendors? Typically, national vendors tend to be fairly regimented in their operations. You will generally know in advance if there is to be any deviation from the norm. On the other hand, what issues might you deal with regarding local program and commercial suppliers?

Promotions/creative service processes: Perhaps the most fluid of these processes would be those related to promotions. Most stations not only have generic promos, but a number of topical ones as well. In a typical operation, several promos are added daily as well as about an equal number must be deleted. Here, the key is determining at what point (day and time) should a particular promo no longer air? What plan or system will the hub use?

4. Standardization of Process

The next step in moving towards centralization is the standardization of regular tasks. These are fairly self-explanatory:

For traffic and sales:
>Show format coordination
>Copy acquisition
>Log editing
>Commercial/political commercial standards
>Log reconciliation

For news and creative services:
>Local breaking news
>Network breaking news

Local cut-ins
Weather crawls and school closings
Promos and snipes

Notice in this step, a candidate for centralization is compelled to establish standard procedures for each of these common activities, and then immerse each spoke within the hub to follow the established standard operating procedures.

5. Standardization of Technology
It makes life much easier to have, if not identical technology at each "spoke" facility, at least very similar technology. These are also self-explanatory:
Automation (A critical element here is the system's initial configuration – similar to establishing your personal computer's operating system preferences – and duplicating it throughout the hub).
Video servers
Communication
Transmitter controls
EAS Equipment/software
Monitoring software

6. Operational Definitions
What is a hub? What is it not?
What does a hub do?
What does a station do in a hub?
How does a station interact with other group stations?
What does a station control?
Who works at a hub?

This may seem rather obvious at first reading, but in talking to non-MCR personnel, it is sometimes amazing to hear what they know about MCR that is, in fact, in error. Perhaps a better title for this section might be Operational Expectations, for some think hubbing a facility becomes a panacea for the station's issues. Centralization can be a very powerful tool, but a potential candidate for hubbing must clearly understand what the process can and cannot reasonably do. Your automation vendor should be able to provide invaluable assistance on this issue.

7. Traffic Needs
With traffic playing a key role in master control operations, it is imperative their needs are fully examined:
Day-of-air changes
Inventory management
Viewing inventory (especially political spots)
Reporting of missing material
Show timing information
Other variables

8. News Needs
With news playing a major role in master control Operations, you also need to clearly define in specific detail how news will carry out the following tasks:

Local breaking news
Wall-to-wall coverage
Weather crawls
Tuning in microwave and/or satellite shots
Topical news promos (producing, turnaround, expiration date/time)
Camera controls (studio cameras, traffic/scenic cameras)

9. Other Master Control Duties

Besides monitoring the air product, these MCR duties are vital to the operation:
- Transmitter Monitoring & Controlling
- EAS Monitoring & Controlling
- Various Specific Station Responsibilities

10. Disaster Recovery

The larger the hub/spoke relationship is, the greater chance for there to be issues. Based on the initial model chosen by senior management, disaster recovery really comes down to two basic questions:

If the HUB is offline, what is the procedure?
If the station is offline, what is the procedure?

14G
APPENDIX: Driving Automation – Screen Shots

There is no replacement for hands on use of software; however it probably is useful to have some familiarity with how the screens look and what the various icons and buttons mean. All automation systems are different, but do have similarities.

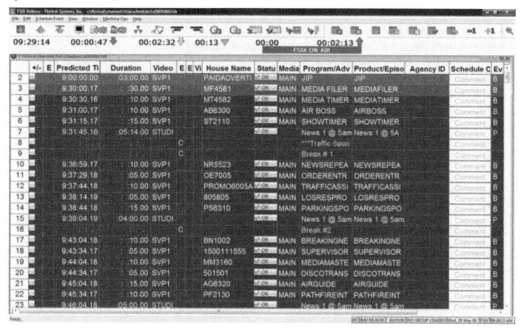

Shown above is an example of an automation playlist. In this case, it is from Florical Systems, though most systems have similar looking playlists. We will break down the purpose of each line.

Title Bar
-*FSIX:* Represents "call letters" of playlist loaded.
-*Airboss – Florical Systems, Inc.*: Application ("Airboss"), by Florical Systems, Inc.
-*C:\florical\channels\fsix\schedules\s0905060.fsh* : The currently loaded schedule.

Menu Bar
Similar to word processing applications, File and Edit perform similar functions (Open File, Save, Print, etc.) and (Undo, Paste, Find, Replace, etc.). Schedule Event allows the MCO to manipulate playlist events. "View" lets the MCO modify the list's appearance. Window allows for multiple open windows to be displayed in various ways. Machine Ops lets the MCO control which equipment will be under automation's control.

Icon Bar

Under the Menu Bar lies an Icon Bar. While automation systems differ, many have icons that parallel commands in the Menu Bar. From left to right the icons for this illustration do the following tasks:

Roll & Take

Return to Last Event

Return to start of Last Event

Take Black

Toggle between Primary & Backup with Automatic return to Primary Source

Toggle between Primary & Backup with Manual return to Primary Source

Take Emergency Source *(Programmed by Facility)*

Take Network Source *(Programmed by Facility)*

Start Secondary Event

End Secondary Event

Stop Down count to Next Event

Resume Countdown

Take Switcher Offline

Put Switcher Online

Insert a "Join In Progress" Event *(Programmed by Facility)*

Insert a Breaking News Event *(Programmed by Facility)*

The right half of the Icon Bar controls the next event by icon:

Hold Next Event

Release Next Event

Skip Next Event

Load Next Event (primarily used with videotape sources)

Cue Next

Ready Next

Preview Next

"-1" Delay (Delay countdown by 1 second)

"+1" Advance (Advance countdown by 1 second)

Timing Bar

Following the Icon Bar is the Timing Bar; you'll notice there are six times listed across this bar. From left to right they represent the following:

Current Time

Down count to Next Event

Down count to Next Program Event

Pre-roll Frames for Next Event

Time Different from Schedule (In this case, the 00:00 indicates NO deviations from the schedule; if there was a time discrepancy, you'd see the word *EARLY* or *LATE* preceded by the amount of time you are early or late.)

Time Into Current Event

Television Operations

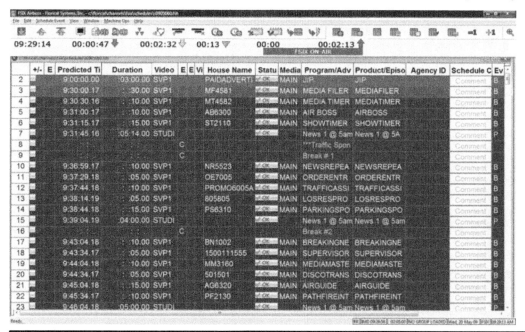

	+/-	E	Predicted Ti	Duration	Video	E	E	Vi	House Name	Statu	Media	Program/Adv	Product/Episo	Agency ID	Schedul
2			9:00:00.00	03:00.00	SVP1				PAIDADVERTI	OK	MAIN	JIP	JIP		Comme
3			9:30:00.17	:30.00	SVP1				MF4581	OK	MAIN	MEDIA FILER	MEDIAFILER		Comme
4			9:30:30.16	:10.00	SVP1				MT4582	OK	MAIN	MEDIA TIMER	MEDIATIMER		Comme
5			9:31:00.17	:10.00	SVP1				AB6300	OK	MAIN	AIR BOSS	AIRBOSS		Comme
6			9:31:15.17	:15.00	SVP1				ST2110	OK	MAIN	SHOWTIMER	SHOWTIMER		Comme
7			9:31:45.16	05:14.00	STUDI					OK		News 1 @ 5am	News 1 @ 5A		Comme
8						C						***Traffic Spon			Comme
9						C						Break # 1			Comme
10			9:36:59.17	:10.00	SVP1				NR5523	OK	MAIN	NEWSREPEA	NEWSREPEA		Comme

Schedule Display

This screen displays the automation *in action*, from top to bottom; it is the road map of what will go to air.

At the very top is listed the *file directory* of this playlist. This is important, as several playlists can be open at the same time.

Below the directory starts the actual *playlist*. Most systems will allow you to change the order of the columns across, or eliminate those that don't apply to your facility. Some facilities like to mirror the playlist to the on air schedule from traffic, especially regarding things like time, event duration, house number, program/episode, advertiser/product, etc. In this example, some columns were *squeezed* so no space was wasted. For brevity's sake, we will limit this to a few, select column headings.

Predicted Time: Time the automation system expects to put event on air. One also has the option of displaying *Scheduled Time*, the time traffic has planned for the event to happen. Sometimes these are correct, other times the times given are merely placeholders for the on air schedule's construction and mean little.

Duration: The total length of the event. While you cannot cut the length of a commercial, you can alter the duration of a show segment. This might be necessary if something earlier delayed your show (obviously, try not to do this often).

Video: The video source (In this case, SVP1, or video server #1).

Event Type: (only E is visible). Next to video source, a column has either no entries (representing

Normal Event) or C (for *Comment*) – a playlist notation that does nothing, and doesn't appear in the as-run log. Other events may be added for the reconciliation process later (e.g.: *Missed Event* – an event that should have aired but did not for some reason).

House Name: (or *House Number*) the primary identifier for a program, commercial, promo, PSA, or any other on air element.

Status: Indicates equipment status (OK -- ready for air, Cued --tape or film, etc.)

Media: Refers to a media source – main or backup -- or name/number of a physical storage medium.

Program/Advertiser: Either the name of the program or advertiser.

Product/Episode: Sometimes a product name, but more often a commercial's agency number, or a show's episode number.

| RR | IMD 09:26:58 | :02:05:00 | NO GROUP LOADED | Wed, 20 May 09 | FSIX | 09:29:13 AM |

Status Bar

Finally, the small bottom bar shows the system's status. We will skip some details specific to Florical Systems and focus on functions common to several systems:

02:05:00: Indicates the next break has 2 minutes, 5 seconds of content.

Wed., 20 May 09: Indicates that day's date.

FSIX: Indicates the call letters for this channel.

9:29:13 AM: Current time. If list plays to another time zone, this is the remote site local time.

15
GLOSSARY

4A: The **American Association of Advertising Agencies** is an American trade association. Founded in 1917, the 4A website says that 4A's membership "produces approximately 80 percent of the total advertising volume placed by agencies nationwide." The association issues annual awards for the best agencies in different categories.

4K: Essentially ultra high definition (UHD) video. Having roughly four times the number of pixels (hence 4K) as an HD image, these formats are currently used in cinema (the resolution is comparable to projected 35 mm film), and moving into broadcast and other distribution.

8-VSB: The abbreviation for Eight-level Vestigial Sideband. The modulation method used for DTV broadcasting in the United States and several other countries mostly in North and South America. Most of the world uses some version of DVB-T with COFDM modulation techniques.

A/53: The ATSC standard for digital television in the United States. See http://www.atsc.org/standards/a53.html for the complete and up-to-date standard.

acquisition: The step in the workflow where the content is brought into the facility in any manner of means.

ad-ID: or Universal Material Identifiers (UMID), identify a commercial uniquely with a number assigned from a central agency.

AES3: Also called AES/EBU. AES is the Audio Engineering Society (A professional society devoted exclusively to audio technology; aes.org). The AES3 audio standard is so common that it is all but synonymous with uncompressed (PCM) digital audio, as in "that patch bay has AES/EBU audio as well as some analog audio."

affiliate: see *network affiliate*.

air chain: For traditional OTA, the equipment path the signal takes from the program source through master control and on to the transmitter.

air check: Most facilities make a continuous recording of their broadcast product. Often this is a device that makes a Web accessible, low-resolution, browser viewable copy of programming and keeps it available for some period of time. On occasion a higher resolution air check is desired, and master control generally makes a DVD, tape, or sets up a capture of the program on an as-needed basis.

ALS: see *automatic logging system*.

ANSI: American National Standards Institute. ansi.org. The organization publishes a suite of standards appears in a wide array of protocols within most industries.

archive: Deep storage for content that is not in current use. Often news, sports, commercials, and some programs are archived for potential future use.

ASI: see *Asynchronous Serial Interface*.

as-run log: Or just *log* is typically generated by the automation system, and shows which elements played, in what order, and the exact time each element aired. Generally, traffic takes the as-run log and reconciles (compares) it against the schedule (see also reconciliation).

assemble edit: A videotape term referring to an edit mode that records video, audio, timecode and control track at once. Assemble edits generally have clean edit start points, but jittery out-points. An insert edit is the alternative.

Asynchronous Serial Interface (ASI): ASI is electrically and optically identical to Serial Digital Interface (SDI) and can use the same cables, routers, fiber, etc. (with one restriction, while SDI video can be inverted without penalty, ASI cannot as it is sensitive to the polarity of the signal). Multiple programs can be carried (multiplexed) within a single ASI bit stream. Unlike SDI, ASI content must be demultiplexed and decoded to be viewable. ASI is often HD, SD and both MPEG 2 and MPEG 4 are common although future compression is also likely to be carried on the ASI physical connection.

ATS: see *automatic transmission system*.

ATSC: Advanced Television Systems Committee. An international, non-profit organization developing voluntary standards for digital television. Based in the United States, in Washington, DC. atsc.org. Although ATSC standards are issued as voluntarily; in the United States the FCC has adopted the ATSC A/53 standard as mandatory for US based OTA TV broadcast. ATSC recommended practice A/85 is the basis of loudness control regulations (CALM Act).

automatic logging system (ALS): The part of a monitoring and control system (in particular in an *automatic transmission system*) that collects data about the operation and status of the system and stores it for inspection and processing at a later date. Alternately, a system that records the audio and video as broadcast, that is available to analyze what actually occurred on air, or verify and prove that a particular piece of content, such as an advertisement, did in fact air at the correct time and in the correct manner. The CALM act often encourages broadcasters to use an automatic logging system to make available proof that loudness remained constant during commercial breaks in order to respond to any complaint.

ATS (automatic transmission system): A system allowed by the FCC to automatically maintain the proper operation of broadcast station power, modulation, and other parameters. See Section 73.1400 of the FCC Rules. azimuth: In satellite reception, along with elevation, azimuth is used to determine where a satellite is located in the sky from a given location. The azimuth is an east-west parameter (see also *elevation*).

azimuth: In satellite reception, along with elevation, azimuth is used to determine where a satellite is located in the sky from a given location. The Azimuth is an East-West parameter (see also elevation).

baseband: In video and audio content, the uncompressed and often synchronous movement of content over analog, SDI digital, Ethernet, or other physical connections. Baseband is far easier to manipulate and process than compressed or encoded content. Baseband by definition requires the maximum amount of bandwidth, so its practical use is limited to the production environment and only rarely seen in the transport and storage environment.

beauty shot: A camera shot requested by either a director, producer or assistant director when they are looking for something pleasing to view that has little to do with the event or game being covered (a.k.a. eye candy).

bird: A slang term referring to a satellite.

bit: Short for binary digit. The smallest unit of digital information. The value of a bit is 1 or 0. Abbreviation: b.

bit-rate: The speed at which bits are transmitted, measured in bits per second (b/s or bps). Also called data rate.

black and code: A videotape term (mostly) referring to an operator routing black into the videotape machine and presetting a certain timecode number to start recording onto a fresh tape; beginning at the start of the tape and going until the tape ended. The result was a collection of black and coded tapes ready for use. It is useful also in some few digital editing environments or projects.

BNC connector: An unbalanced, two-conductor connector with bayonet locking pins commonly used to connect low-power, 75 ohm impedance coaxial cables as used for analog and most digital video and often for digital audio. BNCs may also be used for radio frequency (RF) signals, and can be 50 ohm impedance for such purposes.

BOC: see *broadcast operations center*.

branded feed: Video with graphics, bugs and other items that are keyed into the picture to identify and make the programming unique.

Broadcast Exchange Format (BXF): Also known as SMPTE Standard 2021. BXF is a protocol that makes it easier to integrate the master control automation system with the traffic system. Both the automation and traffic systems must be BXF-compliant. The most common feature of BXF is the ability to make late changes to the broadcast schedule without manual and error prone processes.

broadcast operations center (BOC): The central operations location for a broadcast network, satellite distributor, or centralcasting vendor. Related to TOC (technical operations center), where hands-on processing and procedures occur. Also NOC: network operations center, where equipment and distribution processes are monitored, managed and restored.

BXF: see *Broadcast Exchange Format*.

byte: A group of eight bits. Abbreviation: B.

CALM Act, Commercial Advertisement Loudness Mitigation Act: A law that requires broadcast, cable, satellite and other video providers to keep the loudness of commercials at a level consistent with regular TV programming. The law went into effect December 2012.

catch server: A specialized server (and associated software) designed to receive content sent from a pitch server, usually via satellite or Internet. Content distributors use the pitch/catch server to send programming, metadata and other material in the form of files to a station or facility. The arrangement can be rather sophisticated including error correction, and instructions on content timing (SOM/EOM, etc.) usage and proof of delivery receipts returned from the catch server to guarantee complete delivery.

CATV, cable TV: A MPVD that uses coaxial cables and fiber to reach homes with at least TV services, and more often IP based services (phone, Internet, VOD, security, etc. A subset is the master antenna TV service (MATV) where antennas with only or mostly OTA content are distributed through a multiple residence building or community. Cable systems and telephone companies are the chief provider of Internet services to homes (ISP) in addition to TV.

centralcasting: Hubs perform one or several functions (master control operations, acquisition and possibly traffic) as well as housing most of the hardware, and then distributing the air product to the spokes from the hub.

chief engineer: The person responsible for the proper technical operation of a broadcast station. In some stations, the title of director of engineering (DOE or DE) or VP of engineering is used for essentially the same role.

chief operator: FCC rules require that an over-the-air station designate a person with the primary responsibility for the technical compliance of the station; in particular maintaining the required documentation both public and operational to meet FCC requirements and proper operational practices. Commonly the chief operator role is filled by the chief engineer or operations manager. A posted letter, usually with the station licenses, indicates the chief operator with contact information.

Children's Television Act, CTA: A law enacted by Congress to limit the amount of commercial time for programs aimed at children and to increase the quantity of educational and informational programming aimed at children.

Class A TV station: A low-power TV station that has a primary, or protected, channel allotment. There are approximately 600 Class A TV stations in the U.S. Class A TV stations were not required to terminate analog transmissions on Feb. 17, 2009, the end of the DTV transition period for full-service TV stations in the U.S. A class-A television station may obtain a license to broadcast digitally at not more than 15kW UHF or 3kW VHF, but is not required to do so.

clean feed: Video without graphics and branding.

cliff effect: A characteristic of a DTV signal, where reception tends to either be perfect or not present at all. It is the opposite of the graceful degradation characteristic of an analog TV signal.

clip: A piece of video content, frequently short.

closed captioning (CC): A method for displaying an on-screen visual text representation of the audio portion a TV program for the hearing impaired.

cloud, the cloud: An IT concept where cloud computing refers to services, storage and/or applications based at another location, generally by a third party. The idea is to gain the capabilities, storage capacity, etc. without the need for investing in the overhead, training, or the monitoring and installing of updates generally found with an on-site IT department. Many of the functions of broadcasting can be done in the cloud, and some functions can be improved through the use of cloud technology.

codec: An abbreviation for encoder/decoder. A device or application that converts analog signals to digital (encoder) and then back to analog (decoder).

Code of Federal Regulations (CFR): The Federal Communications Commission's TV rules appear in Title 47 (Telecommunications) of the U.S. Code of Federal Regulations. This Includes Part 73 (Broadcast) and Part 74 (Broadcast Auxiliary) rules. Also referred to as the FCC Rules and Regulations, or just FCC Rules.

compression: Reducing data in digital signals by removing redundant and most often less meaningful information. (See also *lossless, lossy*).

compressor: A device or application that reduces the dynamic range of an audio signal.

content delivery network (CDN): An Internet based-platform that delivers content to individual consumers, often by using broadcast or multicast protocols and/or large numbers of servers. In the media business (specifically in the business-to-business sense) this may refer to a third-party that takes content (either programming or commercials) from various sources and delivers them to subscribing clients (typically television stations). Much of the work can be done by the CDN in the cloud.

control and monitoring (C&M): Where the equipment remains at the station, but the operators control it remotely. The text of this book covers several architectures and the language surrounding them. These are all recently invented terms, and sometimes not clear or unique.

control point: In OTA stations, there is a legal requirement to designate a physical location where transmitter control takes place. As a practical matter, this is usually in master control. The control point may move from the studio to a central hub or even a third party service provider, and this can happen several times a day, but at any given time there must be a single designated control point where control of the transmitter(s) resides.

control track: A videotape control track keeps the videotape playing at a constant rate. There are other components that enhance and stabilize the signal later in the process, but the foundation of tape speed, the heartbeat, if you will, is the control track.

crash record: A videotape term; the crash part of record comes from the fact that when videotape machines are put into record from a stopped position, the point where the recording begins has an uneven, dirty start for a moment.

day-of-air: The concept is that there are things that are done and not done on the day of air. Certain changes might be prohibited; certain QA steps might be mandated day of air. Normally, preparation steps happen before the day-of-air, and everything is locked down by the moment of air.

DBS: see *direct broadcast satellite*.

dead roll: The process of rolling a source (audio or video) tape or playback without taking it to air. Operationally, rolling the last minute of a show's closing theme music exactly one minute before the scheduled show off-time, or if earlier programming runs long (live sporting event, awards show, etc.) dead rolling the next scheduled program at the time it was to begin normally, allows one to join the show in progress (JIP) and thus comes out on time (see also pre-roll, which is similar). Normally, the two key characteristics of a dead roll are: starting the source at a specific time, often so that it ends at a specific time, and NOT immediately taking it to air.

demodulator, demod: The part of a receiver or a standalone device that extracts the information from an RF carrier, often after a demux has selected the desired stream of data. The station's off air demod is a high quality receiver with known characteristics used to receive an over-the-air analog TV signal. Typically used to feed a waveform monitor, vectorscope and other monitoring devices used in an analog TV station master control room.

DEMUX: A device that selects the desired content from a multiplex of content e.g., a satellite receiver or home TV set has a demultiplexer to pull out the desired audio and video from transponders or transmitters with multiple programs. (See also *MUX*.)

device controller, device server: The central hardware for a traditional (not an all-IT system, where this function can be virtual) automation system, all controlled devices typically connect to the device controller via serial or Ethernet/IP connections. The device controller usually hosts the list that is being executed, whether that is called a transmission list or a playlist. Systems that use a transmission list to control devices and a playlist that talks to it (that interfaces to the user and traffic) tend to make this distinction. Systems that use one combined purpose list tend to refer to this as the playlist.

dialnorm, dialog normalization: A Dolby product that has wide acceptance in digital broadcast. Part of the program stream metadata tells the receiver where the normal dialog level is, and lets the device adjust its loudness accordingly.

direct broadcast satellite (DBS): In the United States, a satellite-based MVPD using high-power satellites with high Ku band (frequencies above the FSS, fixed satellite service, frequencies) transponders located 11° apart and small dishes. Two competing systems operate in the United States: Dish and DirecTV. Internationally there are dozens of similar DTH (direct-to-home) MVPDs, including B-Sky-B.

director of engineering: The person responsible for the technical operation of one or more broadcast stations. In many stations, this may be equivalent to chief engineer. See also vice president of engineering and operations.

direct-to-home satellite (DTH): See *direct broadcast satellite*.

disclaimer: An announcement or warning given by a station to provide some kind of indication that programming may be uncomfortable or that the station has no role in endorsing the viewpoint of the program. Violent programming, material not suitable for children, paid programs and infomercials usually are preceded by disclaimers.

discrepancy: Any variation from the program schedule. A discrepancy report (or discrep, or DR) notes any changes, errors, or modifications made to the on air schedule. Reconciliation registers the discrepancy, which allows traffic to adjust billing or reschedule commercials or other program elements.

Designated Market Area, Dominant Marketing Area, DMA: A system of ranking media markets, used by the Nielsen Corporation, other rating agencies, and many others. DMAs are numbered from 1 (largest; currently New York City) to 210 (smallest numbered market; currently Glendive, MT). DMAs generally consist of one or more counties. DMA is a widely used TV industry metric for advertising and governmental regulation, and is similar to an OTA station's coverage area. The FCC uses a very similar term, Television Market Area or TMA that assigns whole counties to each TMA.

drop frame: A variation of timecode that compensates for color television's slightly slower frame rate (29.97Hz) than the original black and white (30Hz) NTSC TV. What are being dropped are some of the timecode labels and not frames of video. To make an hour of timecode match an hour on the clock, drop-frame timecode drops frame numbers 0 and 1 of the first second of every minute, except when the number of minutes is divisible by ten. Some system displays show a colon (:) preceding a non-drop frame number, and a semi-colon (;) preceding a drop frame number (01:00:00:14 would indicate non-drop frame, while 01:00:00;14 would indicate drop frame. Think of the drop frame as having a colon with its lower dot dropping.)

DTV, digital television: Generally used to refer to OTA digital TV.

dub: To make a copy of a piece of video by playing it back in real time and recording it elsewhere.

DVD, Digital Video Disc: An optical disc storage system for digital TV signals. Blu-Ray is a higher density version for high definition, and currently finds increasing use in broadcasting.

EBU: see *European Broadcasting Union*.

edit decision list (EDL): A list found on video and film post-production editing systems. EDLs document the media (or reel) numbers used, timecode start/stop times, edit durations, transitions (cuts, dissolves). An EDL can be generated off-line with low resolution video, and applied to full resolution video when it's time to conform the material for the final version.

EEO: see *Equal Employment Opportunity*.

EIC: see *engineer in charge*.

EIT: see *Event Information Table*.

element: In the context of this text; a video, audio, graphic or other piece that in combination with other elements comes together to form a television show.

electronic news gathering (ENG): A method of relaying breaking news or near real time sporting events from a remote site to a TV station's studio, for editing and broadcast. ENG can use TV Broadcast Auxiliary Service (BAS) microwave frequencies at 2-, 2.5-, 6.5-, 7- or 13GHz, unlicensed spectrum, public wireless networks, or in the special case of satellite news gathering (SNG), satellite space.

Electronic Program Guide (EPG): Metadata included in the PSIP codes that presents the program line-up for a given video service. In MVPDs this refers to the entirety of what is presented to the viewer that looks to their program guide for listings of programs into the future.

elevation: In satellite work, the elevation is the number of degrees a given satellite is located above the horizon from a given location (see also azimuth). 10-degrees elevation would have the antenna pointed just above the horizon.

embedded audio: A means of combining audio and video within an SDI signal. Common in areas like Master Control, where audio/video signals travel, are processed and are switched at the same time. Embedded audio is inherently synchronized to the video.

Emergency Alert System (EAS): In the United States, the FCC required system and practices including tests and logging (part 11 of the FCC Rules). The *EAS TV Handbook*, published by the FCC, summarizes the actions to be taken by television station operating personnel, establishes monitoring guidelines, and gives examples of EAS message scripts. OTA broadcasters, CATV systems and some MVPDs and other communications systems are required to participate or voluntarily are involved with EAS, and/or utilize the Common Alerting Protocol (CAP) to distribute messages and alert the general population of situations where warning can protect life and property.

Enforcement Bureau (EB): The enforcement arm of the FCC. In the field the FCC will call in Federal Marshalls if necessary for security or support should the situation present some danger.

engineer in charge (EIC): The person technically in charge of a physical entity (facility, technical area, remote truck).

ENG: see *electronic news gathering*.

EPG: see *Electronic Program Guide*.

Equal Employment Opportunity (EEO): A government regulatory program applied by the Federal Communications Commission (FCC) to broadcast stations and other entities.

European Broadcasting Union (EBU): Association of broadcast stations and interests from many EU nations that set technical standards and participates in projects for the common good. ebu.ch.

Event Information Table (EIT): Metadata included in the PSIP codes.

Environmental Protection Agency, EPA: epa.gov

error vector magnitude (EVM): An overall signal quality metric for any digital RF transmission, including the 8-VSB DTV signal. On occasion, the operator of a DTV OTA station monitors EVM as the overall best indicator that all is well with the transmitter as virtually any problem shows up as an increase in EVM. MER is a very similar measure of merit used more often outside the US and with DVB-T/T2.

Ethernet: The familiar Cat-5 and Cat-6 four twisted pairs of wire cables with RJ-45 connectors on which most local computer networking is built. Ethernet supports many communications protocols, including some designed to carry real-time video and or audio; however, Internet Protocol (IP) is by far the most common.

evergreen: Any show or element that is not dated and can be run at any time because it has no time specific references in the content. Evergreens are often used when a scheduled program is lost or unavailable.

EVM: see *error vector magnitude*.

exciter: A device at the transmitter designed to take the raw signal sent from the station (usually via STL) and prepares it to be transmitted from the station's antenna.

FEC: see *forward error correction*.

Federal Aviation Administration, FAA: A part of the United States Department of Transportation. Within the context of communications, its regional locations need to know where high-altitude structures (broadcast towers) are located and when there are tower light failures. In most states, the toll-free number 800-WXBRIEF (800-992-7433) will connect you with a local office to report outages.

Federal Communications Commission, FCC: In the United States, an independent agency created by Congress in 1934. The FCC has jurisdiction over all non-federal government/non-military stations, including broadcast stations.

File Transfer Protocol (FTP): A means of transferring files between computers on a network. Video files can be sent simply via FTP. FTP is not a sophisticated protocol, so there are more elaborate and often proprietary protocols to deal with file transfers more securely, flexibly, and efficiently. There are also a myriad of applications that make using and managing FTP user friendly.

flash cam: A camera, usually found in the newsroom, that is usually left on. Its purpose is to allow the news staff the opportunity to instantly put news talent on air without a crew (audio, switcher and director).

flip server: see *transcoder*.

forward error correction (FEC): A means of improving the integrity of one-way digital data, albeit causing a reduction in the data throughput that would otherwise be possible by adding in additional data used to correct errors at the receiver.

frame synchronizer: A device used to synchronize the timing of a video source (frequently from outside the station. A remote or satellite feed) to correspond to the synchronization signal generated from the in-house sync pulse generator.

freeze frames: Some equipment will hold and display the last good frame of video in cases where the video has become corrupted. Sometimes these degradations are minor and a single frame freezes just noticeably, other times the last frame simply sits frozen until the device is reset or service restored. Most equipment resorts to freezing frames only after significant degradation, so the frozen frame often is not totally intact (see the related degradation, pixelization).

FTP: see *File Transfer Protocol.*

full-service DTV station: A DTV station serving a community and assigned spectrum by the FCC. There are approximately 1,700 full-service DTV stations in the U.S.

general purpose interface (GPI): The simplest of all command communications, GPIs and GPOs (outputs) are contact closures like a pushbutton or relay would make. Simple commands like start and stop can be carried by GPI. Complex commands cannot. An "I am running" response is a typical GPO acknowledgement back to the device initiating a GPI trigger.

genlock: Locking a device's timing (for example, a station's master synchronization generator, camera or playback device) to an external reference (for example, a network signal or the station's master timing system). With the proliferation of frame synchronizers, you will not likely be gen-locking your station to an outside source. Almost all video equipment can and is genlocked within a station whether required or not.

good night: When a remote event (a broadcast from outside the studio) has finished the telecast, SMPTE Bars/Tone are traditionally put online (and often key a graphic saying good night from (the location, studio, truck or event that the remote was just broadcast) as an indication that the distribution path can be safely taken down.

graceful degradation: A characteristic of all analog TV transmissions and some very special digital transmissions, where the signal suffers gradual degradation over a wide range of signal to noise (often in excess of 20dB) before reception is totally lost. It is the opposite of the cliff effect characteristic of a DTV signal.

HDMI: see *High-Definition Multimedia Interface.*

head end: The central facility for an MVPD, usually a cable system, where acquisition of content occurs and is processed for distribution. The term is less often used for DBS and centralcasting.

high-definition television (HDTV): Typical formats include 480p, 720i, 720p, 1080i, or 1081p… in other words, a marketing term, which describes all of the formats between standard definition and cinema resolutions which are higher yet.

High-Definition Multimedia Interface (HDMI): Primarily a consumer and prosumer interface used to connect both computer and digital television signals including multiple digital audio channels. HDMI finds significant use in broadcast facilities. HDMI is easily converted to SDI and back, and converters to CAT-6 and extenders for both HDMI and HDMI on CAT-6 are relatively inexpensive compared to SDI reclocking/extenders for situations where a monitor or the like is some distance from the source.

High Definition-Serial Digital Interface (HD-SDI): Similar to SDI, but with a higher bandwidth or capacity to handle the higher data rates needed by uncompressed HD video (see SDI). This is 1.485Gb/s (as opposed to 270Mb/s). To run the higher resolution video formats (1080p, higher frame rates, 4K), more advanced standards such as 3-G-SDI (2.970Gb/s) or dual-link HD SDI (two 1.485Gb/s lines) is needed.

hub, hub and spoke, hubbing: Somewhat of an informal term referring to having multiple stations operated from one location. See also centralcastig, share casting and control and monitoring.

Institute of High Fidelity (IHF): An institute of manufacturers producing equipment for audio recordings. In this context, consumer grade audio generally has RCA connectors with IHF levels, which are considerably lower than the audio levels found in professional environments. An IHF audio device needs an amplifier to feed commercial (line-level) analog equipment properly.

ingest: The content inputting process necessary to enter a program or commercial into a server/ automation system. Involves checking audio and video levels for single-element events (a commercial or promo), and also the start of message and end of message points for a multi-segmented show.

ingest station: Work areas that run an ingest application, and have the necessary hardware, to take in content from tape, live, or data files, and sometimes legacy playback equipment like film and long-retired tape formats. To make this easier and faster, most ingest stations can cue tape decks and communicate with some sources and hardware to start and stop the feed.

insert edit: A videotape term referring to an edit mode allowing the operator to select which tracks to edit (audio/video/timecode), and an in-point and (optionally) an out-point. The only requirement is pre-existing control track. An assemble edit is the usual alternative.

integrated receiver/decoder (IRD): A receiver (normally used with a satellite or fiber linked system) that demuxes and decodes and frequently decrypts a program or content feed.

International Telecommunications Union, ITU: A European, standards-setting organization. itu.int.

interstitial: A short program element placed within a break following a full-length program. Generally found in premium channel and public television facilities only, they are often fill programs (extended length promos, often the making of a production) designed to fill time until the next scheduled program is to begin, usually at the top or bottom (30 minutes past) of the hour.

interruptible foldback (IFB): Foldback is an old audio term referring to sending audio back to the source. If the source is a talent on microphone, the foldback is often interrupted by the producer, engineers, and directors to allow them to speak to the person on mike. If there is a significant delay in the foldback, a mix-minus is sent where the talent hears everything and everyone else on the program but themselves to avoid hearing the distracting echo. If a phone is used for IFB, there is some side tone audio from the phone so the speaker hears a little bit of themselves to avoid hearing nothing which is awkward as we have become accustomed to having some side tone on telephones.

Internet Protocol (IP): A protocol for communicating information across a packet-switched network.

Internet Protocol Television, IPTV: The delivery of a digital TV signal within a Telecom, CATV (as CATV converts to IP), or other IP based distribution network. Web and OTT TV may be IP-based.

ISCI: This once industry standard commercial Identifier has been largely replaced by the UMID universal material identifiers, which identifies a commercial. Only archived material is likely to have an ISCI number in the older format ABCD-1234.

join in progress, JIP: The process of joining a program already begun, generally due to an earlier program running long, or cutting away from programming to air a news bulletin. See also leave in progress.

KVM: An abbreviation for keyboard, video and mouse. A switching device allowing operators to control several computers using just one shared keyboard, video monitor and mouse. Often, several computers need to be controlled from a control room or transmission area. A KVM switch saves valuable real estate in the racks by eliminating the need for multiple keyboards, monitors and mice. Each computer is connected to the KVM switch; the MCO then pushes the designated switcher button to control the computer of his/her choice, needing only one keyboard, video monitor and mouse. The typical KVM command to switch between computers is a double strike of the CMD key.

leave in progress, LIP: The process of leaving a program already in progress, generally due to late-breaking news coverage. (This is a less common term compared to JIP, but is, nevertheless, used in some facilities.) See also join in progess.

LKFS: abbreviation for loudness, K-weighted, relative to full scale. A loudness standard designed to enable normalization of audio levels for delivery of broadcast TV and other video. LKFS is standardized in ITU-R BS.1770.

log: see *as-run log*.

lossless compression: Within the compression/decompression process, there is no loss of data. The reconstituted image is a duplicate of the original.

lossy compression: Within the lossy compression/decompression process, there is some loss of data resulting in an image with less detail and or accuracy than the original.

low noise amplifier (LNA): An amplifier mounted as close as physically possible to a satellite receiving antenna, often in a weatherproof housing at the antenna.

low noise block downconverter (LNB): An LNA that also shifts a band of signals down to a lower frequency. There are far more LNBs than LNAs.

low resolution proxy (also low-res proxy): Both a process and a type of file resulting in a lower quality duplicate file allowing various departments across a computer network to monitor a spot for content, or allow an ingest operator to mark the start of message and end of message points at a location other than the ingest station. The full quality content takes considerably more bandwidth to move conveniently, so the proxy is used for functions where seeing the full quality of the clip is not necessary. One can also make an EDL with just a low-res proxy.

low-power TV station (LPTV): A secondary, low-power TV station, subject to displacement by a full-service TV or DTV station.

make-good: The means of correcting an earlier error in the playing or scheduling of a commercial. If a commercial is either impaired during playback, or did not fully air from start to finish, a make-good is generally but no always desirable.

master control operator (MCO): The person responsible for the moment-to-moment activity in the master control room.

MCR: master control room.

master synch generator: A specialized clock that keeps all broadcast equipment electronically in time with one another so that functions like clean switching and mixing can occur.

metadata: Literally data about data (like the table of contents of a book). In the context of video, this refers to many pieces of information relating to a broadcast signal or a file on a server.

monitoring and control system (M&C): The system or systems that control everything from transmitters, generators, playback equipment, to heating and ventilating. M&C systems can be large or small, enterprise-wide or simply control a transmitter. M&C systems collect information needed to analyze failures and to maintain a record of performance.

mosquito noise: A distortion that appears near the sharp edges of an MPEG-encoded digital signal. This is caused by the lossy nature of MPEG encoding. Mosquito noise becomes more noticeable on larger-screen displays.

Moving Pictures Expert Group (MPEG): Responsible for a family of standards used for coding audio and visual information in a digital compressed format. www.mpeg.org

multicasting: The process of digitally distributing multiple program streams from one point in the Internet or private network that replicates the stream rather than creating a new stream for each user.

multichannel video program distributor (MVPD): Program distributors using the major carriers (legally it is cable television, telcos and satellite; and for all other intents and purposes, the Internet) as a real-time distribution system.

multiplexer, MUX: A device that takes individual program streams, and orders and packages them onto a single transmission stream (TS) for distribution or transport. Multiplexers may also manage encoders (statistical multiplexing) in order to allow all of the programs to fit on a limited bandwidth circuit by limiting encoders output based on the best use of the circuit and dynamically considering the quality needs of the various programs.

multiviewers: Where many video sources are pasted (or mapped) into a larger display. Multiviewers often include alarm functions for loss of (or out of range) video or audio, closed caption, etc. Generally alarms appear on screen as red blinking boxes or the like. Audio levels are often also displayed as VU meters overlaid on or next to the video.

National Television Systems Committee, NTSC: An industry group that created the analog color television system used in the United States. NTSC also refers to standard-definition analog TV broadcasts or signals.

network: In IT communications: networks are simply collections of connected nodes. There are data networks, RF based networks, social networks, etc.,

network: In broadcasting: A television network: is a means of program distribution from the network hub through affiliates to viewers. While most think of a network as the big four (ABC, CBS, NBC and Fox), there can be variations of this: sports networks (a collection of unrelated stations established just for game coverage), cable networks (both basic cable and premium), religious networks, and ad hoc networks formed for a one-time event.

network affiliate: A station that signs an exclusive contract to run programming from one source and is expected to air all or most of that source's output.

network owned-and operated, O&O: In the United States, a station owned and operated by one of the networks. As these stations are generally in the top US markets and generate significant revenue, they play an important role in the profit picture of their owners and tend to have a closer relationship to their network than an affiliate owned by a group or individual.

Nielsen Audio Video Encoder, NAVE: A system/device allowing the Nielsen Media Research Service to more accurately measure the audience by including show data: title, date and time of broadcast, channel information, etc. into the broadcast for detection at monitored households. Broadcasts that are delayed are also reported.

network operations center, NOC: The central operations location for a broadcast network, satellite distributor, or centralcasting vendor, etc. Also see *BOC*.

non-drop frame: A version of timecode used to mark each video frame in numerical order. It is almost never used in standard video systems (See also Drop Frame).

non-ionizing radiation: A form of electromagnetic energy that lacks sufficient power to strip ions off of atoms. All radio frequency (RF) energy is non-ionizing energy. This is important because the lower energy levels of sunlight and radio emissions (radiation) are not similar or as harmful as high energy gamma rays, X-rays, and other ionizing radiation that changes cell composition and can cause sickness and death.

Occupational and Health Safety Administration, OSHA: A U.S. government agency, charged with the protection of worker safety. www.osha.gov

one-time only, OTO: Something that runs just once.

over-the-air, OTA: In this context, the reception of RF signals on a television.

phase reverse: In audio, when a signal is reversed in phase 180 degrees. A stereo audio signal with one channel out of phase will result in a poor audio signal when the stereo channels are summed to mono.

picture line up and generating equipment, PLUGE: Part of SMPTE Color Bars, PLUGE (rhymes with huge) is a strip roughly midway up the screen (in SMPTE Bars) with somewhat reversed colors to the larger bars above. This can be used to correctly calibrate a video monitor and other tests and setups.

pixelization: As a digital signal is degraded, it reaches a narrow range between working and not working. On the edge of this digital cliff, the picture usually breaks up in a block pattern that is tied to the compression. Baseband video usually breaks up a pixel (the smallest bit of video) or lines of pixels at a time. Both are referred to as pixelization. If the signal gets slightly better, the picture returns. If it gets slight worse, the picture will freeze or go away.

plotter: In automated traffic systems, the functionality that weighs the options for placing commercials and other elements, and places them to maximize revenues and minimize conflicts with other competing advertising.

pre-roll: Starting a videotape, film or other playback device rolling a few seconds before taking the source to air. Less true now, but in the past some mechanical devices, in particular tape machines and film required up to several seconds of pre-roll time to come up to speed and stabilize.

professional integrated receiver/decoder, PIRD: The equivalent of a test grade demodulator at an analog TV station, it is used most often as a professional grade monitor for a satellite service.

Program and System Information Protocol, PSIP: A critical portion of a DTV signal. If the PSIP codes are missing or incorrect, most DTV receivers will not recognize the existence of an otherwise useable DTV signal. The primary goal of PSIP is to make DTV viewing simple and intuitive for the viewer, hiding the complex interrelationships between the digital components. PSIP provides capabilities to enable familiar channel numbering, familiar methods of tuning (up-down surfing and direct tuning) as well as an on-screen program guide.

program association table, PAT: Metadata included in the PSIP codes.

program map table, PMT: Metadata included in the PSIP codes that indicate what PIDs are associated with what program audio and video streams.

Public Inspection File: A collection of files that all full-service and Class A TV broadcast stations must maintain and make available to any interested party during normal business hours. The Public Inspection File contains information about a broadcast station and its programming and policies. Commonly, the public file is kept online.

quadrature amplitude modulation, QAM: Cable systems carry either analog or digital signals, or a mixture of both. QAM has many advantages in terms of robustness and bandwidth. A typical QAM signal carries 27- to 37Mb/s in each traditional 6MHz cable slot. Broadcast uses 8-VSB in the United States, and COFDM in much of the world, which are better at over the air transmission, but are not efficient enough for cable use. 8-VSB can only accommodate 19Mb/s in a 6MHz slot.

radio frequency, RF: Electromagnetic spectrum generally from 9kHz to 300GHz. OTA transmitters, cell phones and all wireless devices use RF energy to communicate.

rain-fades: Sometimes occur in Ku-band satellite reception. Rain absorbs Ku frequencies, and heavy thunderstorms between the dish and the satellite can seriously degrade or completely block the Ku satellite signal. Other microwave links commonly used in broadcast TV are also vulnerable, in particular 13GHz and up. That said, even a lower frequency C-band link can also experience rain fade in extreme circumstances.

rate card: The menu listing of the individual costs of placing advertising within various elements of the broadcast/online day. Frequently there are discounts and deals to be made, so these are often flexible.

RCA connector: An unbalanced, two-conductor audio connector commonly used in consumer-grade electronic devices.

real time/non-real time: Any live event, or event viewed as it is occurring (live TV, even if it has recorded elements or was recorded prior to release), even if the latency is several minutes, is real-time. One cannot pause, replay, or skip ahead with real-time viewing, though one can turn it off, or select another program. Non-real-time viewing requires stored video, intentionally delayed for moments (in the case of shifting from real-time viewing to pause or backup non-real-time) or nearly forever (viewing an 1890s Edison film). In general, non-real-time viewing has the advantage of infinite options in what, when, and how to view content, but not the immediacy demanded of breaking news, sports, and event coverage.

reconciliation: the key process of taking the as-run log and comparing it to the program schedule, or program log. Comparing what actually played with what traffic originally scheduled is needed to determine what errors occurred, and in commercial TV, what commercials can be billed for.

Redundant Array of Independent Disks, RAID: A means of separating and replicating data over several physical drives. There are seven main families of RAID, starting with RAID 0, which mirrors data on two drives. RAID 6 is probably the most complicated and utilizes striping and double distributed parity. Any RAID array can lose a predetermined number of drives and once replaced, rebuild those drives.

Reed-Solomon Coding: An extremely common method of improving the robustness of a digital signal. Adding this forward error correction (FEC) allows a signal that is recovered with errors to be repaired within limits.

regional spot: Sometimes called a breakaway spot. A spot (or series of spots) only shown to a specific audience. An example might be for a cable provider wanting to air generic spots for over-the-air viewers (not on cable), while airing special offers to only those viewers watching your channel on cable. OTA viewers would see the spot in your normal on air playlist, while the regional spot would come from a different video server (and possibly a different playlist) triggered to start by a secondary event in the automation playlist and fed to the cable provider by special arrangement.

safe title area: Where on a video screen, one can locate graphics where they will be visible to all viewers. Often a safe title area generator lays subtle lines on a monitor to indicate where the graphics should reasonably be located. In the past, all monitors over scanned to some degree as a limitation of the cathode ray tube. Few modern flat screens have any over scan issues, so safe title is generally to avoid areas reserved for other's graphics or other creative concerns.

satellite news gathering, SNG: A method of relaying breaking news to a TV station's studio, using communication satellites in mostly geostationary orbit. Used when an ENG feed is not possible due to distance or terrain blockage.

SBE Certification: A service provided by the Society of Broadcast Engineers to the broadcasting industry. Created in 1975, it provides multiple levels of operator certification to document professional competence. The program consists of 11 levels of certification and three specialist certifications, with written examinations of increasing level of difficulty. Industry experience is required for the higher certification levels. www.sbe.org/certification

Secondary Audio Program, SAP: This is a term more closely associated with the previous NTSC Standard. SAP provides for a second audio program facilitating audio options, including foreign language translations and descriptive audio narration for the visually impaired. It may be unassociated with the video. Some public stations place radio reading services for the blind on secondary audio channels. Others place a co-owned radio station's audio on a secondary audio channel, primarily to reach hotel rooms and other places where the radio signal is poor or radios nonexistent.

Society of Broadcast Engineers, Inc. (SBE): An organization founded in 1964, dedicated to the advancement of all levels and types of broadcast engineer. www.sbe.org

Society of Cable Television Engineers (SCTE): The cable industry's equivalent of the SBE; however the SCTE is also a standard setting organization. Probably the most recognizable standard is SCTE-35, which is used to trigger downstream insertions in cable, and occasionally broadcast TV. Other popular standards apply to splicing inserts into transmission streams and controlling dynamic advertising. www.scte.org

Society of Motion Picture and Television Engineers (SMPTE): Founded in 1916, they are a major standards organization for image-related industries. SMPTE also organizes some educational programs, in particular the SMPTE conventions. www.smpte.org

schedule (on-air schedule): A listing delivered to master control by the traffic department with all or most of the elements that are to air on a channel. Schedules are generally for one day, but may be continuous.

share casting: Hubs perform the common programming work (as in a television group running the same syndicated programming), while the spokes perform duties related to unique local programming, local commercials, news and emergency operations. Hardware may be shared between hub and spoke.

show format book: Usually this is a book of formats for various regular programs. While the timing of each segment and element might vary, the format generally does not. This is useful to determine how many segments, bumps, intros, spots, etc., there are in a show and in which order.

standard operating procedures, SOP: Also standard operating practices. SOPs are generally collected into a book of some kind, or kept online where it is easier to add to or change the SOPs.

standard-definition television, SD, SDTV: Typically 480i, meaning 480 lines of resolution, interlaced. SD is the direct descendant of analog 525 line NTSC television. The difference in line count is because NTSC used some lines for synchronization and these lines were not typically visible do to over-scan that allowed for a bezel to cover a portion of the picture that often was not pretty on a picture tube.

Serial Digital Interface, SDI: The standard physical interface for broadcast-quality, uncompressed, real time digital video transport within a facility that replaces most analog transport. SDI often includes embedded audio. Generally running 270Mb/s for Standard Definition, or 1.485Gb/s for HD 720P and 1080i, and two physical coax lines in dual-link HD-SDI 1080P or digital cinema; SDI on coax (BNC is the standard connector) is limited to about 300-feet between devices with the best coax, so fiber is common on longer runs.

signal-to-noise ratio, SNR: A signal quality metric, generally expressed in decibels (dB). Larger numbers are better. NTSC signals need an SNR of about 40dB or greater to be useable, whereas DTV signals can be usable with lower SNRs (typically 25dB or better). Satellite links are often peaked for best SNR, or carrier-to-noise (C/N), which is very similar.

slate, slug: Usually text, sometimes with audio, that identifies the content to follow, or inserted into content at a place where a commercial or other item is to be inserted. Metadata is the electronic form of a slate. One might slug a black hole with text saying something like "place commercial here" in continuous programming where a local commercial might be inserted.

SMPTE Bars: The most popular version of the familiar setup test color bars.

snipe: An animated graphic sequence lasting around 5-10 seconds and displayed in the lower portion of the screen over the current program promoting an upcoming program or event. These are typically clever and eye-catching promotional elements.

sound on tape, SOT: Typically found in news programs; a self-contained clip where sound is included in the clip. Its opposite would be a voice-over (VO), where an anchor or reporter voices over video.

spot reel: Usually constructed with a special automation playlist (though it can be done manually on an editor) on a spare playout server port; this is usually recorded to tape or other transportable media. The reel generally contains all the breaks necessary for a live event, local production, or to operate the station while performing maintenance on master control.

standards and practices: A department, generally found only at larger networks, that monitors the acceptableness of content, sets the standards of the company, and then maintains that level on a show-by-show basis. Profanity, sex, and sometimes violence are major concerns of this group.

shared ID: A station ID that includes a shared, brief element: a promotional message, public service message, and occasionally a commercial message.

station identification: The routine identification of an over-the-air broadcast entity. A legal ID must include the call letters and city of license. The only additional information permitted between the call letters and city of license is the TV channel number. An ID is generally required near the top of the hour.

streaming: Video and or audio sent via an IP connection, in any manner or format.

studio-to-transmitter link, STL: The means of communication between the studio/master control facilities and the transmitter. Both dedicated microwave and leased fiber optic based telecom links are popular. A TSL (transmitter-to-studio link) may provide a return path from the transmitter for control and sometimes content (such as news remotes) to the studio.

sub-channel: In digital transmission, the available payload may accommodate more than the primary service. These additional services are sub-channels. Often digi-nets or dot-2 services are sub-channel services (e.g., 44.2, 44.3, 44.4 are sub-channels of virtual channel 44).

Sun-outages: Occur during the first two weeks of March and October in North America. Operators will eventually experience brief interruptions in reception caused when the sun lines up with the satellite at a given location. As the sun appears to pass behind the satellite (solar transit), the signal will become noisy and is often lost in the suns radio illumination. This is not, and there is no such thing, as a "sun fade."

technical operations center, TOC: The location where ingest, conformation, quality assurance take place. Also see *BOC*.

timecode: Each frame of video has a specific time counted in frames, seconds, minutes, hours, and sometimes days. The format is HH:MM:SS:FF so that 1:23:14:22 is read as one-hour, twenty three minutes, fourteen seconds, twenty-two frames.

timing sheet: Whether on paper or not, there usually needs to be a listing of when segments and elements begin, end, and their duration.

total running time, TRT: Generally refers to the sum of segments within a program. Sometimes this is mistakenly used to refer to a segment's duration.

Transmission Control Protocol/Internet Protocol, TCP/IP: While these are two distinct network protocols, they are commonly used together, and have become the standard reference to either or both protocols. The Internet is largely TCP/IP as are any number of other systems.

transcoder: A device used to convert video from one format to another. Generally this is taking one compression format, packaging, resolution, etc., and converting it to another in the digital domain without decoding and re-encoding to reduce impairments.

transmitter-to-studio link, TSL: The link from the transmitter back to the studio/master control area (see related *STL*). Generally the TSL carries command and control for the transmitter site and ENG receive content as most transmitter sites are also excellent ENG receive sites.

transponder: In the satellite domain, transponder is the equivalent of a channel. Satellites have several transponders that, like over the air channels, operate on different frequencies. Satellites often reuse transponder frequencies on different polarities.

transport stream (TS): A TS is the combined packetized data streams (multiplex) necessary to carry one or more video and audio programming as well as the information needed by the television or other display device to present this properly (the right audio with the right video, the right video and audio formats, the right guide data, etc.).

trouble ticket: A means of communicating and tracking within an organization that a piece of equipment is not working correctly. Typically, it is a form (virtual or physical) filled out with the details and given to the maintenance or other department to resolve. Often, the resulting metrics are analyzed to monitor equipment failures, trends, parts inventory, etc. Clarify and Remedy are typical and popular trouble ticket system.

trigger: The command to execute some event or function. Often triggers are imbedded into a program stream. A trigger often indicates the start of a commercial insertion or some other event that a downstream player-inserter must perform.

turn: To bring a program in, turn it around, and send it out. Most MVPDs are composed of many program or content turns. Broadcasting a secondary program without alteration received from a satellite is referred to as a "simple turn."

turn and burn: Content that is brought in, used once, and copies disposed of.

TV receive only, TVRO: Satellite systems that use larger dish antennas (in backyards, they are often called big ugly dishes or BUDS) that often can be steered to multiple satellites, and are used with Fixed Satellite Service (FSS) as opposed to Direct Broadcast Satellites (DBS, or BSS) services. TVROs accessing FSS satellites provide the bulk of TV network distribution to OTA stations, cable systems and other MVPDs.

TV translator station: A secondary, low-power TV station that re-broadcasts a TV or DTV signal on a different channel, and is subject to displacement by full-service TV or DTV stations. There are approximately 4,300 TV translator stations in the U.S.

ultra high definition video, UHD: Having roughly four times the number of pixels (hence 4K) as an HD image, these formats are currently used in cinema (the resolution is comparable to projected 35mm film), and moving into broadcast and other distribution.

universal material identifiers, UMID: identify a commercial.

V-Chip: Circuitry and software added to television receivers that allows parental lockout of programs rated as having excessive violence. This capability is mandatory for all TV receivers sold in the U.S. having screen sizes of 13-inches or larger. www.fcc.gov/vchip

virtual channel table, VCT: Metadata included in the PSIP codes.

vice president of engineering: See *director of engineering, chief engineer*.

video over IP, VoIP: Occasionally confused with IPTV, Video over IP is video in any form, any format, any bit rate, with any resolution, compressed or non-compressed that is passed on an IP switched network. There is generally a division between end user facing IPTV, and more-or-less internally and process/production oriented Video over IP. The abbreviation is somewhat difficult as VOIP, voice-over-IP, was a means of making a telephone call before it was practical to carry video.

voice-over, VO: An anchor or reporter voicing over video.

video on demand, VOD: The viewer selects a program and it starts at their command. Trick modes like pause and fast forward are typical. It may be pay per view (PPV), or subscription, or free.

voltage standing wave ratio, VSWR: A transmitter reading indicating reflected power (undesired) from the antenna. An increase in VSWR indicates a failing or icing antenna system. While a ratio, where 1:1 is perfect or 0% reflected, most transmitters read in percent. Typical good VSWR is less than 4% or 1.5:1.

watch folder: A file folder that is generally empty; however, when a file is placed in the folder, processes that are watching the folder will take that content and process it. Transcoding and QA functions often use a watch folder. Watch folders present some issues, not the least of which is dealing with what happens if files are altered while they are being processed. The basic workflow is noted for producing duplicates, and corrupted output under certain conditions.

WX: Abbreviation for weather.

XLR: A three-pin audio connector widely used in the broadcasting and entertainment industries.

Dedication

Family and friends play important roles in all our working lives. My thanks go to my best friend, both personally and professionally, Mildred Ellison. Also, to each of my co-workers and bosses over the years, from whom I've learned so much. Finally, this book is dedicated to anyone with a passion for great television!

–Nick

Partners tolerate much when someone with a full time career elects to sit down and write a book, so to Jody my wife and partner of 35 years, thank you, and I'll try to make up for this. Also, to Jim Wulliman, an educator first and broadcast engineer who labored tirelessly to bring education to engineers through the SBE. And, Jay Adrick, also an educator and engineer that never failed to bring vendor support to training our industry. And to all the mentors and colleagues who opened the doors behind which all this broadcasting stuff is hidden, in particular; Jim Worthington, Tom Mikkelsen, Peter Douglas, Mark Durenburger, Rod Bacon, John Corstvet, Doug Garlinger, "Chuck" Leonard Charles, Stan Moote, Brian Cabeceiras, Skip Erickson...

–Fred

CPSIA information can be obtained
at www.ICGtesting.com
Printed in the USA
LVOW03*1138310516

490596LV00010B/59/P